F.V.

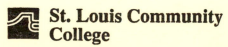

"Law Never Here"

"LAW NEVER HERE"

A Social History of African American Responses to Issues of Crime and Justice

Frankie Y. Bailey and Alice P. Green

PRAEGER

Westport, Connecticut
London

Library of Congress Cataloging-in-Publication Data

Bailey, Frankie Y.
    "Law never here" : a social history of African American responses
to issues of crime and justice / Frankie Y. Bailey and Alice P.
Green.
      p. cm.
    Includes bibliographical references and index.
    ISBN 0–275–95303–3 (alk. paper)
    1. Afro-Americans—Social conditions. 2. Afro-Americans—Law and
legislation—History. 3. Afro-Americans—Civil rights—History.
4. Discrimination in criminal justice administration—United States—
History. 5. Crime and race—United States—History. I. Green,
Alice P., 1946– . II. Title.
E185.86.B25 1999
973'.0496073—dc21   98–38282

British Library Cataloguing in Publication Data is available.

Library of Congress Catalog Card Number: 98–38282
ISBN: 0–275–95303–3

First published in 1999

Praeger Publishers, 88 Post Road West, Westport, CT 06881
An imprint of Greenwood Publishing Group, Inc.

Printed in the United States of America

The paper used in this book complies with the
Permanent Paper Standard issued by the National
Information Standards Organization (Z39.48–1984).

10 9 8 7 6 5 4 3 2

Contents

Acknowledgments

The authors would like to thank the people who contributed in various ways to the creation of this book. Much of the credit for what is good about it belongs to them. The faults are entirely our own.

First, the authors would like to acknowledge the immeasurable contribution of Dr. W.E.B. Du Bois, whose work was both the inspiration and the starting point for our own research. It was Dr. Du Bois who recognized that the "color line" would continue to be a source of contention and conflict in America. It was he who wrote with sensitivity and understanding of "the souls of black folk." During his long life, in his striving for both justice and excellence, he provided an example that we might all seek to emulate.

Of the many others who deserve our thanks, we would like to offer a special word of appreciation to Professor Jim Chambers, who as a reviewer of this manuscript, offered not only incisive criticism, but useful suggestions. Thanks also to the excellent editorial staff at Greenwood Publishing Group, in particular to Acquisitions Editor, Elisabetta Linton, and Senior Production Editor, Bridget M. Austiguy-Preschel.

There are other people who have aided us in our work. We would like to thank the people with whom we did oral history interviews: Doris E. Bedell, H. L. Blassingale, Mattie Blassingale, Geraldine Davis, John Lamar Ford, Sadie Hagood, Fahimah Abdue Khaaliq, Virginia C. Poyer, Yusef Salaam, and Geraldine Paden-Wood. Your memories of African American life in Albany, Harlem, and the South helped us to think through the concepts of memory and history that we deal with in these pages. This book has also benefited from our conversations with Scott Christianson and Joan Potter, both writers and activists in the cause of justice.

Frankie Bailey would like to thank the students in her graduate and undergraduate classes who have challenged her with both their questions and their refusal to accept pat answers. She would also like to thank her research assistants over the years—particularly Tami Beery. Thanks to Graeme Newman and Beverly Smith, former professors, now colleagues and friends, who encouraged her interest in the history of crime and justice. Other colleagues in the School of Criminal Justice, David Duffee, Jim Acker, David Bayley, and Alissa Worden, offered words of encouragement when the manuscript was in its final stages. And Frankie thanks Hans Toch, who has the office across the hall, and who is always there to encourage her scholarship even while chiding her for spending as much time in the office as he does. Due also for her share of credit is Donna C. Hale, Frankie's other writing partner, who listens even when we aren't talking about "our" book. Finally, family members—Frankie wishes to express her appreciation to Thomas Holt, cousin and historian, who has served as a role model for her academic pursuits. And she would like to thank her mother, Bessie Fitzgerald Bailey, who although she might well prefer grandchildren rather than books, has been ever steadfast in her love and support of her daughter.

Alice Green would like to offer her own thanks to Hans Toch, who was the chairperson of her dissertation committee, and is an inspiration for both of us.

Alice gives thanks and praise to her parents. Although they are no longer here, her mother, Annie Mae Paden, and her father, William Paden, live. She continues to be inspired by their spirit of love, sacrifice, resistance, and justice.

Alice would like to thank her husband and best friend, Charles Touhey, for his unbelievable tolerance for the whims of a community activist. He has always been there for her and does whatever it takes to support her passion for justice. Thanks also go to her son, John, for his constant expressions of love and pride in his mother. And finally, contrary to the general stereotype, her mother-in-law, Lila L. Touhey also has always been there for her.

Introduction

The title of this book reflects an inherent historical contradiction—an irony—in the relationship between African Americans and the American criminal justice system. The title comes from a conversation between the landscape architect and journalist Frederick Law Olmstead and a slave he encountered during his tour of the slave states. The slave's name was William. His master, a Louisiana plantation owner, had assigned William, one of his house servants, to drive Olmstead in the plantation owner's buggy. During the course of their twenty-mile journey, Olmstead casually probed William as to his opinions about slavery. William, originally from Virginia, believed that Virginia-bred slaves were far superior to Creole slaves. William also detected some difference among masters, particularly American masters and those of French descent. He found the French masters more severe than Americans. William added that he and the other slaves on Mr. R.'s plantation were fortunate to have him as a master. William explained that French masters sometimes did not give their slaves enough to eat; sometimes they gave them no meat at all. Olmstead told William that "this could not be so, for the law required that every master should serve out meat to his negroes." To this, William responded, "Oh, but some on 'em don't mind Law, if he does say so, massa. Law never here; don't know anything about him." Later in the conversation, William, the slave of a good American master who provided his slaves with ample food and clothing, expressed to Olmstead his own wistful longing for freedom.

> "Well, now, wouldn't you rather live on such a plantation than to be free, William?"

> "Oh! no, sir, I'd rather be free! Oh, yes, sir, I'd like it better to be free; I
> would dat master."
>
> "Why would you?"
>
> "Why, you see, master, if I was free—if I was *free*, I'd have *all* my time to
> myself. I'd rather work for myself. I'd like that better."[1]

William's observation that "Law never here" reflected a fact of life for
African Americans in slavery. Even the slave of a good master was still at
the mercy of the ill winds that might sweep through his master's life and
not only affect the master's behavior but threaten his ownership of his slaves.
Good masters sometimes found themselves in debt. Slaves (sold or traded)
often suffered because of it. For good masters and for bad ones, the law was
a written code. It had little effect on the day-to-day interactions between
the master and his slaves. As William said, "Law never here."

But at the same time—and this was the irony—Law was always there. It
was the laws of Louisiana and of the other southern states, the laws of the
federal government as well, that kept William in bondage. It was the Law
that ensured that if William resisted his status as slave, if he fought back or
ran away, he would be punished. It was the Law embodied in the slave codes
of the southern states and the federal Fugitive Slave Law and the decisions
of courts, local, state, and federal, that gave legal form to the hostile environment in which William and other black Americans lived.

It is this irony of Law as omnipresent (as restrictions and punishments)
and all too often absent (as justice and equity) that is the theme of this book
about African Americans and their relationship with the criminal justice system. The focus here is on how African Americans during their history in
this country have responded to issues of crime and justice.

ENDURING THEMES

This book began with our own search for answers. As African Americans
we were seeking answers to the questions we had been asking ourselves about
race and crime. Our search for answers has convinced us that many African
Americans perceive a great divide between the American creed of "justice
for all" and our own treatment in this country.[2] However, our research has
also made us aware of the variety of life-styles and experiences and the wide
range of opinions about almost any issue to be found within this group
known collectively as "African Americans." In fact, the long and sometimes
raucous debate within this group about what people of African heritage
should be called—"African," "Negro," "colored," "black," "Afro-
American," or "African American" (with or without the hyphen)—is one
indication of the diversity to be found among us.[3]

However, when we examine the responses of African Americans to issues of crime and justice, several themes do emerge. These themes weave their way through the social history of African Americans and through our discourses among ourselves and sometimes with the larger society. These themes have to do with how African Americans perceive American society and ourselves, and by extension the interaction between race and crime.

1. America is a "hostile environment" in which African Americans have been assigned the status of inferior beings who are to be kept in their "place."
2. African Americans need to find both physical and psychological "safe spaces" in which to exist and to grow.
3. African Americans share a cultural heritage and a collective experience and memory of oppression that bind us together as a unique "community."
4. Within this community there are internal divisions among those of different skin color, class, and gender that reflect the history of African Americans in this country.
5. The strategies adopted by individuals and by groups in response to the hostile environment in which African Americans live reflect these divisions.

In exploring these themes, we find that "place" and "space" are linked. As Harris (1982: 16) observes:

The concept of physical space—and attendant psychological implications—has as its basis the broad concept of place for all Blacks. Place can refer to status, to physical location, or to both. Place in any context espouses the hierarchy of masters and slaves, owners and owned, privileged and nonprivileged.[4]

Nowhere is this more clear than when we examine the African American conception of that place we call home.

In the Afro-American cultural vernacular home was always more than the house in which one lived. Home was the household and the community; home was a shared culture and a shared culture of expectations; home was the community of origin and the community of residence; home was a state of mind and the link between the past, the present, and the future. (Lewis, 1991: 33)

It is this meaning of space and place as both physical and psychological locations that we will evoke. It will be reflected in our discussion of how African Americans relate to each other and to their communities and how they think of those places that they left and to which they sometimes return (as in the recent backward migration of some African Americans to the South).

We should note here that in our analysis, we will treat race, class, and gender as "social constructs" that acquire their meanings in the context of human interactions. We will discuss the role of African American culture[5] in shaping black perceptions of race, class, and gender. We will also look at the roles played by dominant society institutions such as the media in the social construction of race. In this regard, we will examine the "war of images" (e.g., Giroux, 1996) in which African Americans have historically felt compelled to participate. White racial stereotypes in the mass media, in social science, and elsewhere required a response by African Americans.[6]

With regard to class as a social construct, we should explain that the application of the concept of class to African Americans is rather complex. On the one hand, there is the matter of how African Americans are perceived by non–African Americans. On the other hand, there is the matter of how African Americans perceive each other. In his study of the black elite, Birmingham (1977: 65) writes, "The phrase 'middle-class' has a special meaning to blacks. To whites, it is essentially an economic consideration. But in black America, class is a question of dignity, and more important, stability." This explains why in the 1920s and 1930s, railroad sleeping car porters were perceived by the black community as having a higher status than that attributed to them by whites. As Birmingham (22) states:

> To be a Pullman car porter in those days was a mark of great status for a black man; to work the Pullman cars, a man had to be trustworthy, a "gentleman," the work was steady and the pay, with tips, was good; similarly, it was a mark of status to work for the Post Office.

Yet, even a job such as that of a Pullman porter, which gave a black man status in his own community, must be evaluated against the overall status of blacks as laborers. The steady work of the Pullman porter often involved putting in four hundred hours on the job in a one month period, travelling as much as eleven thousand miles (Gutman, 1989: 306). The tips were good, but the pay was so bad that the tips were necessary for a man to support his family. The status of the railroad porter—with his steady job and his uniform—was higher than that of the many common laborers in the black community. Relatively speaking, it was a good job. Therefore, "many of those who took porter jobs were highly able, politically sophisticated, well-educated men, often leaders in their community" (Gutman, 306). But by the whites he served in the Pullman sleeping cars, the porter was often viewed as nothing more than a servant who catered to their every whim with a pleasing blend of subordination and style.[7] Hence, the complexity of class as it relates to black Americans.

We should register here our discomfort with the concept of "the underclass." Our concern is that it is one of those concepts that in their use have become "loaded" with racial meaning. As Inniss and Feagin (1989: 14) state: "The concept of the 'underclass,' as it has developed in the last decade in the United States, is not only ahistorical and noncomparative, but highly ideological and political." The term is sometimes used in such a way that real distinctions among lower class black Americans are ignored. In fact, "the underclass" is sometimes used to describe all African Americans who live in "inner city" neighborhoods (i.e., ghettos). Our own perception is that this characterization, which often amounts to stigmatization, is inaccurate.

Now that we have introduced and offered some explanation of the themes that will concern us, we will discuss the major influences on our research and writing.

WHERE WE STARTED

We began with W.E.B. Du Bois, the African American sociologist, historian, and civil rights activist. Du Bois's life began in the midnineteenth century (1868). It ended on the eve of the March on Washington (1963). In *The Souls of Black Folk* (1903), Du Bois wrote, "The problem of the Twentieth Century is the problem of the color line" (xi). In addressing the status of blacks in America, he described the "double-consciousness"—"this sense of always looking at one's self through the eyes of others, of measuring one's soul by the tape of a world that looks on in amused contempt and pity" (45). What we found even more thought-provoking was Du Bois's assertion that because of their experiences as slaves and during the post–Civil War era, "Negroes came to look upon courts as instruments of injustice and oppression, and upon those convicted in them as martyrs and victims" (201).

We asked ourselves if it were that simple. Did this sense of injustice explain why ex-mayor Marion Barry received a warm welcome from his supporters when he returned home from prison? Did it explain why the black people we saw on live television news reports cheered when the not guilty verdict was read in the O. J. Simpson murder case while the white people we saw reacted with anger and incredulity? Was it that simple?

In another essay, in *The Souls of Black Folk*, Du Bois had written that the responses of a group to oppression might take three main forms.

> a feeling of revolt and revenge; an attempt to adjust all thought and action to the will of the greater group or, finally, a determined effort at self-realization and self-development despite environing opinion. The influences of all of these attitudes at various times can be traced in the history of the American Negro, and the evolution of his successive leaders. (84)

If these were the three main forms that African American responses to oppression had taken, then this statement should also (in terms of Du Bois's earlier assertion) describe responses by blacks to issues of crime and justice. We decided to test Du Bois's thesis.

As we reviewed what we knew about African Americans (Du Bois's "black folk") as a people, we began to think about "community"—about the ways in which community has historically been perceived by black Americans. As we talked about this matter of community, we began to think about African Americans within the context of the larger "American" community. In their best-selling book *Habits of the Heart* (1985), Bellah et al. describe the American "national identity" as being shaped by the beliefs that Americans share. These beliefs are a part of our shared American culture. They are the starting points for the "dramatic conversations" that daily engage us. As Americans we are members of a "community of memory" linked by shared traditions, rituals, feasts, and holidays that bring us together and sustain us as a people. But as Bellah et al. point out, this concept of a "community of memory" is equally, in fact particularly, relevant to the ethnic and religious communities that make up our larger society.

> People growing up in communities of memory not only hear the stories that tell how the community came to be, what its hopes and fears are and how its ideals are exemplified in outstanding men and women, they also participate in the practices—ritual, aesthetic, ethical—that define the community as a way of life. (Bellah et al.: 154)

As Americans, African Americans share in the national identity. African American share (and hold dear) many of the same values as other Americans.[8] As members of a racial/ethnic group that has been oppressed, African Americans also share much in common with other historically oppressed groups.[9] At the same time, African Americans constitute and consider themselves a part of an ethnic community that is a unique "community of memory." The choices made by African Americans as individuals and as members of groups in response to oppression form a significant aspect of the lore of that community of memory.

In this regard, the feminist scholar bell hooks argues that the African American past should be put to use in understanding and dealing with the dilemmas of the present. Evoking Foucault's description of memory as "a site of resistance," hooks asserts that for African Americans, the telling of our history will allow not only theorizing but political "self-recovery" (hooks, 1995). Other scholars have examined this nexus between history and memory. In an edited volume titled *History and Memory in African-American Culture* (1994), O'Meally and Fabre apply the French historian Pierre Nora's concept of *lieux de memoire*—sites of memory—to African American history and culture. They use the concept to provide a framework for an interdisciplinary collaboration of scholars who come together to examine the multifaceted interaction between memory and African American history. O'Meally and Fabre note in their introduction to the volume that this linking of history and memory has long been an underlying theme in the writings of African American philosophers and historians and novelists.

We will argue that at the "folk" level, history as memory is also operable;

in fact, it is vital to understanding how African Americans perceive their interactions with the American criminal justice system.

HISTORY, MEMORY, AND BLACK LEADERS

In their acknowledgments in the volume discussed, the editors, Fabre and O'Meally, thank the W.E.B. Du Bois Institute for Afro-American Research at Harvard University for serving as host for their faculty working group. As one contributor, David Blight, illustrates in his chapter "W.E.B. Du Bois and the Struggle for American Historical Memory," it was appropriate that the conference should have taken place at an institute that bears Du Bois's name. Blight reminds us that on the occasion of the hundredth anniversary of Du Bois's birth, Martin Luther King, Jr., praised Du Bois's achievements as a scholar. King described Du Bois as a debunker of traditional historical accounts of African Americans that had distorted the truth and served to poison the "collective mind of America" (Blight, 1994: 45).

One of Du Bois's missions was to reveal and clarify the history of African Americans. Du Bois saw the educating of both black and white Americans about that history as a part of his role as a race leader. He saw himself as a member of that well-educated, elite group for whom he coined the phrase "the Talented Tenth." It was the Talented Tenth who would develop the strategies for dealing with oppression and lead the masses. In short, Du Bois was an "elitist." He was also a complex man who—like other "race leaders" such as Frederick Douglass, Martin Luther King, Jr., and Malcolm X—cooperated with or clashed with the people who came within his orbit. He sometimes seemed to contradict himself. He changed his mind and modified his position. He was flawed—in short, he was human. We make this point about Du Bois because we want to make clear the necessity of taking into account the hopes, dreams, and fears—and, yes, personal quirks—of the individuals who have spoken as race leaders. This does not mean we are arguing for microlevel history or asserting that African American social history must be understood in terms of individual biography. It does mean that we have come to believe that knowing that Du Bois grew up in a village in New England and was educated at Harvard is essential to an understanding of what Du Bois believed were appropriate responses to crime and justice issues.[10]

However, even as we examine the individual responses of black leaders and their influence on their followers, we are also interested in understanding the masses. We will discuss the clues to interpreting the collective memories of African Americans as a group to be found in cultural artifacts such as songs, ballads, and folktales.[11] Particularly during the last three decades, scholars from a variety of disciplines have been involved in collecting and analyzing these cultural artifacts. We have turned to the works of these scholars in our exploration of African Americans' responses to crime and justice.

DEFINING CRIME AND JUSTICE

There is something else we should make clear. As with race, class, and gender, we treat the concepts of "crime" and "justice" as social constructs. We begin with the assumption that definitions of crime and justice will reflect the interactions of groups in relationships of dominance and subordination, power and relative powerlessness. We do not assume that these definitions were based on consensus. In fact, we assume conflict. For example, what colonial Europeans saw as the process of acquiring a labor force, enslaved Africans saw as kidnapping, unlawful imprisonment, forced labor, assault, rape, and sometimes murder. But it was the Europeans who enacted their perceptions into law. For the Africans, it meant that justice was by statute absent from their lives.

The legal scholar Donald Black (1993) has described law as a form of "social control." He argues that in the absence of perceived access to the law and perceived influence on the outcome of the criminal justice process, individuals and groups may engage in "violent self-help." This self-help spans the gamut from duels, brawls, and feuds to riots.[12] We suggest that this concept of self-help might be usefully applied in understanding such events as Nat Turner's rebellion or an urban riot. Moreover, this concept is in keeping with Du Bois's thesis concerning possible responses to oppression.

We will argue that during the era of slavery—when blacks found themselves in a situation in which not only was their sense of justice violated but they had little control over their lives—a pattern of action–response–action was established. This pattern would continue in the postbellum era and to the present. To illustrate, during slavery, the action–response–action sequence looked like this:

—Government action: The use of black (African) labor in the colonies

—Black response: Self-assertion in the form of actions that were perceived as social threat (e.g., forming alliances with white bondservants)

—Government action: Codification of status of blacks as slaves with distinctions drawn between black slaves and white servants

—Black response: Challenges to status as slave

—legal—petitions, court cases, and so on.[13]

—illegal—running away, rebellions, and so on.

This conflict over definitions of crime and justice and regarding the status of blacks was waged within the institutions of American society—family, church, school, politics, economics, and mass media. In fact, African Americans came to define this matter of crime and justice broadly. They perceived criminal justice as subsumed by and inseparable from social justice. Because these two streams have historically flowed together in African American thought, our approach here will be "holistic." That is, we will analyze responses to all forms of oppression (social, legal, economic, political) as a part of the overall effort by African Americans to deal with a hostile environment and to obtain justice (fairness and equity). African Americans have perceived the criminal justice system as essential to the creation and maintenance of this hostile environment. Therefore, we look at responses to issues of crime and justice within the larger context of responses to oppression and the fight to obtain social justice. We argue here that criminal justice must be examined under the rubric of social justice.

We should state here that although we are aware of the importance of examining "black-on-black crime" and its impact on African American communities, that is not the focus of this book. We focus here on how African Americans—finding themselves in a hostile environment—have responded over several centuries to white social and legal oppression. Rather than look inward at black communities and black crime, we will look outward from those communities as African Americans attempt to deal with the injustices that have a profound—and negative—impact on their lives.[14]

We have tried to limit ourselves as much as possible to those episodes in African American social history that culminated in one way or another in an encounter between the participants and agents of criminal justice. However, African Americans often sought relief from racial oppression by bringing civil actions and petitioning state and federal courts. When they failed to obtain relief, they then sometimes engaged in acts that defied the existing law, thereby bringing themselves into contact with the criminal justice system. Therefore, any racially oppressive law created a situation that was ripe for black resistance and white response.

Finally, on the subject of historical context, we should note here our intellectual debt to the Baptist minister and Princeton Ph.D. Michael Eric Dyson. In *Race Rules* (1997), a collection of essays, Dyson argues that with events such as the O. J. Simpson trial and the case of Tawana Brawley (the teenager who accused white law enforcement officers of rape and abuse), there is the possibility—indeed the likelihood—of an underlying racial context, subtext, and pretext being played out. We will address Dyson's thesis again in our final chapters. However, we should note here that we agree with Dyson that misinterpretation and confusion over what is historical context, what is subtext, and what is pretext are obstacles to reasoned discourse among African Americans and non–African Americans.

CONCLUDING THOUGHTS

As we have described, our thoughts have been informed by the works of a variety of scholars from a number of disciplines—historians, anthropologists, sociologists, psychologists, and others. Our thoughts have also been shaped by the voices of ordinary men and women whose perceptions are captured in folklore and oral histories, in blues and in spirituals. We have tried to hear those voices too and represent their perspectives here. We have also tried to listen to the youth of each generation, who, socialized by their elders to share their beliefs, often instead challenged their teaching. This matter of African American youth and "youth culture" becomes especially relevant in the last decades of the twentieth century. We address youth culture toward the end of the last chapters.

Regarding organization, generally the chapters proceed in chronological fashion from the colonial period to the present. That is, we start with slavery and move forward. However, we are particularly concerned with symbolic events that had meaning for the African American community and how these events affected their interpretation of the past. Therefore, we sometimes foreshadow an event or frame a discussion with reference to a later event. We take this liberty with the time–space continuum because we are discussing history as memory and because in presenting our analysis of events in each era, we have drawn on the work of later scholars. These scholars sometimes disagree. Because of these disagreements, we occasionally find it useful to depart from a chronological approach to examine the disputed ground of later interpretation. We are, in fact, more interested here in analysis than in a recitation of events.

In this book we have tried to understand and then convey to you, the reader, the sense of history that shapes African American responses to issues of crime and justice. The title *"Law Never Here"* reflects our awareness that many African Americans—perhaps most of us at one time or another—have felt some ambivalence about our relationship to the criminal justice system. As criminologists, we find it particularly troubling that American justice has not always been just or fair or equal. Perhaps it is naive of us to expect this. Many Americans have experienced oppression and injustice based on ethnicity, class, gender, religion, or sexual orientation. African Americans are not alone in this respect. But, having the collective memory of slavery, African Americans are profoundly aware of the sometimes great distance between the American creed of "justice for all" and the actuality.

In this book, we will focus on African Americans not as victims of oppression but as participants in the drama of American history. Like other Americans, we have sometimes been heroes, at other times fools or even villains. At all times, we have been people seeking our place and space in American society.

NOTES

1. Frederick Law Olmstead (1959), *The Slave States (Before the Civil War)*, Harvey Wish, ed. (New York: G. P. Putnam), 4th ed., 118–125. As Wish, the editor of this compilation of Olmstead's trilogy of books about the South, notes, Olmstead's own feelings about slavery must be taken into account when making use of Olmstead's works. Olmstead was opposed to slavery, but at the same time, he hoped for some peaceful resolution of this American dilemma. He was hopeful that southern slave-holders could be brought to see that the system should not be preserved. But even with the biases that are reflected in his work, as Wish writes, Olmstead has been recognized by historians "as an acute social critic of the Old South" and a sharp-eyed observer (7).

2. See Gallup poll results in McAneny (1993) and Wheeler (1993).

3. Smitherman (1994: 11) observes that name change debates "come to the forefront during crisis and upheavals in the Black condition." In the 1920s, as the National Association for the Advancement of Colored People (NAACP) pursued justice through litigation; it also conducted a successful campaign to have the media capitalize *Negro* (Smitherman, 14). Concerning the name issue, 103 year old Bessie Delany, the first black female dentist in New York City, remarked:

> I don't use the word very often to describe myself and my sister. To us, black was a person who was, well, black, and honey, I mean *black as your shoe*. I'm not black, I'm brown! Actually, the best word to describe me, I think is colored. I am a colored woman or a Negro woman. Either one is OK. People dislike those words now. Today they use this term *African American*. It wouldn't occur to me to use that. I prefer to think of myself as an American, that's all! (Delany et al., 1993: 107)

Delany touches here on the "color" issue as well. As she recalls, "There was an attitude among some Negroes that to be light-skinned was more desirable" (106). This was reflected in the preference for one (race) name rather than another. It was also reflected in the interactions of African Americans with each other and with whites, including those in positions of authority.

4. Also see Patricia Collins (1990) and bell hooks (1995). We also will have in mind as we discuss space and its use the research by psychologists such as Edward Hall (1969) focusing on the psychological aspects of social and personal space. With regard to black migrants to urban areas, Hall writes about the "special problems" of adjustment of lower class Negroes to "city living" (165): "Public housing constructed for low income groups often dresses up and hides but fails to solve basic human problems" (insert, plates 23 and 24 in Hall, 1969). Hall's discussion of use of space by African American migrants is instructive not only because of the point he is making about the psychological aspects of how different groups use space but because of the picture he paints of the black migrant as an urban misfit.

5. There are numerous definitions of culture. For example, Swidler defines culture as a "tool kit of symbols, stories, rituals, and worldviews, which people may use in varying configurations to solve different kinds of problems" (quoted by Conrad, 1997: 140). We refer to this tool kit possessed by African Americans as a "culture" rather than a "subculture" for two reasons. First, even though African Americans share in the common culture of all Americans, they also possess their own unique

and equally important culture shaped by their shared experiences as a people. Second, in this book we will view the world from the perspectives of African Americans. To speak of an African American subculture reinforces the perception of the political and social dominance of European American culture as well as the perception that a subculture is by definition less important and/or inferior to the dominant culture. As will become clear, we will make a very different argument here. Speaking of African American culture, Nobles (1989: 106) states:

> Culture is important. In fact, many students of liberation struggles have noted that culture serves as a weapon in a people's struggle. . . . Culture is the process that gives people a general design for living and pattern for interpreting their reality.

6. Discussing race and popular culture during the 1980s Reagan administration, Gray (1995: 14) asserts:

> Through the discursive production and organization of television news images and reports about black welfare "cheats" and moral panics about black "family disintegration" and epidemic drug use and violence in the nation's cities, race and popular media . . . were central to the consolidation of a conservative cultural and political hegemonic bloc.

7. See Perata (1997/98) on the working conditions of Pullman porters. We will return to this topic in our discussion of the role of A. Philip Randolph and the Brotherhood of Sleeping Car Porters as a part of the larger movement to obtain social and economic justice for blacks.

8. However, see, for example, Bender (1989) for the debate concerning American values. We assume here that what those values are and what they should mean in our civic lives are at the heart of the "dramatic conversations" we have as Americans.

9. See, for example, Takaki (1979). Also see Franklin (1984), in which he discusses the values shared by oppressed groups.

10. In his third autobiography, Du Bois acknowledges the influence of his upbringing in shaping his perceptions. For example, "It was not good form in Great Barrington to express one's thoughts volubly, or to give way to excessive emotion" (Du Bois, 1968: 93). Other life experiences would have their impact, but in many ways Du Bois remained true to his upbringing.

11. Osunleye (1997: 435) describes folklore as "an invaluable framework for insight into the history and worldview of African Americans." But also note Osunleye's comments about the misuse of folklore by some scholars who have focused narrowly on folklore related to sex and violence and presented those tales as representative of the whole.

12. The inclusion of duels in this list reflects the fact that—although men of money and standing had the ability to influence the criminal justice process—the interpersonal conflicts that brought them to the "field of honor" were matters that they chose not to pursue in a court of law. These "gentlemen" were willing to disobey the laws banning dueling in order to confront each other over perceived insults to honor and reputation. As we will discuss, among elite southern slaveholders rituals of honor were played out not only on the dueling field but in their relationships with their slaves.

13. For example, Bailey (1979: 44) finds that in eighteenth-century Virginia, although denied "elementary political rights" such as voting and holding office, "on a few occasions even slaves used petitions to communicate with the legislature. This

was especially common after 1776, when the Assembly assumed the power to authorize the manumission of slaves."

14. Books that deal more extensively with theories of black criminality include Chambers (1995), in which he "examines some of the social forces that influence Black responses to differential societial conditions" and discusses the issue of "social exchange" and its impact on both blacks and whites (xii). Other works by social scientists on this topic of blacks and crime will be mentioned later in this volume.

CHAPTER 1

Of Natural Rights and Social Death

Slavery was a form of legal oppression. Slavery existed in Africa, Europe, and Asia long before the European colonization of the land that would become the United States of America. That fact cannot be disputed. What have engaged historians and others are the similarities and differences between slavery elsewhere and slavery as it developed in the Americas. Another matter that has generated heated debate is that of the evolution of slavery in the British colonies. Did the colonists in Virginia, for example, eagerly embrace the concept of African slavery because of their need for labor? Or was slavery, as Thomas Jefferson would later assert, forced upon the colonists by the royal government? In this chapter, we will address these questions. We will also examine the legal aspects of slavery and the sometimes illegal (i.e., lawbreaking) responses of Africans (later African Americans) to bondage.

LABOR AND BONDAGE

Regarding labor and bondage in the New World, Rice (1975: 2) writes:

However much European serfdom might have weakened by the time of the American discoveries, the whole heritage of the West (and the East) sanctioned the use of unfree labour. The use of slaves to colonise the Americas was not an aberration.

Rice continues, "The construction of a slave system based strictly on race was a new development," even though "the use of slavery itself was not" (3).

But in the beginning a system of indentured labor by white servants existed side-by-side with the enslavement of Indians (Native Americans) and Africans. As Daniels (1990: 30) observes: "Since about half the Europeans and all the Africans were, to one degree or another, unfree, the free immigrant was in the minority during the colonial period." The presence of white indentured servants had a profound impact on the evolving institution of slavery. Prior to 1660, "white labor under indentures lasting several years made up the bulk of the labor force in Virginia and Maryland" (McColley, 1986: 11).

From 1619, when the first Africans arrived in Jamestown, Virginia, until 1660, the slave trade was dominated by the Dutch (McColley, 18). Many African slaves were sold to the Caribbean sugar planters, who were better able to pay for them than were the colonists on the North American mainland. Because it was "relatively difficult to acquire blacks before 1660 . . . generally speaking, those Virginians who owned them were among the wealthiest, the most powerful, and the most resourceful people in the colony" (McColley, 18). It was also the wealthy and the powerful who were best able to purchase the labor of white indentured servants.

The demand for labor in Virginia during its "boom period" as a tobacco colony encouraged the creation of a system of indentured labor, "which, while short of slavery, was also some distance from the freedom that Englishmen liked to consider as their birthright" (Morgan, 1975: 123). Even if they were not physically abused, "Englishmen found servitude in Virginia more degrading than servitude in England" (Morgan: 127). The labor system that existed in Virginia was one of "exploitation." But

> the very imbalance of sex and age that made Virginia's servants highly exploitable made them potentially dangerous when freed. Bachelors are notoriously more reckless and rebellious than men surrounded by women and children, and these bachelors were a particularly wild lot. The way they got to the colony helped to guarantee they would be so. (Morgan: 235–236)

The "wildness" of these servants and the fact that they were potentially dangerous would not have come as a surprise to the masters who purchased their indentures. In England, the social class from which these servants were drawn was considered the "dangerous class." Workhouses and poorhouses had been established to deal with members of the lower class and their offspring. The poor as a class were considered in need of control and discipline.[1] Initially some of the same stereotypes were applied both to white indentured servants and to black slaves. Both were perceived by their masters as "shiftless, irresponsible, unfaithful, ungrateful, dishonest; they got drunk whenever possible; they did not work hard enough or regularly enough" (Morgan: 319).

In the case of the white indentured servants there was the added problem that eventually their indentures ended and they became "freedmen." Once servants gained their freedom, instead of working for established planters, they preferred to strike out on their own. They were able to do this because of the cheap public land that was still available (Morgan, 215). As farmers, freedmen not only were removed from the labor market but also offered some competition as tobacco growers.

One solution to this problem—one mechanism for retaining the labor of servants—was by finding a way to lengthen their terms of indenture. Between 1658 and 1666, the Virginia assembly took action to create new laws that would apply to servants who arrived in the colony "without an indenture in which the terms were specified" (Morgan, 216). The assembly also created new laws that prolonged the period of indenture of servants who were convicted of crimes, particularly "the servant's favorite vice"—running away (Morgan, 217; also see Sellin, 1976).

There is some disagreement among historians about the eagerness—or lack thereof—with which planters moved from a predominantly white indentured labor force to a labor force made up mainly of black slaves.[2] The creation of the Royal Africa Company (1663) marked the official entry of the English into the slave trade. Over a hundred years later, as they moved toward revolt against England, the colonists would allege that the British government was responsible for the proliferation of slavery in the colonies. In his draft of the Declaration of Independence, Thomas Jefferson accused King George III of

> [urging] cruel war against human nature itself, violating its most sacred rights of life and liberty in their person of a distant people who never offended him, captivating and carrying them into slavery in another hemisphere, or to incur miserable death in their transportation thither. (quoted in Hornsby, 1972: 7)

This accusation by Jefferson was not completely disingenuous. In the decades prior to the Revolutionary War there was a perception in the colonies that England was the source of colonial depravity—the source of the taste for spending and consumption that seemed to be permeating the colonies (Shi, 1985).

Whatever England's role, as the colonists moved toward the use of slave labor, they begun to create the legal infrastructures required to hold blacks in perpetual bondage. By the second half of the seventeenth century, Virginia and the other colonies had begun to draw legal distinctions between black and white, slave and free.[3] Concerning the legal aspects of the slaves' status in the colonies, Finkelman (1993: 2068) states:

> Initially blackness did not lead to a presumption of any particular status. Early in the colonial period this changed, however. Throughout the South color led to the development of a presumption that all blacks had a certain status at law.

This was the equivalent, in criminal law terms, to what might be called a presumption of guilt based on race.

Because blackness was linked to the status of slave, "if a black was found away from the control of a white, the black was presumed to be guilty of something: travelling without a pass, running away, or being in rebellion" (Finkelman, 2069). This presumption of guilt was extended to free blacks, who had to prove their status by carrying "free papers" (Finkelman, 2069).

Higginbotham (1996: 30) points out that the slave statutes that were compiled into codes between 1705 and 1865 provided both substantive and procedural law:

> The substantive statutes defined the parameters of slavery, regulated the behavior of slaves, and regulated the behavior of free people interacting with slaves. Procedurally, they set up a separate judicial system for slaves, defined their punishment for various crimes, and turned them into a commodity in the economic system. No aspect of the lives of slaves and free African Americans was too sacred or mundane not to be regulated by the codes.

Criminal justice, particularly in the South, but also to some extent in the North, was color-coded.

THE NATURAL RIGHTS OF FREE MEN

On March 23, 1775, at St. John's Church during the Second Virginia Convention, Patrick Henry made the speech that figures prominently in any account of Virginia's role in the American Revolution. In a rousing call to arms, Henry told his listeners, "I know not what course others may take, but as for me, give me liberty or give me death."

After serving five terms as the governor of Virginia, in 1794 Henry retired to his plantation, Red Hill. Tobacco was the chief crop grown there, and Henry was "among the 100 wealthiest landowners in Virginia." He owned "21 horses, 167 cattle, 155 hogs, and 60 sheep." He also owned "66 plantation slaves" (*Historical Almanack*, Patrick Henry: 2).

Patrick Henry was not the only "founding father" who owned slaves—so did George Washington and Thomas Jefferson.[4] At the time when he wrote the draft of the Declaration of Independence, Jefferson was the second largest slaveowner in Albemarle County, Virginia, holding 175 slaves (O'Reilly, 1995: 20). This is the contradiction that historians have struggled to explain—that men who could speak so eloquently and fight so bravely for their own freedom could at the same time hold other humans in bondage.

At the time of the American Revolution, "20 percent of the overall population in the thirteen colonies were of African descent" (*Historical Almanack*, Introduction: 1). Slavery existed not only in the southern colonies but in the

North as well. During and in the aftermath of the conflict with Great Britain, there was some sentiment for the abolition of slavery. Jefferson, who would later accuse George III of such a grave wrong toward Africans, had attacked slavery in his pamphlet *A Summary View of the Rights of British America* (Miller, 1995). In his draft of the Declaration of Independence, he "amplified the charge that the king was responsible for the perpetuation of slavery and the slave trade" (Miller, 7).

But it was an embarrassing situation. As Dr. Samuel Johnson had asked, "How is it that we hear the loudest yelps of liberty from the drivers of Negroes?" (quoted in Miller, 8). Whatever Jefferson and his compatriots might say about how slavery had come to exist in the colonies, the plain fact was that much of the wealth of the planter class—and of others who profited from the African trade—was bound up in slaves.[5] Miller (1995: 13) writes:

> One third of the signers of the Declaration of Independence were slaveowners, most of whom had no intention of sacrificing their rights to hold human beings in servitude upon the altar of American freedom simply because the Declaration asserted the ideal equality and universal rights of abstract man.

Nash (1990) states that several factors in the 1770s and 1780s "made this the opportune time for abolishing slavery." These factors included the strong sentiment for ridding the country of the "peculiar institution." There was also the vulnerable position of the lower South, which made it unlikely that the region most inclined to resist abolition would attempt "to break away from the rest of the states" (6–7). Religion, the rise of evangelical Christianity in the South, was another factor lending momentum to abolition sentiment (Nash, 14). During the early 1730s, the southern colonies had experienced "The Great Awakening"—"a spontaneous series of revivals . . . that . . . quickly spread up the Atlantic Coast" (Shi, 1985: 23). The lingering effects of this evangelicalism were still being felt during the Age of Revolution.[6]

But as Nash (1990: 35) observes:

> Two main problems confronted those who thought about ending slavery in America. The first was economic: how would slaveowners be compensated? The second was social: how would freed slaves be fit into the social fabric of the new nation? Solutions to these two thorny problems hinged, in turn, first on a willingness to make economic sacrifice, and second, on an ability to envision a truly biracial republican society. Northerners as well as Southerners . . . lost the abolitionist fire in their bellies on both of these cardinal points.[7]

The failure to abolish slavery during this opportune period would have consequences for the Africans and their descendants who would remain enslaved or be born into slavery. It would also have consequences for both white Americans who owned slaves and those who did not. For whites, the consequences of African slavery included a "Herrenvolk democracy"[8] that was in direct conflict with the American creed. The existence of slavery also contributed to the creation and perpetuation of a caste–class hierarchy and a violent "culture of honor" in the South. Slavery required the creation of a dual system of justice.[9] It also required its defenders to develop elaborate philosophical arguments to justify its existence. Eventually it would require them to risk their lives in a war about the way of life that slavery had spawned.

But perhaps, as Thomas Jefferson argued, the most profound consequence of slavery for white Americans was that those who lived within its sphere were corrupted by it. In *Notes on Virginia* (1785), Jefferson wrote about the cruelty, pride, and mindless brutality slavery engendered in both slaveholders and their children (Miller, 41).[10] Looking at the institution of slavery, Jefferson feared divine retribution—perhaps in the form of a bloody slave revolt. He wrote, "Indeed I tremble for my country when I reflect that God is just: that his justice cannot sleep for ever" (Jefferson, 1955: 163).

Yet while despising slavery and its impact on white Americans, in the end Jefferson, like many other slaveholders, lacked the will to give up the lifestyle it provided. Moreover, as a pragmatist, he was unwilling to risk the political capital he possessed in what he considered a futile effort to abolish slavery. As an optimist, he believed that eventually some solution would be found. That solution must involve the transportation of the freed slaves out of the country, for Jefferson was convinced free blacks and free whites could not live together in peace. In 1820, having retired to Monticello, Jefferson looked at the situation and observed: "We have the wolf by the ears; and we can neither hold him, nor safely let him go. Justice is in one scale, and self-preservation in the other" (quoted in Miller, 241).

For blacks, the injustices of slavery were many. In 1857, as he delivered the opinion of the Supreme Court in the case of Dred Scott, Chief Justice Roger Taney declared:

> The unhappy black race were separated from the white by indelible marks, and laws long before established, and were never thought or spoken of except as property. (quoted in Bardolph, 1970: 18)

The chief justice concluded that Dred Scott and other slaves were "so far inferior, that they had no rights which the white man was bound to respect" (Bardolph, 18)

Orlando Patterson (1982) argues that, as did slaves elsewhere, slaves in the United States experienced not only the loss of freedom but "social death": a status of legal "kinlessness" and exclusion from the political process. Slaves were classified as legal nonpersons.[11] But in small ways and large, slaves resisted their assigned status as "chattel property."

Resistance by slaves involved responses to their bondage that were perceived as "crimes" by those who enslaved them.[12] Addressing this point, Byrne (1994) writes: "If everything normal and human is illegal, it then becomes necessary to break the law in order to assert one's humanity" (353). Frederick Douglass wrote from the slave's perspective, which was distinctly different from that of those who made the laws. When Douglass broke the law by running away, he regarded himself as "a fugitive, not from justice but from slavery." In his narrative, *My Bondage and My Freedom* (1855: 191), Douglass writes:

> Slaveholders have made it almost impossible for the slave to commit any crime known either to the laws of God or the laws of man. If he steals he takes his own; if he kills his master, he imitates only the heroes of the revolution.

This matter of perspective is crucial to understanding the responses of slaves (and their allies) to the criminal justice system during the colonial and antebellum eras. A slave could "steal himself" by running away.[13] He (or she) could engage in acts of "day-to-day resistance" such as deliberately breaking a tool or feigning illness. He (or she) could even engage in a conspiracy or a revolt. A slave could do these things and still perceive himself as having, if not the law, at least justice on his side.

SLAVE REBELS

The historian Eugene Genovese (1979: 11) has observed, "No slave revolt that hesitated to invoke terror had a chance." In 1831, a slave named Nat Turner led a revolt—an "insurrection"—in Southhampton County, Virginia, in which fifty-seven white people were killed.[14] Nat Turner's Rebellion was the "largest and bloodiest slave revolt in American history" (Bennett, 1968: 83).[15] Nat Turner's revolt invoked widespread terror among southern whites.

In 1829, a firebrand black abolitionist, David Walker, had published in Boston *Walker's Appeal*, an antislavery pamphlet in which he urged slaves to rise up and seize their freedom. The pamphlet had circulated in the South, and might have been smuggled into southern ports by black seamen.[16] Although he was literate and a student of the Bible, there is nothing to indicate that Nat Turner had read Walker's call for armed resistance by southern slaves. However, in 1968, looking backward at the two men and their individual attacks on the institute of slavery, Lerone Bennett, Jr. (1968: 83), declared, "Nat Turner was David Walker's word made flesh."

In 1831, southern slaveholders called Nat Turner a fiend. In the North, white abolitionists hesitated to voice support for a bloody slave rebellion. However, these abolitionists did not hesitate to point out to slaveholders that this was what they had been warning them about.[17] Even earlier, during the Revolutionary era, Thomas Jefferson had warned his fellow slaveholders of the retribution they might well face for the South's "peculiar institution." In fact, the fear of retribution in the form of a slave insurrection had plagued slaveholders since Africans were placed in bondage. During Bacon's Rebellion (1676) in colonial Virginia, the arming of slaves and indentured servants and the subsequent refusal of a group of them to surrender stirred concerns among plantation owners about white–black collusion against those in power. But the fear of slave conspiracies was not restricted to the South.

As Painter (1996: 9) states:

> Slavery was an important part of northern life before 1800, however latter-day historical symbolism may have erased its stigma from the North. . . . Only Charleston among American cities had a larger black population than New York, and New York City's 5,865 blacks . . . accounted for about 10 percent of the total population.

In New York City, in the eighteenth century, concerns about the growing slave population (the largest in the North) were reflected in laws aimed at both controlling slaves and punishing them.

> An act of 1705 decreed death for any slave from Albany city or county found north of Sarachtoge (Saratoga), that is escaping to French Canada with which the British were at war. A more general law of 1708 was the first to mention slave conspiracies. . . . Entitled "An Act for Preventing the Conspiracy of Slaves," it authorized death of any Negro or Indian slave who purposely killed any of "her Majesties Liege people not being Negroes, Mulattos or slaves." (Mackey, 1982: 14–15)

After the discovery of a slave conspiracy in New York City in 1712, eighteen slaves and nine whites (coconspirators) were executed. Four of the slaves were burned alive, perhaps reflecting a need not only to punish the slave conspirators, but to destroy the devilish evil they embodied.[18] In the aftermath of the uprising, the laws governing slave behavior were made more rigorous. But this did not prevent a recurrence of slave unrest.

In 1740, the population of New York City was about twelve thousand people, about two thousand of whom were slaves (Daniels, 1990: 106). It was in this setting that the slave conspiracy of 1741 was uncovered.[19] The response by the government was aimed not only at punishing those who were said to have conspired, but at reducing the likelihood of future conspiracies. Thirty-one slaves and five whites (coconspirators) were executed.

Daniels (1990: 106) observes that "New York's brief code was nearly as strict as those of the Deep South." During this period when the presence of large numbers of slaves was a concern, slaves in New York were subject to "unique capital laws" (Mackey, 1982: 19). That is, they could receive the death penalty for offenses that were related to their status as slaves—for example, "the mutilation or dismember of free citizens" (Mackey, 14–15). However, the 1780s and 1790s brought reforms in New York's slave laws. In 1813, the New York legislature—following a "gradual manumission" process—declared July 4, 1827, as the day when slavery would end in the state. Although New York would continue to be implicated in the illegal slave trade,[20] like the other northern states, it was now free of the fear of slave insurrections.

The South was not. By 1831, there had been several major scares, such as the Stono Rebellion in South Carolina in 1739. In the wake of this rebellion

> which confirmed white fears of the potential for a massive slave revolt, most colonies passed laws designed to crush even the possibility of slave rebellion. As a part of the deterrent process, the southern colonies also created elaborate surveillance systems . . . local militia units. (Frey, 1991: 16)

But in November 1775, a proclamation by Lord Dunsmore, the British governor of Virginia, that offered freedom to those blacks who would join the British war effort, "raised the specter of a wholesale flight of slaves to the British colors." The proclamation caused slaveowners to fear "slave mutinies and massacres" (Mullen, 1973: 13). Then in 1800, whites in Richmond, Virginia, were shocked by the discovery of conspiracy led by a black man named Gabriel. In 1822, ex-slave Denmark Vesey plotted a rebellion of slaves in Charleston, South Carolina. And finally came Nat Turner's Rebellion—the event that would send shock waves through the South.[21]

Since the Revolutionary War, when the British had done the unthinkable by offering slaves who would fight for the loyalist cause both arms and their freedom, the South had lived in dread that the slaves would form alliances with outsiders—foreign governments, Indian tribes, northern abolitionists. The slave revolution in Saint Domingue (Haiti) that had toppled the government there was seen as a vision of what could happen in the South.[22] But the allies available to the slaves on the North American mainland were reduced as France and Spain ceded the territories that they held. Slaves had sometimes found refuge with Native American tribes,[23] and the alliance of the Seminoles with black slaves in Florida proved the United States government with one of its costliest campaigns (see Frey, 1991). But although the Seminoles and the blacks who had found sanctuary with them offered a spirited resistance, the general threat of black–Indian alliances was reduced with the removal of the Native American tribes to lands west of the Mississippi River.

Escaped slaves sometimes managed to create pockets of resistance in "maroon" communities. These communities of runaway slaves "harassed the slaveholders in the Old South from the seventeenth century to the end of their regime" (Genovese, 1979: 68). From these encampments, they engaged in guerrilla warfare against area plantations and farms. But because of the topography of the southern United States, these communities were more difficult to maintain than those that had been established by escaped slaves in the mountains and jungles of Latin America. Escaped slaves were able to establish strong guerrilla bases in the Dismal Swamp, along the Virginia–North Carolina border, in the seventeenth century.[24] But by the late antebellum period, these communities had "shrunk to the status of a nuisance." Following a similiar pattern, in Georgia and South Carolina during the eighteenth century, small groups of escaped slaves waged "sporadic warfare, suffering blows, and regrouping without being able to develop and consolidate major war camps like those of Palmares or the interior colonies of Jamaica, Surinam, or Saint-Domingue" (Genovese, 67–68). In the nineteenth century, maroon activity in the United States was focused in Louisiana and Florida, "where the Seminole Indians offered refuge to fleeing blacks and produced a major confrontation with white power" (Genovese, 68–69). However, other than during the Seminole Wars, maroon activity seems to have been longest lived and most effective during periods of upheaval such as that created by the Revolutionary War (see Frey, 1991).

At any time, a black man or woman or a group of blacks who considered active resistance to enslavement had to weigh the cost. Keve (1986: 12) writes:

> The crime by slaves which brought the greatest fear to whites was any type of insurrection whether by groups of slaves or just solitary attacks. The laws allowed, and the courts freely ordered execution of any slave who attacked his master.

Or her master—in 1746, the governor of Virginia commissioned a court of oyer and terminer to hear the murder charge against a slave named Eve, accused of poisoning her master's milk. Although the court believed she had been "led and seduced by the instigation of the Devil," they, nevertheless, found her guilty. Eve had not been allowed representation. No one spoke for her before she was sentenced to "be drawn upon a hurdle to the place of execution and there to be burnt" (quoted in Keve, 13).

A frontal attack on the system was a risky business. As we will discuss in the next chapter, after weighing their options, many slaves chose a less direct approach.[25]

CONCLUSIONS

Describing the oppression of African Americans during slavery, a former slave said, "The white man was the slave's jail" (Rawick, quoted in Schwarz, 1988: 12). The institution of slavery was supported by a legal system that made African Americans not only unfree laborers, but prisoners in a world in which all white men (until proved otherwise) stood as their guards and wardens. In this system, on the large plantations, overseers and drivers supervised the slaves. As Schwarz (1988: 10) observes:

> The latter men resembled policemen on the beat. . . . All of them would keep their jobs, maintain their "professional" reputations and retain their privileges only as long as they controlled the slaves.

If the overseers failed to control the slaves, there was the militia and—as a last resort—the power of the federal military. It was a brave slave indeed who dared challenge the walls of his prison by rising up and striking out at the system. Cunning was required. Nat Turner, who in the memory of African Americans symbolizes the slave rebel, was a master of this necessary cunning. He was "Preacher Nat" to his fellow slaves.

> Around whites he cultivated a different veneer, playing the roles . . . which whites expected of slaves. So long as Nat appeared the gifted fool, the harmless "dreamer of dreams," as one white man called him, then the whole white community would leave him alone to preach. (Oates, 1975: 39)

But what Nat Turner was preaching was the gospel of freedom. He led an insurrection of slaves whose goal was to tear down the walls of their prison.[26] This bold path was not the one most slaves chose. However, as Genovese (1979: 1) observes:

> Nothing could be more naive—or arrogant—than to ask why a Nat Turner did not appear on every plantation in the South, as if, from the comfort of our living rooms, we have a right to tell others, and retrospectively at that, when, how, and why to risk their lives and those of their loved ones.

Armed resistance was one choice African Americans slaves could make. However, another form of resistance—day-to-day resistance—was often a more realistic response in a world in which "the white man was the slave's jail."

NOTES

1. See, for example, Hay et al. (1975) on crime and society in eighteenth-century England and the conflict between the ruling class and the masses.

2. However, Boles (1983: 18) argues that with improved survival rates (i.e., as the populace of the colonies became more adept at surviving disease, starvation, and other threats to life), masters reached a point at which they found it more cost-effective to buy a slave and have his or her labor for life than to purchase the temporary labor of an indentured servant.

3. Also see Frey (1991: 14–15). Roger Daniels (1990: 106) states:

Although the English common law did not recognize slavery and in the celebrated Somerset case, Lord Mansfield, a British judge, ruled in 1772 that all slaves held in England must be set free, with the double standard that came to characterize British imperialism on racial matters, slavery in British colonies took on the full color of law.

4. According to Davis and Graham (1995: 2), "More than one fourth of the delegates to the constitutional convention . . . owned slaves."

5. For a discussion of "the economics of slavery" and its relationship to American capitalism see Ransom (1989, chapter 3). Also see Fogel (1989).

6. As F. Woods (1990) points out, religion would later be used to develop one of the arguments used in defense of slavery. In the nineteenth century, proslavery advocates would argue with reference to biblical scripture that

the transatlantic slave trade appeared to be a reenactment and fulfillment of ancient law; it was the Africans' status as "strangers," that is, *outsiders*, that made them ideal candidates for bondage. (Woods, 45)

Also see Schwarz (1988: 12) concerning the attempt by Baptist and Methodist denominations to "justify their failure to abolish slaveholding among their white members by claiming to be the special means of morally uplifting the slave members."

7. For discussion of manumission of slaves by masters in post-Revolutionary Maryland see Phillips (1993).

8. A "Herrenvolk democracy" is a concept formulated by the sociologist Pierre L. van den Berghe "to explain the reconciliation of racist and democratic ideologies in America." Such a society operates democratically for the master class and tyrannically for other groups (Berzon, 1978: 18).

9. See for example Hoffer (1984) on the pressure placed on courts in early eighteenth-century Richmond with "full deployment of a chattel slave system and a flood of black slaves into Richmond County." Hoffer describes local justice as "buckling under the strain" (vii). As the system of slavery evolved, legislatures in South Carolina, North Carolina, and later Georgia created "freeholder courts" that tried slaves without a grand jury or a trial jury (Hoffer, xiv–xlvi).

10. Written in response to queries from the secretary of the French legation in Philadelphia, rather than for his fellow Americans, Jefferson's *Notes on Virginia* was published first in Paris (1785), then in London (1787), and then a "pirated edition" made its way to Philadelphia (O'Reilly, 1995: 21). See Jordan (1968) on attitudes of Jefferson and other white colonials toward blacks. Also see Snowden (1983) for discussion of what he describes as a period "before color prejudice."

11. However, as Oakes (1990: 7) points out,

the legal kinlessness of the slaves created special problems in the Old South precisely because slaves did form strong family ties, and because those family ties formed the nucleus of a slave community and the culture that resisted the intrinsically dehumanizing tendencies of slavery itself.

12. See Frey (1991) on the creation of laws as a reaction to behavior by slaves.

13. See Morris (1996) on the use of the concept of a slave's stealing himself by two scholars, Peter Wood and Philip J. Schwarz, and the way the offense was actually defined by southern lawmakers.

14. As is common in violent events such as rebellions and riots, there is minor disagreement about the actual number of people killed. For example, Stone (1992)

places it at "fifty-seven whites murdered in the three-day revolt." Stone states that "[a]ll sources agree" that a young woman named Margaret Whitehead was "the sole person that Nat Turner himself killed" (10–11). Among other scholars, Parker (1993) agrees with the figure of fifty-seven whites killed. However, Axelrod and Phillips (1992) report that the rebels committed "sixty murders and sent bolts of terrors throughout the slave South." They add that in response "whites went on their own rampage, killing and torturing innocent blacks. Turner and about fifty of his rebels were caught in the avengers' net and twenty were quickly convicted and hanged" (110).

15. According to Oakes (1990: 153–154), "New World slave rebellions usually reflected the African tribal loyalties that survived within the slave community. . . . With slaves born in the Americas—creoles—the ethnic identities that sustained organized revolt diminished." Oakes suggests that this "is probably the most significant reason for the differences between patterns of rebellion in the South and other New World slave societies." In the South, by the nineteenth century, many slaves were American-born.

16. Slaveholders placed a bounty on Walker: "A reward of one thousand dollars was offered for Walker's head and ten times that amount was offered if he was captured alive" (Mays, 1969 [1938]). Distribution of his pamphlet in the South was made a crime (Hornsby, 1972: 15). Even before the Walker episode, southern cities had placed restrictions upon black seamen who arrived on ships in their ports. It was a matter of concern that the black seamen, if allowed to mingle with the slave population, might have an undesirable influence (Bolster, 1990). As for David Walker, when he died of a sudden and mysterious affliction, "[a]lmost all of black Boston was convinced the dauntless crusader had been poisoned" (Harding, 1983: 94). However, Hinks (1997) points out that although there is "a great body of lore" about David Walker's death, apparently no one has checked such claims against death records for the city of Boston, which list Walker as dying of consumption. Hinks asserts that the available sources "strongly support a natural death from a common and virulent urban disease of the nineteenth century" (269–270). As for the matter of whether or not black seamen were involved in the distribution of Walker's pamphlet in the South, Hinks argues that it was more likely that the pamphlets were distributed by sympathetic white seamen because in cities such as Charleston, black sailors were under too much surveillance to be able to distribute such materials (145–149).

17. As Crunden (1994: 84) states, "For the abolitionist leaders, sin and evil were the real issues, and Christian conversion the goal." In other words, they saw slavery as a sin, and their goal was to cleanse the land of this sin—ideally, by convincing the slaveholders of the evil inherent in holding blacks in bondage.

18. See McMillan (1994: 113) for his discussion of white fear of the "magical powers of Blacks." He asserts, "Burning was not a punishment for White arsonists, nor was it used against Whites who participated in uprisings against the enslavement of Africans. . . . The punishment of immolation was reserved for the so-called satanic Blacks." He adds, "In white ideology, Blacks were morphologically and culturally associated with Satan." McMillan's article focuses on witchcraft in colonial New England, where blacks were accused of witchcraft but none was executed. We should note here the presence of several black women among those accused in the Salem witch trials of 1692. There has been some scholarly controversy around the racial identity of Tituba, the first person to be accused. Although in the late nineteenth

and early twentieth centuries, she was identified by historians and novelists as African American or at least part Negro, recent research indicates she was Carib Indian. See works of Petry (1964), Starkey (1950), and Breslaw (1996). Feminists scholars have claimed Tituba as a symbol of resistance; see Breslaw (1996) and Condé (1994).

19. Acts of arson had been occurring in the city. However, Genovese (1979: 4) argues that the conspiracy "seems largely to have been a figment of white hysteria."

20. See Vinson (1996) on the arrival and departure of slave ships from New York harbors and the response of magistrates.

21. See Oates (1975). Also see Boney (1984: 110–111) on white reaction to the rebellion and the factors that served to "moderate" their responses.

22. Slaveholders were uneasy about the arrival of white émigrés from Saint Domingue who brought their supposedly loyal black servants with them.

23. Regarding these slave–Indian alliances, Franklin (1956: 29) writes:

> Whites on the Southern frontier not only lived under the constant fear of Indian attacks, but also were distressed by the presence of fugitive slaves among the Indians. . . . The presence of Indian tribes near the plantations created an aggravating situation which the planters were determined to eradicate. This constituted an important motive of their support of the federal government's removal policy.

24. See also Leaming (1995) on maroon communities in Virginia and the Carolinas.

25. See Aptheker (1977) on slave rebellions. Also see Palmer (1994) on resistance among the first blacks in the Americas.

26. In the 1960s, during the civil rights era, the white writer William Styron's novel (1966) about Nat Turner drew the wrath of some African American scholars (Clarke, 1968), who asserted that Styron had sullied the image of an authentic African American hero.

CHAPTER 2

The Slave Community

In the years following the Civil War, white southerners remembered with nostalgia and affection "Mammy," the faithful female slave who had been "like one of the family." She had nursed white babies, cared for white adults in sickness and death, been always loyal to her beloved mistress and master. In collective white southern memory, she stood in the doorway barring the marauding Yankees from the plantation house.[1] But the plantation house had fallen on hard times. The South had lost a war and a way of life. Rising battered from defeat, the postwar South embraced "the cult of the Lost Cause" (Ely, 1991: 17). Among the saints of that religion was the black "Mammy." Every religion requires its mythical figures.

This is not to say that the black mammy never existed. Of course, there were female house slaves who served the white family. Of course, these slave women sometimes developed ties of affection to members of the family. But the image of Mammy that became a part of postbellum Civil War mythology was a creation of the white southern mind. Like other slave "types"—Uncle Tom, Sambo, Topsy, Jezebel, even Nat—the mammy became a stereotype of literature and minstrel shows.[2] These stereotypes supported the South's postwar ideology. They also reflected the lack of knowledge that had existed among slaveholders about the interior lives of their black slaves.

THE WEARING OF THE MASK[3]

Southern slaveholders wanted to believe that they knew their slaves. One of their abiding fears was that they did not. The obstacle slaveholders faced was that their slaves did not wish to be known. As Olaudah Equiano[4] wrote in his 1789 autobiography:

When you make men slaves you deprive them of half of their virtue, you set
them in your own conduct an example of fraud, [plunder], and cruelty and
compel them to live with you in a state of war. (Equiano, 1789)

Only occasionally did this war erupt into violent rebellion by the slaves.
In tranquil times, it appeared to be no war at all. Yet there was always
uncertainty—the fear that even the most trusted slave might be a "domestic
enemy"—a "Jacobin" plotting an attack on the institution of slavery.[5] However, this element of deception in the master–slave relationship might flow
in both directions. Greenberg (1996: 32) observes:

Consider the issue of lies in the relationship between masters and slaves. We
know a great deal about the way slaves undertook the activity of "puttin' on
ole massa," but we have paid less attention to the ways the master engaged in
"puttin' on ole slave." Some slaves believed that masters generally told the
truth, but most understood that masters were not always what they seemed.

The lies the master told included broken promises to allow a slave to
purchase himself or not to sell a slave's child or to free a slave on the master's
death. The slave knew that much of the power in the relationship resided
in the hands of the slaveowner, who had both law and custom on his side.
Our focus in this chapter is on these interactions between black slaves and
elite white slaveholders. As Wilson (1978: 13–14) states:

Because white laborers lacked power resources in the southern plantation economy, their influence on the form and quality of racial stratification was minimal
throughout the antebellum and early postbellum periods. Racial stratification
therefore reflected the relationships established between blacks and white ar-
istocracy, relationships which were not characterized by competition for scarce
resources but by the exploitation of black labor.[6]

In his interactions with this exploited black labor, the gentleman slaveholder endeavored to characterize his behavior as honorable. An "intimate
relationship" existed between "honor and power in white male Southern
culture" (Greenberg: 25). Honor meant that the slaveholder was careful of
the image he projected to the world. To maintain his honor, the southern
gentlemen wore a "mask" that concealed his true feelings (Greenberg: 25).
At the same time, he possessed the power to "forcibly and publicly . . . dis-
honor [his] slaves" (Greenberg: 33).[7]
This dishonoring involved all of the rituals of degradation that not only
stripped away the slave's mask of deception but often literally stripped away
the slave's garments to expose the naked body to the eyes, touch, and whip
of the slaveholder. In her narrative, Harriet Jacobs, who resisted the advances
of her lustful master, relates to her readers the tale of this pursuit. It began
when she was fifteen. Her owner, a fifty year old doctor, began to whisper

to her of his intent: "He told me I was his property, that I must be subject to his will in all things" (quoted in Greenberg, 37).

The knowledge that even a benevolent master believed his slaves "subject to his will" and might under circumstances in which his authority was challenged use the whip provided slaves with justification for engaging in deception. "Fooling old master" was perceived not only as a battle of wits, but as a matter of physical and psychological survival. As the words of an old slave song said:

> Got one mind for white folks to see,
> 'Nother for what I know is me;
> He don't know me, he don't know my mind. (quoted in Levine, 1977: xiii)

In this battle of wits, to keep his or her mind sacrosanct was key to the slave's psychological survival.

Yet, even if he was aware of a deception by a slave, a slaveholder might be willing to indulge it. This was especially the case if the slave's mask was one of "subservience" (Greenberg: 33). Such accommodation by the master of the slave's deception should not be interpreted as altruism. Indulging the deception allowed the "benevolent" master to avoid dealing with the matter of punishment of the slave's misdeeds. It allowed him to take part with the slave in the rituals of domination and subservience that reinforced the master's status as a man of honor and the slave's status as an inferior. These rituals were displayed in the distribution of rations, clothing, and occasional gifts by the master to his slaves (Joyner, 1984: 109–110). They included the presence of the master and his family at the slaves' funerals, weddings, and holiday dances and the performance by the master of burial services and wedding ceremonies. These rituals and others established the power of the master and the dependence of the slave (Greenberg, 1996; Wyatt-Brown, 1982).

But even when such rituals were routinely engaged in, even when the slave showed subservience and the master benevolence, there was still the matter of the mask. Did the master always know when the slave was deceiving him? Could the slave trust even the most kindly master? Both master and slave thought not.

SUBVERTING SLAVERY

Frey (1991: 12) writes, "For the slaveholding elite, the central dilemma was how to defend slavery against slaves." The elite white slaveholders possessed power. They had a criminal justice system and a political system that supported the institution of slavery. Aside from the whips in their own hands, they were able to call upon the coercive force of overseers, black drivers, "paddyrollers," local and state militias, and the federal military.[8] But controlling slaves remained a problem. Slavery—even in the South—was never a "total institution."[9] From the beginning, slaves and their allies challenged the system.

The Achilles heel of the institution of slavery was that although slaves were legally "property," they persisted in asserting their right to possess themselves. They continued to behave like men and women and in doing so forced the slaveowner and the criminal justice system to acknowledge their humanity. Rendered "kinless" by law, they persisted in forming families and creating communities. The slave community provided a base from which to challenge the institution of slavery.[10]

THE SLAVE COMMUNITY

"Sometimes I feel like a motherless child," goes a line from a Negro spiritual.

The escaped slave Frederick Douglass related that his father was thought to have been his white master, his mother was a slave woman:

> My mother and I was separated when I was but an infant—before I knew her as my mother. It is a common custom, in the part of Maryland from which I ran away, to part children from their mothers at a very early age. (1845: 24)

After this separation, Douglass saw his mother only four or five more times—when she stole away to see him at night. She walked twelve miles each way, knowing that she risked a whipping if she were not in the field at sunrise (Douglass, 25).

Eventually, Douglass had a final parting from his mother. But he, like other motherless children in the slave community, was not alone. The community provided an extended family made up of blood relatives and of "fictive kin"—pseudo aunts, uncles, grandparents, and cousins.[11] These other adults and children provided the motherless child with love and care (see Gutman, 1976: 217–226).

There is some historical debate about how effectively the slave community functioned and the degree of cohesion and unity it was able to achieve.[12] The nature of the community depended on the nature of the environment in which it developed. The slave community in America developed slowly. During the seventeenth century, the slaves imported into the colonies were predominantly young males. They often shared living quarters with white indentured servants. They worked with them, ate with them, sometimes had sex with and became runaways with them.

Those slaves who entered the mainland colonies from the West Indies had already been "seasoned"—acculturated—to the slave system. They spoke some English and would have been able to communicate with the white indentured servants and free laborers with whom they worked. But even the slaves who came directly from Africa into the North American colonies lived with white servants and white masters in situations that made it difficult to establish African communities. During the seventeenth century, many slaves lived on isolated farms and plantations. There was also a gender imbalance of male slaves outnumbering females (Boles, 1988: 6). This imbalance continued until the eighteenth century.[13]

When the slave community did begin to evolve, its structure was affected by factors such as the agriculture, geography, and racial demography of the region. In the lowcountry of South Carolina and Georgia, malaria and other diseases were prevalent. It was not an environment that whites considered healthy. Therefore, blacks were often left under the supervision of overseers and black drivers. The task requirements of growing rice were different from those of tobacco growing in the Chesapeake and Piedmont regions. The black population, particularly in South Carolina, outnumbered the whites. In the South Carolina lowcountry, the slaves were able to form communities on the plantations in which many of the aspects of African culture were incorporated into the architecture of slave villages, the food cooked, and the creole language (Gullah) spoken.[14] In areas such as Williamsburg, Virginia, the situation of the slaves was different and the nature of the community reflected the closer interaction of the slaves with whites.

But for all of the African slaves and their descendants a "creolization" process took place as they engaged in cultural exchange with the Europeans and with Native Americans.[15] A new people, African Americans—with a culture that reflected both their African heritage and their acculturation to America—was being born. This African American culture was reflected in the speech, music, religion, folklore, and even the dress of the slaves.[16]

Their African heritage and the shared experience of bondage provided cohesion to this ethnic community. At the same time, there were forces that threatened its unity. As in any small community, tensions and jealousies existed in slave communities. Because of the unique position of the slaves, these tensions and jealousies were sometimes related to differences such as skin color (and white parentage) and status. Much has been made of the divisions that existed between house slaves and field hands. One argument advanced is that the house servants—some of whom were the mulatto relatives of the white family—enjoyed not only higher status but better food, clothing, and living conditions than the field hands. The argument goes that because of their close association with the white family, the house slaves developed loyalties to the family. For this reason, they could not be trusted by the slave community. House slaves were—to put it colloquially—the "white man's niggers." They were his spies and informants.[17]

However, recent historical research suggests that the life of the house slave was sometimes more oppressive than that of the field hand. The house slave was under the watchful eyes of the mistress of the house. He or she was subject to the abuse of the master. In the case of the female slave, the sexual abuse of the master sometimes prompted the jealous rage of the mistress (Weiner, 1996: 286–287). Even in those conditions where no ongoing physical and sexual abuse occurred, the house slave was constantly at the "beck and call" of the white family. By contrast, the field hand—although he or she worked long, hard hours—could usually count on escaping to the relative privacy and freedom of "slave row" come sundown.[18] The house slave's day might sometimes extend long into the evening hours—particularly if he or she was a personal servant who lived in the master's house.

However, there is evidence that some house slaves used their positions for the benefit of the slave community. In intimate contact with the white master and his family, they were able to serve as the eyes and ears of the slave community, providing information not only about the master's plans but about changing political conditions that might affect the slaves. This was especially the case when whites became so comfortable with the presence of black servants that they were rendered "invisible."[19]

In their constant contact with the white family, some house slaves became valued and trusted servants. Because of this some white masters and mistresses broke the law by teaching a favored servant to read and write. This knowledge allowed house slaves not only to read the newspapers that came into the house but to forge passes for themselves and for other slaves. A slave who could read and write was in a position to create or seize an opportunity to obtain freedom for herself and others.

Sometimes a house slave gave whites reason to doubt the wisdom of living on such intimate terms with blacks. Sometimes a house slave slipped poison into the soup or took part in a conspiracy to revolt. Sometimes a trusted house slave—the family's carriage driver or the children's mammy—was not as loyal or as devoted as the mythology of the postbellum South would have us believe. House slaves often had ties of blood and kinship to the slaves who toiled in the fields. The house slave like the field slave was faced with the dilemma of bringing children into a world in which they would live in bondage.

RAISING THE SLAVE CHILD

Even though the life expectancy for both whites and blacks showed a steady increase during the era of slavery, the mortality rate for black slave children remained high. In the correspondence of slave masters there are references to "overlaying"—cases in which a slave mother, sharing her bed with an infant, rolled over on the baby during the night and smothered it.[20] The slave masters and their overseers complained of the carelessness of the slave mothers. Modern medical knowledge would suggest, however, that many of these cases might have been not the carelessness of an exhausted woman but sudden infant death syndrome (SIDS).

Perhaps some of the deaths of infants were deliberate. Perhaps some slave mothers made the choice to kill a child. A few cases in which slave mothers were accused of the murder of a child were prosecuted in southern courts. However, most mothers did not make that choice.[21] Despite high rates of mortality, enough slave children were born and survived to make the slave population in the United States self-sustaining. In fact, after the end of the foreign slave trade in 1808, enough slave babies were being born to support a domestic slave trade.[22]

But from the time of conception, the slave child was at risk. This was so even when the master placed enough monetary value on slave offspring or was simply humane enough to reduce the work load of a pregnant woman. The slave child was born to a mother who was often suffering from malnutrition or disease related to the environment in which she lived. Into the nineteenth century cholera epidemics caused by inadequate waste disposal and contamination were common and affected both blacks and whites. Less deadly, but chronically debilitating, was infestation by intestinal parasites. Slaves often went barefoot because of ill-fitting shoes and were exposed to the human waste–infested soil around their dwellings. From this exposure, they acquired the worms that caused intestinal diseases (Savitt, 1978).

If the slave child survived the health risks of early childhood, there were other dangers ahead. In order to survive in the hostile environment of slavery, black children born into bondage had to learn the lessons that socialized them into the slave system; they had to learn its intricate rituals. There was often a period of grace when slave children—because of their relative uselessness as field hands—were allowed to be children. While their parents were in the field or at work in the master's house, younger children were cared for by an elderly slave or perhaps one of their siblings[23] They ran and played—sometimes with white children. Often slave children were assigned as companions to the master's children, who might have no white children with whom to play. In this situation, a slave child might for a brief period be able to share some of the schooling that his white companion was receiving. The white child might even take it upon himself to instruct his slave.[24]

But as ex-slaves recall in their narratives and in oral testimony, for the slave child there eventually came a day when he or she was expected to begin to work. The slave child would be assigned duties in the household or assigned to the field (as "half a hand") to learn the work required under the watchful eye of an adult slave. Some slave children—having observed their parents and the other slaves—were eager to make the transition from childhood to adulthood.[25] For others, the transition from carefree child to laborer came as a shock.

Even before they began to labor in the field or in the master's kitchen, slave children had to learn other vital lessons—"survival tactics" (King, 1995: 67). A slave child had to learn his place. He had to learn that as a slave he was not to "talk back" to white folks. He had to learn the rules of etiquette that required that he always take off his hat before a white man and never look him directly in the eye. He had to learn that he was always to go to the back door of a white man's house. He had to learn to say "yes, sir" and "no, ma'am" not only to his elders but always to white people (King, 68; Doyle, 1971). He had to learn that he must never repeat what he heard the grown-ups say. Such learning was vital to his survival and crucial to the safety of his parents and the slave community.

Like all children, slave children sometimes misbehaved—or violated one of the norms that were specific to their status as slaves. Some masters were indulgent of children, seeing them as harmless, lazy, funny "pickaninnies." Others were as inclined to punish children as adults—believing that the control of the slave population was paramount.[26] This matter of the punishment of the slave child was particularly difficult for the parents. Ex-slaves remember the tears of their parents forced to stand helplessly by as they were whipped by a master, mistress, or overseer. On some occasions, slave parents intervened. Sometimes they were able to prevent the whipping of the child. More often they themselves were punished for their defiance.[27]

It is conceivable that the male parent found it particularly difficult to stand by while his child was punished. This is not to suggest that mothers loved their children less. However, universally, one aspect of the concept of "manhood" is that the male define himself as the protector of his children and his wife. As their postslavery testimony indicates, to watch a child or a wife being punished was difficult for black men. By the same token to have their children and their wives witness their own punishment was also bitter.

However, as a part of his socialization into the world of the slave, the child also would have learned that one of the ways in which his father—who might not always be able to defend himself or his family—could express his love for that family was by providing for them (Blassingame, 1979: 178). The hunting, fishing, and trapping that the slave man was able to do supplemented his family's diet. The produce grown in his garden plot provided the family with the vegetables that the master might not provide. Moreover, the father could teach his child the skills he himself possessed. He could teach him how to be a field hand or a craftsman.[28]

But what the child also learned was that sometimes his father, no matter how much he loved him and his mother, was unable to prevent the family from being separated. There is a great deal of debate among historians about the rate of family separation among slaves. What we do know is that economic, social, and political changes that affected certain regions of the South had an impact on rates of white migration, which in turn affected the stability of slave families. For example, in the nineteenth century many of the younger sons of white plantation owners headed west to find land that was unclaimed and had not suffered the soil erosion that had occurred in the Chesapeake and Piedmont regions. When they migrated, they took slaves with them (Goodstein, 1989: 74). Slave families were broken up, often permanently. Another common cause of slave family separation was a pressing economic situation faced by the master. The fall of tobacco prices in the Upper South left plantation owners with debts and surplus slaves. These slaves were often sold to the cotton growers in the Lower South. And then there was the disruption that was likely to occur when a master died and his estate was sold or divided among his survivors. Slaves were a part of that estate. Slave children learned early that they might be separated from their parents. This was a fear that dogged the days of the slave family.[29]

It was also one of those areas in which some negotiation with, or manipulation of, the slaveholder was possible. Slaves were sometimes able to persuade masters not to break up their families, not to sell a wife without her husband or children without their parents.[30] This type of negotiation was sometimes available to a slave who was hardworking, valuable for his or her special skills, and/or well liked by his master or mistress. The correspondence of slaveholders indicates they could sometimes be persuaded that it was in their vested interest not to separate a family and thereby upset a valued slave. Sometimes humanitarian instincts could be appealed to.

Of course, it is true that some slave masters as a matter of policy tried never to separate slave families. But expediency was often the deciding factor. During the post-Revolutionary and antebellum eras, the country experienced economic upswings and occasional depressions. These depressions could be particularly severe in the South, where the fortunes of tobacco, wheat, cotton, and rice determined the fortunes of both poor farmers and wealthy plantation owners. For plantation owners such as the former president Thomas Jefferson, who was debt-ridden but slave-wealthy, selling off slaves became a way of maintaining economic viability.

For a slave who was about to be or had been separated from family members, there was another strategy that was sometimes successful. He or she could run away. This was one way in which a slave was sometimes able to manipulate a master. When a slave ran away to join a loved one or was about to avoid being sold, the master might decide to keep the family together or to sell the slave and family to the same master or at least to the same neighborhood (Blassingame, 1979: 171). Such a strategy required that the master recognize that the slave was engaging in a form of negotiation.

The act of running away was sometimes a facet of the ongoing interplay of power and accommodation between the master and the slave community. Some slaves ran away seeking freedom. Other slaves ran away temporarily—to express their feelings about a proposed sale or to escape punishment or because they were angry at an action taken by the master (Boles, 1983: 177–178). In these cases, the runaway sometimes hid in the woods nearby. Members of the slave community might provide him with food (Litwack, 1979: 230). Another slave might act as a go-between for the master and the runaway slave. In fact, some masters took it for granted that slaves would sometimes be temporarily "absent without leave"—that they would run away and

eventually return. For example, the plantation owner James Hammond incorporated this idea into his policies for plantation management (Faust,
1992: 68).[31]

Witnessing such interactions between master and slave, the slave child
learned that for each slave the experience of bondage was different. Masters
and slaves were people who interacted within the limits of their prescribed
roles, but the personality of each was important. The slave child learned that
some slaves were more effective in engaging in acts of "day-to-day resistance" against the institution of slavery than others. Some slaves could feign
illness ("malingering"). Other could engage in "Samboish" ineptness that
resulted in broken hoes and injured livestock. Some could listen as the overseer told them how he wanted a task done and then do it their own way and
still escape punishment. Other slaves could steal the master's potatoes or his
liquor and not be detected.[32]

The slave child learned that his parents and other adults who were too
pragmatic to engage in violent and reckless acts could engage in subtle forms
of self-assertion.[33] These acts included matters as fundamental to self-esteem
as naming practices. When a master insisted on naming a child to suit his
own fancy, the slave parents might simply give their child another name that
reflected his ancestry or that was significant to the parents. That name might
be used only in the slave community, but it became the name by which the
slave child identified himself. It was his name, given to him by his parents,
not his master.[34]

The slave child learned that such psychological triumphs over the system
were important in surviving it. He also learned that his parents and other
adults found subsistence in their culture. They worshipped in the religion
services that the master approved. Often the minister was a white man who
told the child and his parents that the Bible said a servant should obey his
master.[35] But there were other services that the child was warned not to
speak about—services conducted by black preachers. These services com-
bined the religious practices and beliefs of the child's African ancestors with
those of the Christian church. The result was a religion that promised the
slaves they would be rewarded for their suffering in the hereafter. But the
religion of the black preachers also presented the slave child and his parents
with images from the Bible of which the master would not have approved—
images of warriors who led their people out of bondage.[36] The spirituals the
child heard were both comforting promises of a better life after death and
invitations to "slip away" to freedom.[37]

The spirituals were like the stories and folklore the child heard in his
cabin at night. On one hand, the tales of Brer Rabbit were about an animal
trickster who used cunning and guile. Brer Rabbit was often mean, sometimes cruel, in his dealings with other animals. But the Brer Rabbit tales also
showed the child that the weak could defeat the powerful.[38] The folktales
and the stories of John and Ole Massa provided the slaves with a humorous

release of anger and frustration (Joyner, 1984: 187–194; Levine, 1977; Earl, 1993). These stories also reminded them that knowing one's opponent was all-important. Understanding how the master thought could sometimes provide the means to get the upper hand. "Sambo" in his grinning mask might have the last laugh.

But the slave child also knew or heard stories of slaves who refused to smile. Sometimes in one reckless act of defiance, these slaves stood up and fought back. These were the slaves that the community both admired and feared: admired for their courage, feared for the wrath they might bring down on the heads of them all. But still the black men who delivered a blow for freedom were the folk heroes of the slave community. The child heard his elders whisper of Gabriel and Denmark. And about Nat Turner who had led a rebellion.[39]

CONCLUSIONS

Dillon (1990: 88) writes:

> By its very nature, slavery involved a contest of wills. The will of the owners who were intent on commanding respect, subservience, and labor from their slaves, were constantly pitted against that of the bondsmen, who were struggling to retain control of their own persons and to establish bearable conditions for survival.

The communities established by the slaves helped to make their lives bearable. Within this precariously held physical and psychological space, slaves were able to be men and women, fathers and mothers. Even though slaves, such as Frederick Douglass, suffered losses and separations and witnessed brutality, they also had the opportunity to draw strength from other slaves. The slave's honor—dismissed as nonexistence by the slaveholders—was preserved in his or her interactions with others in the black community. Even in servitude, many slaves found ways of preserving their dignity and their sense of themselves as people held in bondage rather than human chattel.

This struggle to maintain dignity and sense of self was waged in an environment in which the laws offered no protection for the slave family. It was an environment in which marriage between slaves was subject to the whim of the master, in which the status of the child followed that of the slave mother,[40] in which the slave who came to the defense of a spouse or a child risked punishment that might entail sale or even death. In this environment, in which they were legal nonpersons, the slave family and the slave community contrived to survive.

NOTES

1. See Turner (1994) for discussion of this image of the black mammy in the film *The Birth of a Nation* (1915).

2. Boskin (1986: 86) reports that minstrel shows were performed in the 1930s in the Federal Industrial Institution for Women (federal prison) in Alderson, West Virginia: "Directed by the authorities, the inmates enacted such shows as *Wotta Night* (1933) and *Down in Haiti* (1935)." A prison official noted on one occasion that "the colored girls gave their customary good entertainment."

3. This theme of wearing the mask is one that continued to appear in African American folklore and literature even in the aftermath of slavery. For example, Paul Laurence Dunbar titles a poem "We Wear the Mask."

4. Equiano escaped from slavery and eventually joined the British abolitionist movement.

5. In the wake of Nat Turner's rebellion, one white southerner described Negroes as the "Jacobins of the country"—"anarchists" (Oates, 1975: 43).

6. See also Bolton (1994) on poor whites in the antebellum South as tenants and laborers. Regarding white southern laborers, Chambers (1993: 136) writes:

> Confronted, on the one side, with competition from black labor and, on the other with some influx of foreign immigrants and Northern labor, the position of white labor in the South steadily deteriorated in the ante-bellum period. The editor of the *Charleston Mercury* wrote that slavery was the natural condition of all labor. He was hung in effigy for his honesty.

7. In fact, Greenberg asserts, slaves were seen as lacking honor. Along this same line, Patterson (1982: 78) writes, "The idea that a person's honor is more valuable than his life, and that to prefer life to honor betrays a degraded mind, comes close to being a genuinely universal belief. It is a theme that haunts Western literature." The slave was by this standard degraded because "it was the choice of life over honor that the slave or his ancestor made." However, slaveholders—who prided themselves on their possession of honor—sometimes took to the dueling field to avenge perceived wrongs that (even by contemporary standards) were hardly worth dying over. The concept of honor in this slave culture became distorted.

8. See Franklin (1956) on "the militant South."

9. Stanley Elkins's (1963) comparison of the southern system of plantation slavery to a concentration camp and his description of the obedient, nonresisting "Sambo" personality produced by this system has generated a great deal of debate among historians.

Regarding the behavior of slaves on lowcountry rice plantations, Joyner (1984: 89) finds that the slaves "were neither Sambos nor Horatio Algers. If they were efficient workers *within* the system of paternalism, they were also effective workers *of* the system, and they knew how to work it for their own ends."

See Parish (1989) on the historiography of slavery.

10. Martin and Martin (1985: 18) state:

> Four crucial elements of family life among the slaves were key to the development of caregiving in the slave community: (1) the breakdown of patriarchy and the concomitant rise of black male–female equality and cooperation, (2) the mutual aid network, (3) the prosocialization of children, and (4) status-group cooperation.

Later in this book, we will return to Martin and Martin's argument concerning the "helping ideals" that developed in the African American slave community.

11. See Genovese (1976 [1972]): 493) on the "surrogate father."

12. Aside from the disruptions in the community caused by sales, there were other

possible sources of dissension such as the differing statuses and job assignments of slaves. For example, some slaveholders used black "drivers," who were usually supervised by white overseers but who themselves supervised the work of other slaves. Joyner (1984: 67) concludes that on lowcountry rice plantations, drivers often "attempted to mediate between the other slaves on the one hand and the masters on the other."

13. See Boles (1983) on factors affecting black population growth and the emergence of black slave communities. See also Klein (1995) on African women in the Atlantic slave trade.

14. See Joyner (1984) for discussion of a South Carolina slave community.

15. See Ferguson (1992) on the archaeological reconstruction of slave communities in South Carolina and Virginia. See also Gutman (1976: 332), Mintz and Price (1976), Joyner (1984), and Sobel (1987). Sobel argues that in colonial Virginia an intense interaction occurred between the slaves and whites, masters and others, with whom they worked and lived. This interaction resulted in a creolization of the worldviews of not only the slaves but the whites. For example, perceptions of time and of work held by the whites were modified by their interaction with slaves.

16. See White and White (1995) regarding slave hairstyles.

17. See Smitherman (1994). In the 1960s, Malcolm X would use these terms to describe his contemporaries.

18. Even the slave's cabin was not always a safe place. It too was subject to intrusion by the slaveowner and other whites, such as overseers. A slave woman might be raped in her own cabin. See McLaurin (1991) for the case of Celia, a slave woman charged with the murder of the master who had purchased her when she was fourteen, raped her repeatedly, and forced her to bear two children. Pregnant with her (and her master's) third child, Celia resisted her master's advances, killing him in the process. Celia was convicted of murder. Her execution was delayed until after her child was born. The child was stillborn. Celia was hanged. See also Higginbotham (1996: 99–101).

19. Frey (1991: 50) writes:

> Table talk listened to by domestic slaves, conversations overheard by slave attendants or musicians, was quickly carried back to the slave quarters and was rapidly disseminated through the cross-quarters underground to other plantations, even to other colonies.

20. Savitt (1978) suggests that the fact so few cases of overlaying by white mothers are recorded may reflect the social stigma attached to this form of infant death. Cases involving white mothers may have been described in other terms.

21. Genovese (1976) suggests that among slave mothers infanticide occurred "only in some special circumstances" (497).

22. See Abreu (1996) on the debates in Rio de Janeiro over the "Free Womb" law. She discusses the slave mother's womb as "female space" the master sought to control.

23. See Blassingame (1979:181) and Mellon (1988). However, also see Savitt (1978) on the dangers to the young child who was cared for by a not much older babysitter.

24. See Mabee (1979) and Webber (1978) on the education of slave children.

25. King (1995:26) describes one of the reasons slave boys were often eager to make the transition from childhood to the world of work. Until they began to work,

the boys often were given nothing more to wear than "shirts that did not hide their nakedness." When they began to work in the fields, they were given pants.

26. Ayers (1984: 133) states:

> Masters hesitated to punish respected slaves who could foment resistance among other slaves, but hastened to make examples of troublemakers. Unfortunately for the master's consistency, however, these two kinds of slaves were not mutually exclusive.

27. Such incidents appear often in the narratives of escaped slaves and in oral history interviews with former slaves.

28. For the slaves' participation in commerce see Boland (1995), McDonnell (1988), Walsh (1995), Whitman (1993), Wiggins (1985), and Wood (1995). This was an area in which slaves were able to carve out some independent space for themselves. They could do this by hiring their labor out for money or by becoming entrepreneurs, selling produce and other goods (to their master or at market). Each of these activities had both legal and illegal possibilities. For example, a master might allow a slave to hire himself out but not comply with an ordinance requiring the master to purchase the slave a badge that would indicate his status. Or a slave might steal his master's goods to sell or trade to a willing white accomplice. Bynum (1992: 4–5) asserts:

> Illegal gambling, trafficking in illegal goods, and competing for women provided some black men with a sense of mastery over their own world and sometimes over portions of the world of their masters. Achieving success through underground commerce brought status in African American communities, particularly when it undermined white control.

29. The threat of sale and family separation was one mechanism the slaveholder could use to control an unruly slave (Jones, 1992). However, this threat was not always effective (see Starobin, 1974: 55–56). Of course, sale also could be used as a form of punishment—as in the case of slaves who were "sold down the river" to the Deep South.

30. Since marriages between slaves were not recognized by law, the master was under no legal obligation to respect the union. Black men and women whom God had joined together were often put asunder by white masters.

31. A South Carolina planter, James Hammond, master of 10,808 acres and 147 slaves, kept "extraordinarily detailed records" (Faust, 1992: 55). His plantation diaries over a twenty-year span offer clear examples of the process of resistance and accommodation engaged in by both master and slaves. Among the issues over which Hammond and his slaves struggled were the existence of a slave church, the theft of plantation goods, and the slaves' use of a black healer or of folk cures. Faust concludes, "Resistance was a tool of negotiation, a means of extracting concessions from the master to reduce the extent of his claims over black bodies and souls" (Faust, 65).

32. Regarding theft by slaves for survival, Frederick Douglass recalled:

> I had no bed. I must have perished with cold, but that the coldest nights, I used to steal a bag which was used for carrying corn to the mill. I would crawl into this bag, and there sleep on the cold, damp clay floor. (quoted in H. Bruce Franklin, 1978: 51–52)

Also see Savitt (1978: 97), who observes, "Part of the reason for food theft was, obviously, hunger." Savitt also provides a discussion of slave illnesses, real and feigned, and the efforts by masters to develop a scientific approach to the punishment of slaves (i.e., painful without causing permanent damage).

33. See Byrne (1994) on the limits of slaves' independence and slave crime in Savannah, Georgia. Whites were concerned about illegal activities by slaves, which included drinking and gambling.

34. Also see Blassingame (1979: 182), Boles (1983: 43), and Sobel (1987: 156–157). See Joyner (1984: 217) on the giving of "basket names" to be "used only among kin and friends." Joyner notes that this giving of two names not only reflected competition with the master over the right to name but followed "traditional African double-naming customs."

35. See Ayers (1984: 123–125) on church discipline of the slave who committed offenses. Also see Jones (1990).

36. Regarding the African survivals to be found in slave religion and the slaves' adaptation of the Christian faith to their needs see Genovese (1991) and Earl (1993).

37. See Mays (1969: 19–24) and Joyner (1984: 144). See F. G. Wood (1990) on the passages of the Bible favored by masters versus those favored by the slaves. For essays on slaves, masters, and religion in the South from 1740–1870, see Boles (1988). Also see Jones (1990). Regarding the slave preacher, Genovese (1991: 203) states:

> The black preachers of the Old South were of many kinds. In the cities especially we find men who . . . were in effect regular denominational ministers, at least as well trained as their white counterparts. Then there were the innumerable class leaders or assistants or prayers leaders—those who ostensibly assisted a white minister but who, more often than not, did most of the actual or at least the effective preaching to the blacks. And then there were the exhorters of all kinds, especially on the countryside—men who got the spirit and preached the Word with or without any training or guidance at all.

38. Turner (1994: 113) states, "Brer Rabbit symbolized the most successful slave, the one who could minimize his workload, maximize his food intake, and all the while escape punishment."

39. See Boles (1983:179–180) on slave types; also see Sobel (1987: 41) on the adjustment of slaves. Parish (1989: 9) states, "Among the slaves, unyielding rebelliousness or utter docility were both exceptions to the general rule; the great majority of slaves maneuvered in the broad ground between these extremes."

40. Regarding parentage, Davis (1983: 72) points out, "Birth records on many plantations omitted the names of the fathers, listing only the children's mothers. And throughout the South, state legislatures adopted the principle of *partus sequitur ventrem*—the child follows the condition of the mother."

CHAPTER 3

Free Blacks and Slavery

In both the South and the North, the destiny of free blacks was inextricably linked to that of slaves. In the North and in the Upper South and in cities of the Lower South such as Charleston and New Orleans, free blacks had established striving communities. In both North and South, a well-to-do elite maintained a "respectable" life-style. However, many other free blacks were poor. Class—and color—divisions existed within free black communities.[1] But in spite of their differences, most free blacks believed that their fate was tied to that of black slaves. Laws controlled the mobility and the status of free blacks.

This was particularly true in the South. After 1790, southerners "were less worried and irritated by Negro slaves than by Negroes who were not slaves" (Jordan, 1968: 406). In their effort to control free blacks, southern legislatures enacted laws: "Everywhere in the South the free Negro was pelted with restrictions, miscellaneous in character, growing in severity, and similar in underlying intent." In 1806–1808, Georgia mandated that free blacks would be "tried for felonies in the same manner as slaves; that in major towns they were subject to slave laws" (Jordan, 408).

Outside the South, free blacks were also under restrictions. For example, between 1804 and 1807, legislation enacted in Ohio required

blacks entering the state . . . to register themselves and their families with country clerks, to carry certificates attesting to their freedom, and to post $500 bond within twenty days of arrival in Ohio. Whites employing unregistered blacks or harboring fugitives from slavery were subject to criminal prosecution. (Gerber, 1976: 4)

Although such laws in Ohio and elsewhere were "unwieldly and generally unsuccessful in limiting black population growth," they did provide "an excellent weapon in the periodic harassment of black residents" (Gerber, 4). The mechanisms used to control free blacks also included the differential application of certain laws. Bynum (1992: 100) finds that in three counties in central Piedmont North Carolina

> more free black than white women lost custody of their children through the apprenticeship system. An unmarried mother of a black or mulatto child could certainly expect her child to be apprenticed. Between 1850 and 1860, black and mulatto children accounted for 61 percent of the children apprenticed . . . even though free black women made up only 9 percent of female-headed households.

Bynum (99) asserts that, as practiced, the apprenticeship system in these North Carolina counties functioned as both "an early attempt to institute a system of social welfare for the poor" and "an instrument of racial control."

Faced with such legal and social policy, by the nineteenth century, free blacks were engaged in a dual struggle to improve their own legal, economic, and social position and to bring about the end of slavery. Their own position had always been tenuous. In the eighteenth century most whites were inclined to believe "that Africans were by nature inferior . . . and had been so degraded under slavery that they were unfit for freedom" (Nash, 1988: 13).[2] Because of their racial heritage even light-skinned ("all but white") mulattoes were identified with the "degraded" black slave.[3] In the decades following the Revolutionary War, free blacks found themselves required to prove their worth. Because of Pennsylvania's striving black communities, both Americans and Europeans looked to "the fate of Pennsylvania's free blacks as a litmus test of environmentalist theory regarding racial differences" (Nash, 13).[4]

In urban centers such as Philadelphia, free blacks worked to create social institutions, which included independent black churches, schools, businesses, and voluntary associations. In 1816, free blacks in Philadelphia organized their first independent black church, the African Methodist Episcopal church. The church was led by Richard Allen, who had been born a slave in Philadelphia. After a humiliating experience in the white church to which they belonged, Allen and other black members withdrew to organize a church of their own.[5] Economic activity also flourished. Free black businessmen such as James Forten, a shipbuilder who employed both black and white laborers, were prosperous members of the community. Voluntary groups, such as fraternal organizations and benevolent associations, facilitated social interaction and provided "mutual aid"—such as death benefits—to members and their families (Rury, 1985; Winch, 1988).

In Boston, blacks organized themselves "to deal with local and national problems." Although the community was small in population, it was active in dealing with issues.

> Because those who constituted the community were largely poor and were excluded from many of the social services of the city, informal, cooperative solutions were found to their problems. This cooperation, which was in some ways a reaction to discrimination by the white society, became an important factor in the development of black social activism. (Horton and Horton, 1979: xi)

This activism by Boston blacks ranged from communal self-help to protest meetings and participation in the rescue of fugitive slaves. It included challenges to the segregated school system. One judicial case, *Roberts v. City of Boston*, argued by the white abolitionist Charles Sumner for the black father of a five year old child named Sarah, anticipated the arguments that would be made over a hundred years later in *Brown v. Board of Education* (Horton and Horton, 72).[6] Other responses to oppression by the African American community in Boston included the formation in 1826 of the Massachusetts General Colored Association. This association numbered among its members the fiery David Walker. In the mid-1830s, the association engaged in collective legal action "to protect black seamen travelling to slave states."[7] In 1842, African Americans in Boston founded the Freedom Association; membership was "widely representative of the community." The activities of the association "were clearly illegal, and at times violent. . . . Yet, members saw the Freedom Association as legitimate antislavery work. Funds for its operation came from black contributions" (Horton and Horton, 99). The mandate of the association was to provide "food, clothing, shelter and other aid" to escaped slaves. Members engaged in such dramatic feats as the rescue of an escaped slave named Shadrach from a courtroom where his hearing was taking place. Federal charges were brought against the two leaders of the rescue. They were defended by Richard Henry Dana and John P. Hale. The jury was unable to reach a verdict in the case of one of the men and acquitted the other. "Years later Dana learned that at least two jurors had refused to convict the defendants" (Horton and Horton, 105).

In Boston, Philadelphia, New York City, and other urban centers, an emerging black press served the needs of the ethnic community, addressing the social and economic issues that were of concern to the middle class. These newspapers also instructed readers in self-improvement and behavior (Hutton, 1993). However, the abolition of slavery was a key concern. For the black middle class, "the advancement of the race" depended not only on factors such as the education of black youth but, crucially, on the abolition of slavery. In May 1827, in New York City, the first black newspaper, *Freedom's Journal*, was founded in response to the treatment African Americans were receiving in the white press. Mordecai Manuel Nash, the publisher of an influential newspaper, *The New York Enquirer*, had been using his newspaper to air his proslavery views. He "consistently vilified blacks in every possible form of human degradation in the press" (Senna, 1993: 15).[8] A small group of free blacks decided to publish their own newspaper so that they would have a forum in which to speak for their race. The editors of this newspaper were the Reverend Samuel Cornish and John B. Russwurm. In the prospectus announcing the newspaper, the editors wrote:

> Daily slandered, we think there ought to be some channel of communication between us and the public through which a single voice may be heard in defense of five hundred thousand free people of color. (quoted in Senna, 1993: 16)[9]

In the South, this newspaper was considered "subversive literature." Blacks could be arrested if found with a copy (Senna, 18). As with other steps toward institution building, the creation of the black press took place in an atmosphere of racial hostility.

Regarding this hostility, in the early nineteenth century "Negrophobia" was emerging as a potent force in urban life. However, white dislike and fear of blacks were not new phenomena. In 1726, white Philadelphians had expressed their unease about the free blacks who lived among them with an "Act for the Better Regulating of Negroes in This Province." The preamble to the act stated, "'Tis found by experience that free negroes are an idle, slothful people and often prove burdensome to the neighborhood and ill examples to other negroes [slaves]" (quoted in Nash, 1988: 35).

This attitude toward free blacks was echoed in other cities, North and South. In southern cities such as Charleston, free blacks and urban slaves enjoyed more freedom and mobility in the cities than did blacks who lived in rural areas. They often worked alongside white laborers and sometimes lived in poor, racially mixed neighborhoods. But by the nineteenth century, free blacks and slaves who hired themselves out or were hired out by their masters were becoming an economic threat to white laborers, some of whom were themselves recent immigrants.[10]

In northern cities, the sporadic racial violence between blacks and whites often seemed to be lower class clashes along boundary lines between groups competing for both space and jobs. But, as Nash (1988: 223) notes of Philadelphia, Negrophobia was supported by the attitudes of white politicians and intellectual leaders who were also hostile toward blacks.

The response of well-to-do free blacks to this hostility was to seek respectability.[11] For example, in 1809, the Society for the Suppression of Vice and Morality was established by the black elite in Philadelphia. Aware that they were being judged by the worst element of their race, they felt growing concern about some of the new arrivals to the city. These newcomers spoke in southern dialect, drank and gambled, dressed flamboyantly, sometimes ran afoul of the law, affected a body language—the sauntering gait, unrestrained singing, and laughing, and exuberant dancing that set them apart from the "respectable" black society. (Nash, 219)

Ministers such as Richard Allen lectured their congregations about moral behavior. In the fashion of the ministers of Puritan New England, Allen in 1808 used the occasion of the execution of a black murderer to "thunder" at his people about their immoderate behavior. The man who was executed had come to Philadelphia from Maryland. He had killed a white woman while he was drunk (Nash: 221) His behavior was not to be emulated. But the efforts of the black upper class to uplift the lower class and to improve themselves did little to defuse the racial situation. In 1825, a stove in Richard Allen's church that had been rigged with cayenne pepper and salt exploded. Two people were killed. During the next decade "black churches would become the special targets of racist white attacks" (Nash, 227).

In 1831, in the aftermath of Nat Turner's rebellion, a bill was proposed and debated in the Philadelphia legislature to bar migrating blacks from the state and repeal the legal protections offered to fugitive slaves. Free blacks led by the businessman James Forten protested the bill (Nash, 225). In Philadelphia and the other urban centers, free blacks found themselves engaged in an ongoing battle to protect the space they had carved out for themselves. This meant that they must fight for the rights of all blacks because their own fate was so closely tied to that of the slaves. Free blacks were active participants in the abolition movement, forming their own organizations as well as working with whites in racially mixed abolitionist societies.

However, not all free blacks identified their interests with those of the antislavery struggle. Among those who did not were those few who owned slaves.[12] For example, William Ellison of Charleston had been born a slave. After obtaining his freedom, he became a cotton gin maker and the owner of a plantation. Ellison was "one of the wealthiest free persons of color in the South and wealthier than nine out of ten whites" (Johnson and Roark, 1984: xi–xii). Ellison owned "more slaves than any other free person of color in the South outside Louisiana, even more than all but the richest white planter" (xi–xii).[13]

Ellison, the former slave, was a mulatto "man of color." He did not think of himself as black. In fact, he was one of the founding members of an exclusive society that accepted as members only those of mulatto heritage. Ellison and the others in his circle of relatives, friends, and acquaintances lived well and traveled freely. As the Civil War approached, Ellison and his friends were reluctant to leave Charleston and the property they had acquired. Prior to the war, they had been able to avoid many of the more humiliating aspects of being free blacks because of their wealth and their connections with elite whites (Johnson and Roark, 1984).

Less privileged Charleston blacks suffered through the recurring episodes of legal oppression that accompanied insurrection scares. The rebellion leader Denmark Vesey had been active in the African (AME) Church of Charleston. When his conspiracy was revealed, official attention turned to this black church, which had separated from the white Methodist church in 1818. Charleston authorities "harassed the black congregation and finally closed the church in 1821" (Johnson and Roark, 38).

Free blacks in Charleston (and in other southern cities) also found themselves subject to "guardianship laws," which required that they have a white sponsor. There were also "registration laws" and "capitation tax laws." The first required the free black person to register with the local authorities. The second required free black men and women to pay what amounted to an annual tax on themselves. These laws were often not fully enforced. However, free blacks were always in the "anomalous position" of a suspect group—"Free people were supposed to be white" (Johnson and Roark, xiii).

Free black survival in the South depended on the tolerance of whites. Each time there was an outbreak of slave violence or a rumor of rebellion, attention turned not only to the slave population but to free blacks. Denmark Vesey[14] had plotted an insurrection. Other free blacks might do the same. Even if they didn't, they were a bad example for slaves. The American Colonization Society encouraged free blacks in both the South and the North not to stay where they were not wanted. The society worked to interest blacks in emigrating to Africa. It was instrumental in establishing Liberia and sending American blacks there to colonize the country. But for the most part—in spite of recurring discussion—free blacks did not eagerly embrace the colonization movement.[15] In fact, African Americans began organizing to resist this movement. As Hinks (1997: 98) observes, "The slow but steady reaction of numerous black communities against the rise of the American Colonization Society (ASC) began to weave these strands [of Masonic, religious, and benevolent ties] into an organized network."

In the decades before the war, free blacks in northern cities participated in the Negro convention movement. Meeting in locations such as Philadelphia, New York City, Rochester, and Buffalo, these conventions allowed black leaders to come together to discuss the issues that concerned them. V. P. Franklin (1984: 90) describes the conventions as having three major objectives:

> [F]irst, the organizing of free black opposition to the "black laws" being passed in several northern states; second, the examination of test strategies for advancing the free black population; and third, the discussion of the ways of bringing about an immediate end of slavery in the United States.

Black leaders such as Henry Highland Garnet saw the right to vote as crucial to black advancement and achievement of justice. In 1841, Garnet appeared before the judiciary committee of the New York assembly, "stressing the blacks' claim to full citizenship by virtue of services rendered to the country in wartime and peacetime." He asserted that the damaging effects of black disfranchisement were "discouragement, pauperism, and crime" (Swift, 1989: 125–126). This sentiment would be echoed by Frederick Douglass when he addressed the United States Congress in the aftermath of the Civil War.

However, Douglass and Garnet, in spite of their shared sentiments about the citizenship rights of blacks, were sometimes in less agreement about the most appropriate strategy for dealing with the slavery problem. In the 1840s and 1850s, the Garrisonian position of moral suasion became less acceptable to some black leaders. Douglass, who was identified with the Garrison faction, found his position challenged by Henry Highland Garnet.[16] In his 1843 "Address to the Slaves of the United States of America" before the black convention in Buffalo, Garnet (who like Douglass had been born a slave) cried, "Resistance! Resistance!" Evoking the memory of the heroic black rebels Denmark Vesey, Nat Turner, Joseph Cinque, and Madison Washington, Garnet proposed that the slaves rise up and "Strike for your lives and liberties." He urged the convention to go on record as supporting armed resistance by black slaves. The motion—opposed by Douglass, who thought the speech contained "too much physical force"—was narrowly defeated (Swift, 1989: 135–138). [17] But Douglass himself was gradually moving away from his more moderate position.[18] He could see that moral suasion had not worked. The South was becoming more intransigent on the subject of slavery. Both free blacks and fugitive slaves were in greater jeopardy than they had ever been.

In the South, white slaveholders sensed what they described as a growing restlessness among their slaves. Because of this they increased their preparedness for defense against insurrection. Militia units received more funding for new equipment; new units were formed; young white men were drilled in public squares as both black and white citizens looked on (Franklin, 1956).[19] In cities such as Charleston and New Orleans, travelers noted the overlap between the militia and the police. Throughout the South, police departments had been formed in part because of the need to provide patrols to control the activities of blacks (e.g., Rousey, 1996).

In these cities, the activities of free blacks in the South were coming under increasing scrutiny. Free blacks were subject to arrest on a variety of charges, including vagrancy. Southern states moved to make manumission more difficult and to require blacks who had been freed to leave the state within six months or a year or face reenslavement. Some free blacks in the South headed north.

So did some slaves.

NORTH TO FREEDOM

In 1849, Harriet Tubman, a Maryland slave, escaped to freedom. Tubman became known as the female Moses. Returning to the South again and again (at least twenty times), she led more than three hundred other slaves to freedom (Hornsby, 1972: 20). Tubman was one of the "conductors" on the famous Underground Railroad.[20] Abolitionists and sympathizers provided the "stations," the safe stopping places along the way, as slaves fled northward.[21]

Other slaves found their own way—in a box, in a disguise, with a forged pass. Several of these escaped slaves became important figures in the abolitionist movement. Frederick Douglass, Ellen and William Craft, and others went on the lecture circuit, speaking to white northern audiences about their experiences. They became symbols of the wrongs of slavery—living refutation of the southern claim of black degradation and ignorance.

These fugitives also wrote about their lives. These "slave narratives" were accounts of the fugitive's experiences in "the house of bondage" and his or her escape to freedom. The narratives became best-sellers during the antebellum period (Foster, 1994: ix) and would later influence postbellum black autobiography and prison literature (Franklin, 1978).

Foster identifies four major reasons for the popularity of this genre. The narratives: (1) were useful "for the religious and moral education and persuasion of their readers"; (2) "provided details about the life-styles and attitudes of southern whites and blacks"; (3) satisfied the public's appetite for sensationalism; and (4) were financially advantageous to publishers, who "encouraged sales through various promotional techniques" (Foster, 20–21).

Many people who read the narratives were not committed to the antislavery cause. But the narratives, along with antislavery tracts, pamphlets, and newspapers, fueled the sectional debate. The South retaliated with its own outpouring of proslavery literature. The rhetoric escalated. Eventually, Harriet Beecher Stowe, who modeled her Uncle Tom on an escaped slave, would enter the fray with her *Uncle Tom's Cabin*.[22]

At the same time, the political situation was worsening. In the 1830s, there was increased racial violence in the North, at its worst in Philadelphia in August 1834. At the same time, antiabolitionist riots occurred in several cities (Morris, 1974: 62). These riots reflected the attitude of President Andrew Jackson, who branded abolitionist literature "unconstitutional and wicked." In 1836, Postmaster General Amos Kendall authorized southern justices to fine local postmasters "who did not immediately burn the 'incendiary publications' " (Morris, 62). But the Compromise of 1850, which included a tougher version of the 1793 Fugitive Slave Act, was interpreted by many white northerners as an infringement on the rights of free men, white as well as black.[23] Northern states responded by enacting "personal liberty" laws.[24] The South challenged the constitutionality of these laws in a southern-dominated Supreme Court. In the North, interracial vigilance committees were formed to "rescue" fugitive slaves from jails and courtrooms before they could be sent south.[25]

In New York, the black abolitionist David Ruggles,[26] who published an abolitionist newspaper, was also the founder of the New York Committee of Vigilance. In Philadelphia, the General Vigilance Committee led by William Hill was active (Cheek, 1970: 28). These vigilance committees in New York, Philadelphia, Boston, and other northern cities, which began to appear in the mid-1830s, were "organized efforts to aid runaways" (Cheek, 28). With funding from contributions, they provided services that included food, clothing, shelter, legal aid, help in finding a job, or forged freedom papers (Cheek, 28). In engaging in these activities, they—like the members of the Underground Railroad—were breaking the law. Ruggles's committee claimed to have rescued three hundred people during the five years when he was its leader (Goodheart, 1984: 13). Young (1994: 58–59) describes the "genius" of Ruggles's "practical abolition" as his ability

> to combine goals that the mass of blacks could relate to with methods with which they felt comfortable. . . . These methods included using small working groups to collect funds and police the black community and the willingness to use violent means to interfere with the law.

In 1850, as the Fugitive Slave Act was about to be signed into law, black abolitionists and their white allies expressed their intention to resist it. In Cazenovia, New York, at a gathering called by the New York State vigilance committee, those present resolved to "stand by" runaway slaves and started a fund for the defense of William L. Chaplin, who was facing charges in Washington and Maryland for the aid he had given runaway slaves. The fugitive slaves who were in attendance at the convention drafted a letter to the slaves in the South urging them to flee north, telling them New York State was "the safest place to steer" (Swift, 1989: 261). A year later at a black state convention in Albany, New York, the Committee on the Fugitive Slave Act reported that the liberties of black citizens of New York were "fearfully endangered" by the act. The delegates to the convention "declared the Fugitive Slave Act to be a gross violation of the Bible, of the Declaration of Independence, and of the federal Constitution" (Swift, 1989: 261). This sense of the Fugitive Slave Act as not only unjust but unlawful fueled the actions of blacks in the North.

Desperation and a desire to maintain the freedom they had obtained fueled the actions of escaped slaves who resisted being taken back into slavery. This resistance was sometimes violent. In Christiana, Pennsylvania (1851), a Maryland slaveowner was killed by armed black resisters when he and a small group of men attempted to storm a house to retrieve his escaped slaves. Most of the resisters escaped to Canada. A white neighbor who had been caught up in the episode when he rode over to see what was happening was placed on trial, but he and the others were acquitted. This episode fueled the growing certainty among southerners that abolitionists were engaged in a full-scale assault on the institution of slavery and that neither government officials nor the judiciary in the northern states could be trusted to control them (Slaughter, 1991).[27]

By fits and starts the two sections and their sympathizers in Kansas, Nebraska, Texas, and California moved toward war. Slavery was not the only cause, but it became a symbol of the differences that separated North and South. John Brown's raid on the federal arsenal at Harper's Ferry became a gauntlet thrown down, another episode edging the country closer to war.[28] Robert E. Lee, a slaveholder, reluctantly took up arms in defense of the South. Lee's slaves undoubtedly greeted the war with more eagerness. Like the Revolutionary War and the War of 1812, this war offered them another chance for freedom. This time their hopes were high.

CONCLUSIONS

In 1856, in Ohio, a committee of ten black men addressed a resolution to the state legislature. In this resolution, they warned:

> If we are deprived of education, of equal political privileges, still subjected to the same depressing influences under which we now suffer, the natural consequences will follow, and the state, for her planting of injustice, will reap her harvest of sorrow and crime. She will contain within her limits a discontented population . . . ready to welcome any revolution or invasion as a relief, for they can lose nothing and gain much. (quoted in Cheek, 1970: 34)

In the antebellum era, free blacks found their fate intertwined with that of black slaves. They were constricted and restricted by the legal system and by the norms of race relations in both the North and the South. To strive for the freedom of African American slaves was to strive for their own freedom. At the same time, within the limits of the social structure, African American free people strove to create and sustain black communities. Writing of the small upstate New York community of Geneva, Grover (1994: 5) notes that even in the face of white racism, blacks managed to create a vibrant community life. For African Americans in Geneva, "the inculation and management of knowledge about whites became a practical and necessary life skill." They used this skill

> to carve a reasonably secure, if not especially or always comfortable, spot for themselves in local society. The fact that overt racial conflict was rare in Geneva just as likely suggests how sophisticated their understanding of local society was as it does their supposed passive accommodation to it. (Grover, 5)

The free African American citizens of Geneva faced problems that were both similar to and different from those faced by free blacks in New York City or Philadelphia, Charleston or New Orleans. In each city, free blacks were faced with the task of challenging racial mores and legal restrictions while avoiding the wrath of the whites who had fixed ideas about the place of blacks in the scheme of things. Free blacks had the difficult task of achieving "racial betterment" while resisting the stigmatization of all blacks that was the inherent by-product of slavery.

NOTES

1. Frazier (1932: 12) writes: "The most striking characteristic of the free Negro communities was the prominence of the mulatto elements. About thirty-seven per cent of the free Negroes in the United States in 1850 were classed as mulattoes."

2. See Rowe (1989) on blacks in the criminal courts in late eighteenth-century Philadelphia. Rowe concludes: "The fact that blacks historically were associated with property offenses, and that property crimes came to loom larger in the concerns of white Philadelphians . . . constrained the court's capacity for objectivity" (706).

3. In a city such as New Orleans, with its French heritage and Creole population, distinctions based on skin color and heritage were more exacting than in an Upper South city such as Richmond, where more of the free black population were darker in color. Regarding the development of color distinctions among African Americans see Russell, Wilson, and Hall (1993).

4. See Newman (1995) on African American women in Philadelphia during the Revolutionary era and the impact of the Gradual Abolition Law on their lives.

5. While on their knees at prayer, Allen and his friends were ordered to move from the new gallery of St. George's Methodist church, which they thought had been set aside for black worshippers (Winch, 1988: 9).

6. In the *Roberts* case, the court ruled in favor of the school board committee (Horton and Horton, 1979: 73).

7. In the wake of the Denmark Vesey conspiracy, black seamen arriving in ports such as Charleston were held in local jails for the duration of their stay to prevent them from interaction with (and agitation among) local blacks. In 1824, the Supreme Court had declared the law invalid; however, the practice continued (Horton and Horton, 97).

8. In the August 1, 1826, issue of his newspaper, Nash asked, "What do our colored citizens do but fill our almshouses and prisons and congest our streets as beggars?" (Swift, 1989: 24).

9. Swift (1989: 28–29) finds that the *Journal* gave prominent attention to (1) coverage of activities in the black community; (2) biographies, history, or current events highlighting black accomplishment; (3) editorials exhorting black self-improvement; and (4) literature of protest against white attitudes and treatment of blacks.

10. In Charleston, white workers started petitions aimed at barring blacks from certain jobs (Johnson and Roarke, 1984).

11. In his recent book, Randall Kennedy makes reference to the "politics of respectability" historically practiced by blacks (Kennedy, 1997).

12. Some African Americans purchased family members to remove them from the control of white masters and to eventually secure their freedom. Jordan (1995: 210) observes, "One of the more curious aspects of the free black existence in Virginia was their ownership of slaves. Black slave masters owned members of their family and freed them in their wills." Regarding black ownership of slaves Berlin (1974: 273) writes:

> Economic success in the South depended largely on the ownership of slaves, and free Negroes were no more exempt from this than whites. Although most free Negro slaveholders were truly benevolent despots, owning only their families and friends to prevent their enslavement or forcible deportation, a small minority of wealthy freemen exploited slaves for commercial purposes. This small group of free Negroes were generally the wealthiest and best-connected of their caste.

13. Cyprian Richard of Louisiana was said to have assets of $225,000 and own "no less than 91 slaves" (Birmingham, 1977: 117). This was at a time when most slaveholders owned fewer than ten slaves and many only one of two. Large slaveholders were the exception rather than the rule.

14. Denmark Vesey had been a slave. He purchased his freedom with fifteen hundred dollars he won in a lottery. "The judge who sentenced Vesey after his failed rebellion was puzzled that a man who was free and rich would have risked life, liberty, and personal prosperity in this way" (Fabian, 1990: 126–127).

15. See Streifford (1979) for discussion of the impact of the abolitionist movement on colonization efforts.

16. See Stuckey (1987) on Henry Highland Garnet. He discusses Garnet's rejection of materialism and his differences with Frederick Douglass. Also see Mays (1969 [1938]: 45), who describes Garnet as "one of the few leaders of his time who advocated any means whereby freedom might be achieved even to the point of violence and bloodshed."

17. In 1848, Garnet published his address in a volume that included David Walker's 1829 "Appeal to the Colored Citizens of the World."

18. In a July 5, 1852, oration in Corinthian Hall, Rochester, New York, Douglass described slavery and slaveholding as "the whole system of crime and blood" (in Hord and Lee, 1995: 215). Stetson and David (1994: 132–135) discuss the legendary exchange between Douglass and black female abolitionist Sojourner Truth during the anniversary meeting of the Western Anti-Slavery Society in Salem, Ohio in August 1852. After hearing Douglass's speech advocating violence as sometimes more effective than moral suasion, Truth was reported to have stood up and asked of Douglass, "Is God Dead?" (or "Is God gone?)." Although Truth would eventually abandon Garrisonian nonresistance, at the time, the exchange was widely reported. Stetson and David assert:

> By reducing the historic exchange between two courageous black speakers on the most critical issue of their time to a personality conflict, self-interested white critics denigrated Douglass in a way that was also denigrating to Truth. . . . In canonizing this phrase ["Is God dead?"] from an instance of black-on-black conflict, white people in the nineteenth century awarded transcendent value to the concept of black non-resistance." (135)

See Walters (1976) for discussion of the abolitionist movement after 1830, when the attack on slavery became more intense and factions within the movement became more obvious.

19. See also Goodstein (1989) concerning race relations on the Nashville (Tennessee) frontier. After an initial period of fairly easy racial relations, white citizens began to move toward a defensive stance. Patrols were started to deal with concerns about arson and about the Sunday activities of blacks.

20. See Blockson (1987) for narratives of slaves who escaped from various states via the Underground Railroad.

21. Between 1830 and 1860, nearly nine thousand runaways are reported to have entered Philadelphia. Some stayed; others stopped en route to Canada (Okur, 1995: 537). In 1840 when Cinque and the other Africans who had revolted on the Spanish slaveship *Amistad* were brought to Philadelphia, African American residents were involved in raising funds for them and speaking in their support (Okur, 553). For an account of the *Amistad* mutiny see Jones (1987). The recent film and the historical project to build a replica of the ship have spurred interest in—and awareness of—the episode.

22. Although the book was widely despised by southerners, Stowe was writing within the literary genre of the romantic melodrama. The difference was that her heroine and hero were black (mulatto). Her Uncle Tom was not so much an accommodationist of slavery as a Christian saint. Her villainous Simon Legree was a northerner by birth, was more weak than evil. For more on this book and its impact see Gossett (1985). On the literature and narratives depicting the "suffering of slaves" see Clark (1995).

23. As Genovese (1979: 114–115) asserts, in the eyes of its critics, the defense of the social order of the South "increasingly required the suppression of elementary civil liberties not only in the South but throughout the United States": the "gag rule" limiting debate on slavery in Congress, the interference with the mails, southern demands for the suppression of free speech and assembly by abolitionists, and, finally, "the contempt for home rule implicit in the Fugitive Slave Law's administrative provisions." The critics of the South "associated slavery with an arrogant and reactionary social class."

24. The due process procedures that were a part of the personal liberty laws provided a person who had been seized with an opportunity to challenge the seizure in court. This was important not only for escaped slaves but for free blacks, who with enforcement of the Fugitive Slave Act were at increasing risk of being "kidnapped" and sold south into slavery before they could prove they were free. However, the personal liberty laws ran head on into the federal requirement that northern states provide southern masters with assistance in recovering their "property." For discussion of specifics of these laws in key northern states see Morris (1974).

25. In his study of nineteenth-century policing in Boston, Lane (1967) finds that slavery as a political issue during the 1830s and 1840s involved the police in "serious controversy" because of the "deep divisions" in the city (51). Not everyone supported the activities of the abolitionists or their rescue operations. But see Horton and Horton (1979: ch. 8) on the response of the black Boston community to fugitive slaves.

26. Young (1996) has a chapter on Ruggles. Young looks at the meaning of manhood for the black abolitionists and concludes that it was defined in terms of humanity, freedom of movement, knowledge (learning), and political uses. He asserts that if the African American leaders "squabbled among themselves, and they did, the reason was the underlying tensions associated with maintaining their manhood" (81).

Young argues that the African American working class had a different definition of manhood, so the opposition of black middle class men to "parties, drinking, fancy clothes, freer sexual behavior . . . must have seemed a denial of a large part of what they [working class men] understood as manhood" (82).

27. See Finkelman (1988) for some volumes of pamphlet literature on fugitive slave cases. Also see Cheek (1970: 30–32) on the Christiana raid and black response to the Fugitive Slave Law, including "slave rescue cases" such as those of Shadrach, Thomas Sims, Anthony Burns, and Jerry.

28. See Du Bois's biography of Brown. As John David Smith notes in a new edition of this volume (1997: xiii), reviewers have taken Du Bois "to task for errors of fact and interpretation." However, the volume is particularly useful because of the black perspective Du Bois offered of John Brown and because of what it tells us about Du Bois's own evolution into a scholar who was also an advocate for civil rights.

CHAPTER 4

The Trials of War and Reconstruction

In July 1863, the New York City "draft riots" occurred.[1] Blacks on the streets, on streetcars, and sometimes in their own homes were attacked by white mobs. During these riots, "more than 105 people, most of them black" were killed. The rioters, "chiefly young unmarried males liable to be drafted, beat blacks, shot blacks, and hanged blacks from lampposts" (Brandt, 1996: 19). Some black New Yorkers sought protection in police stations or fire-houses. Many fled to the woods surrounding the city. A few were sheltered by white neighbors. Some fled to the relative safety of New Jersey or the city of Brooklyn.

A Merchants' Committee was formed "for the Relief of Colored People Suffering from the late Riots in the City of New York." This committee of white merchants raised $40,779 for the victims of the riots and hired colored pastors to assist in reaching the displaced African American residents. In its report, the Executive Committee noted, "We aimed to produce a moral effect upon them, as well as to relieve their wants. One thing is certain, that in a few days our streets and wharfs were again filled with colored people going about their accustomed work" (Report of the Committee of Merchants: 3). One of the members of the committee observed during another meeting:

> Those who know the colored people of this city can testify to their being a peaceful, industrious people, having their own churches, Sunday-schools, and charitable societies; and that, as a class, they seldom depend upon charity; they not only labor to support themselves, but to aid those who need aid. This is their general character, and it is our duty to see that they are protected in their lawful labors, to save themselves from becoming dependent on the charity of the city. (3–4)

As a part of its activities, the committee solicited the testimony of those African Americans who had been caught up in the riots, which they thought would be of interest to the readers of the report. The testimony included tales of brutal assaults and murders by the white rioters. However, the merchants reported that this "unprovoked persecution" of black New Yorkers had worked "to the final advantage of the people abused." Since the riot, African American servants had been in high demand among employers.

On August 22, 1863, after the crisis had passed, a delegation of black leaders delivered an address to the committee. After thanking the merchants for their "Christian kindness," the delegation ended with the request that if the merchants were concerned for "our future destiny in this our native land," then they should "give us a fair and open field and let us work out our own destiny, and we ask no more." That is, they asked only for the space in which to achieve self-determination.

Unfortunately, Mr. J. D. McKenzie, the chairman of the Executive Committee, seemed to miss the hint embedded in the delegation's words. In his response, he mixed praise with paternalism. He assured the delegation that the question of the Negro "engages our thoughts I am well convinced for [sic] more than it possibly can your own." After describing black Americans as "the innocent cause of untold woes [the war]," he counseled the delegation to remember "that true liberty is not licentiousness, it is obedience to law" (27–29).

No response by the African American delegation is recorded, but one suspects they left the meeting with somewhat mixed feelings about the merchants. However, the merchants had shown them and their people kindness. This was something they had not received from the white rioters in the streets (Report of the Committee of Merchants).

The riots had occurred as young white men in the North were protesting the draft. Draft protests spun off from the racial antagonism that already existed between white immigrants and blacks. In Toledo and Cincinnati, Ohio, in 1862, riots had broken out between white "largely immigrant Irish" dockworkers and black laborers. Blacks were beaten and property in the black areas near the docks was destroyed (Gerber, 1976: 29). However, such interracial conflict did nothing to deter the eagerness of many young black men to volunteer for combat. African Americans saw the war as directly related to their own freedom. Whether free or slave, they knew that the outcome of the war would determine their future. But the Union Army was no more eager than the Army of the Confederacy to send black soldiers into battle. However, after the first two years of the war, it became obvious to Union officials that additional fighting men were needed. There was also the concern that the South was using slave labor to support its activities. As a military matter, the emancipation of slave property in those southern states that were waging war against the Union became expedient. So did the use of black soldiers in the Union fighting force.[2]

However, the enthusiasm of black troops was dampened by the discovery that they were to be led by white officers. The disillusionment was complete when the black soldiers found that they were not receiving adequate clothing or food or arms. Their salaries were less than those of their white counterparts.[3] They were being used as laborers. In addition, the Confederates gave violent form to their displeasure when they found themselves facing black soldiers. Those taken as prisoners of war faced southern retribution for their audacity. In April 1864, at Fort Pillow, Tennessee, General Nathan Bedford Forrest's Confederate forces massacred the black soldiers who had surrendered to them (Hornsby, 1972: 25). Aware of this massacre, black regiments such as the 1st U.S. Colored Troops "used 'Remember Fort Pillow' as a battle cry" (Angell, 1992: 57).

In the South, some black male slaves made their way to Union lines. Some of them became soldiers. During the war, those slaves who had not yet fled their bondage waged their own war of attrition on their master's home front.

OF SLAVES AND MISTRESSES

> Somebody must take them in hand [,] they grow worse all the time [.]
> I could not begin to write to you . . . how little they mind me.
> —Lizzie Neblett to her husband, Will Neblett,
> November 23, 1863 (quoted in Faust, 1992: 182)

Lizzie Neblett's husband, Will, was a soldier in the Confederate Army. In her letter, she explained to him why she had been forced to call upon a neighbor to assist her in managing their slaves. In Will Neblett's absence, the slaves had become disobedient. One particularly rebellious slave named Sam was whipped by Coleman, the overseer who worked for Lizzie's mother. Neither Lizzie nor Sam was pleased that it had come to that. Eventually, through messages conveyed by a house slave named Sarah, Lizzie Neblett and her slave Sam were able to reach a truce (Faust, 182–183). But it was an uneasy truce. Lizzie Neblett, like other southern women who found themselves in the same position, felt betrayed.

> Throughout the history of the peculiar institution, slave mistresses had hit, slapped, even brutally whipped their slaves—particularly slave women. But their relationship to this exercise of physical power was significantly different from that of their men. No gendered code of honor celebrated their physical power of dominance. (Faust, 189)

White women such as Lizzie Neblett had been taught to expect protection and care from their men. These women were not weaklings (Clinton, 1984), but their place in the scheme of things had not prepared them to employ the violence that was required to keep a resisting slave population under control and at work. Lizzie Neblett, frustrated in her dealings with her slaves, "turned to abusing her children" (Faust, 190). Other slaveholders' wives, after an initial period of disorientation, made a somewhat better adjustment to their new responsibilities. A few even engaged in the business related to the purchase and sale of slave property.

But as the war wore on, more and more southern white women experienced emotions ranging from cynicism and disillusionment to outrage and anger. In Richmond, wealthy society matrons defied the calls for patriotic frugality by indulging in lavish entertainment. The poor women of Richmond took to the streets in "bread riots."

Even some black southerners greeted the war with mixed emotions. Not all blacks rushed to cast their lot with the Union. Free blacks such as William Ellison of Charleston found it expedient to side with the Confederacy. Reluctant to leave his home and his property, Ellison converted his plantation to the growing of food crops and became a supplier to the Confederate Army (Johnson and Roarke, 1984). There were also slaves who actually did remain loyal to their masters, and thereby to the Confederacy. But other slaves waited only for the moment when they could flee to the Union lines.

The slaves had been encouraged in the hope that reaching Union lines would mean freedom by what had happened at Fortress Monroe, where fleeing slaves had found asylum with the Union Army. However, the matter was more complex than it seemed. Neither President Abraham Lincoln nor the Union Army commanders had entered the war with a clear policy regarding the slaves. As a result, on several occasions, commanders allowed slaveowners to reclaim their fleeing property. However, on May 9, 1862, Major General David Hunter issued a proclamation "declaring *all* the slaves of South Carolina, Georgia, and Florida free men, on the grounds that these states were under martial law and that 'slavery and martial law in a free country are altogether incompatible' " (Rose, 1976: 146). Three days later, President Lincoln, not yet ready to act with regard to the slaves, revoked Hunter's order (Rose, 150).

As a matter of policy, Lincoln was unwilling to deprive the southern slaveholders of their property without providing compensation. He proposed a plan to Congress that would provide compensation to the slaveholders, but the plan was too costly. Convinced that the slaves, if freed, should be colonized elsewhere, Lincoln began to look for locations to which they could be sent. He invited a group of black leaders to the White House to discuss his plans for colonization. They were not enthusiastic. No suitable location or plan could be worked out. His hand forced by the fortunes of war, Lincoln reluctantly issued the Emancipation Proclamation in 1863.

As historians have pointed out, the proclamation was limited in its impact. But blacks greeted it with joy and thanksgiving.[4] What was important was what the Emancipation Proclamation symbolized. However, symbolism aside, for the black noncombatants in the South, the war became a prolonged struggle for survival. Many lingered on farms or plantations waiting until the Union Army approached so that they could flee to the Yankees. But often they did so with little more than the clothes on their back. They fled to what amounted to refugee camps. And the Union officers were ill prepared to deal with these refugees who had attached themselves to their armies. They called the fleeing slaves "contraband"—confiscated property.

THE CONTRABAND OF WAR

In May 1861, General Benjamin F. Butler and his Massachusetts volunteers secured a base for military operations in the Tidewater section of Virginia. The base was at Fortress Monroe, and the federal patrol set about securing the countryside around the village of Hampton.

> On every estate they encountered disconcerted whites and exhilarated but cautious slaves. The soldiers, after all, had not come to deliver the slaves from bondage, and it was not yet clear to the troops, the slaves, or the local slaveholders what effects federal occupation would have. (Gerteis, 1973: 12)

During the war years, Hampton, Virginia, would serve as the site for an experiment in race relations. Between 1861 and 1865, the town was the site of three major developments:

> In Hampton, Southern slaves carried out their first mass escape of the Civil War; the Union military first developed the labor and race control policies that it would apply to the ex-slaves . . . and finally, the first Northern missionaries . . . initiated their efforts to aid ex-slaves. (Engs, 1979: xvii)

In Hampton, Samuel Chapman Armstrong, a former Union officer, would later found Hampton Institute, where Booker T. Washington, the "wizard" of Tuskegee Institute, would receive his own education and his indoctrination into the philosophy of agricultural–industrial training for blacks. But that would come later. During the Civil War, Hampton, like Port Royal, South Carolina,[5] was one of the laboratories in which the Union experimented with different strategies for dealing with the Negro problem it had acquired. What soon became clear was that the agendas of slave refugees and free blacks were not necessarily the same as the agendas of the Union officers and northern missionaries.[6]

By December 1863, Hampton had 5,401 black refugees who were receiving government rations. Many of them were unemployed women and children, the families of black soldiers (Engs, 39). Some blacks had claimed the land abandoned by whites who had fled from the Union Army. However, these blacks were coming into conflict with soldiers who "engaged in re-

peated rampages of pillaging, looting and rape in freedman's settlements"
(Engs, 35). The blacks armed themselves to fight back.

The white authorities began to consider ways to move some of the refugees out of Hampton. They examined the possibility of sending freedmen
north to work for white families, but the plan was difficult to implement
because of the reluctance of the freedmen to migrate and because of the
problems with the placement system.

When northern missionaries arrived, they began to establish schools and
to provide the freedmen with both secular and religious instruction. However, the ideas about morality preached by the missionaries did not take into
account the poverty and disorganization that the refugees were facing. Both
black crime and white violence plagued the settlements (Engs, 88–89). During the war and in its aftermath, black church and political leaders "joined
forces with the Freedmen's Bureau and even the civil authorities to bring
peace to their settlements" (Engs, 40).

The Freedmen's Bureau (the Bureau of Freedmen, Refugees, and Abandoned Land) had been created by Congress in March 1865 in the War
Department. Its mission was to help the former slaves adjust to their freedom. The bureau assumed the role of guardian to the black freedmen; although it was in charge of confiscated Confederate lands, President Andrew
Johnson's pardon of southern planters meant that the planters were often
able to reclaim their lands. The bureau became a broker of contracts between
the planters and the former slaves they wanted to hire as laborers. Its duty
was to draft the contracts so that the freedmen received a fair wage.[7]

Among the bureau's other charges was that of overseeing the administration of justice in cases involving freedmen in the postwar South. However,
as Litwack (1979: 284) states:

> While in many ways fairer toward the freedmen, the quality of that justice
> varied according to the competence and commitment of the particular officers
> and depended on their success in securing the cooperation of the Union Army
> to enforce their decisions.

As Litwack observes, the efforts of the Freedmen's Bureau aside, "After their
initial experiences with the judicial system, many freedmen found little reason to place any confidence in it" (284). The Freedmen's Bureau was limited
in its ability to protect freed blacks from southern courts that "upheld a
double standard of justice" (284).

In this area as in others, the work of the bureau was complicated by its
own bureaucracy, by the racism of some bureau officials, and by what was
perceived as the "willfulness" of the freedmen, who did not always cooperate
with the plans made for them. One plan involved an effort to deal with the
problem of landless, unemployed blacks by sending some of them out of the
South. The Freedmen's Bureau was joined in this effort by no less a figure

than Sojourner Truth. In 1864, Sojourner Truth, the black abolitionist, moved to Washington, D.C., to help in the war effort. Truth felt it was important that the freedmen become self-supporting. She, herself, had taken a winding path from her birth as a slave in New York State, to her involvement with a religious "cult," to her work as an abolitionist and crusader for women's rights.[8] Between 1864 and 1868, she "worked in the refugee relief camps for the National Freedmen's Relief Association, a private organization, and for the Freedmen's Bureau" (Painter, 1996: 213). In the fall of 1864, she worked in the freedmen's camp at Mason's Island on the Potomac and later at another camp in Arlington Heights, Virginia.

When Truth discovered the Freedmen's Bureau was trying to find jobs for the freedmen in the North, she became active in recruiting northern employers. She went to Rochester, New York, and placed ads in newspapers there. However, even though she was able to find white employers who wanted to hire black servants, the bureau and Truth's colleagues in Washington were unable to supply the black freedmen. Truth went back to Washington to recruit blacks to come to Rochester. She made several trips back and forth, escorting less than a dozen freedmen each time. She was never able to meet the demand for servants. Finally, she gave up in frustration and returned to Battle Creek, Michigan. As Mabee (1990) observes, Truth's primary concern had been to get freed slaves "off dependence on government" and into jobs in the North. Truth was apparently "not particularly concerned with such matters as what their pay would be or how their exploitation could be prevented" (Mabee, 19). On the basis of what she had seen, she thought that the freed slaves would be better off in the North than where they were.

But many southern blacks had not yet reached that conclusion. The South was their home. With the war over, they hoped to claim their "forty acres and a mule" and to begin their lives as free people.

BLACK RECONSTRUCTION

For many freedmen, their first priority was to find family members from whom they had been separated during slavery. Much of the roaming that blacks were said to have engaged in during this period had as its goal the reestablishment of families. Freedmen advertised in black newspapers. They sought help from the Freedmen's Bureau. They even asked help of former masters (Litwack, 1979, 1986). Freed slaves also made use of the black press.

> Until well into the 1870s and 1880s, the newly established black newspapers, both in the South and in the North, abounded with advertisements in which relatives requested any information that might assist them [in finding family members]. (Litwack, 1979: 232)

When family members were found, often the reunions were joyful. But such reunions could be wrenching if a spouse discovered his or her mate had taken another partner or parents found that a child had bonded with another family. Such cases sometimes brought the freedmen to the courts presided over by the Freedmen's Bureau for help in resolving the problems created by the enforced breakup of their families during slavery.

Other freedmen sought help from the bureau in making their marital relationships legal. As the black Texas newspaper *The Freedmen's Press* wrote in an 1868 editorial, during slavery, "lawful wedlock was unknown and relations of husband and wife, parent and child" were not protected by Southern law" (quoted in Crouch, 1994b: 335). In Texas, the freedmen, concerned with "the legitimization of their marital and parental prerogatives," were able to obtain within the 1869 state constitution an article that made their marriages legitimate (Crouch, 345):

> All persons who, at any time heretofore, lived together as husband and wife, and both of whom, by the law of bondage, were precluded from the rights of matrimony and continued to live together until the death of one of the parties, shall be considered as having been legally married, and the issue . . . shall be deemed legitimate. (quoted in Crouch, 345)

This constitutional enactment gave "future generations a legal family foundation" (Crouch, 346). Black Texans were no longer legally "kinless."

However, black families in Texas and elsewhere in the South still faced other barriers to full enjoyment of their freedom. These barriers included the "black codes" enacted by the southern states after the war. Quarles (1996: 154) writes, "The Black Codes, passed in the fall and winter of 1865–66, were designed to take the place of the defunct slave codes, and the two had some features in common." Like the slave codes, the Black Codes cast the black laborer in a role that limited both mobility and choices. The economic relationships between blacks and potential white employers were circumscribed by vagrancy ordinances that punished blacks who were not employed. The codes also forbade blacks from joining the militia, possessing firearms, voting, or testifying against whites in court. They could, however, own property and make contracts, testify against other blacks, and legally marry (Quarles, 130).

The codes were struck down by a Republican-controlled Congress. The federal government moved to enact the Thirteenth Amendment, the Civil Rights Act of 1866, and the Fourteenth Amendment. Technically, blacks in the South and elsewhere were now citizens who enjoyed the same rights and privileges as whites. But even during the federal military occupation of the South, racial violence was already occurring. In 1866, a race riot in Memphis, Tennessee, left forty-eight persons dead. Most of them were black. "Negro veterans were special targets" (Hornsby, 29).

> Contemporary observers attributed the violence to the unruly conduct of black soldiers in Memphis and to the long standing animosity between blacks and the Irish, who competed for work as manual laborers. (Hardwick, 1993: 109)

Military occupation was made more bitter for southerners when black soldiers were among those sent to keep order. The black soldiers "empowered" by their experiences were less inclined to show deference to white southerners than in the past. At the same time, the soldiers provided aid and comfort to the black migrants who congregated in cities such as Memphis when the fighting stopped (Hardwick, 111).

In Memphis, the Union officers shared some of the white southerners' concern about the presence of large numbers of displaced blacks.[9] In fact, they made a largely unsuccessful effort to persuade the ex-slaves to relocate to the countryside (Hardwick, 112). But they also sent black soldiers out to provide security at black public meetings. Such assignments, as well as their patrol duties and their off-duty recreation, brought black soldiers into contact with black civilians. Their activities also led the soldiers into confrontations with the police and other whites. In Memphis, all of the ingredients were present for the riot that erupted. That same year, a riot in New Orleans had a death toll of thirty-five, with over one hundred wounded.

In 1867, the Ku Klux Klan held its first national convention in Nashville, Tennessee. Not coincidentally it was also in 1867 that Frederick Douglass addressed his plea to the United States Congress for the enfranchisement of black males. He made his argument in the context of an analysis of not only racial but class and labor issues. Douglass asserted:

> The South fought for perfect and permanent control over the Southern laborer. It was a war of the rich against the poor. They who waged it had no objection to the government, while they could use it as a means of confirming their power over the laborer. They fought the government . . . because they found it, as they thought, in the way between them and their one grand purpose of rendering permanent and indestructible their authority and power over the Southern laborer. Though the battle is for the present lost, the hope of gaining this object still exists. (4)

Douglass argued that to ensure the preservation of the Union and to bring the South into the national mainstream black men must be given the right to vote so that they could defend not only themselves but the Union against white southern insurgency. Not to give black men the vote, Douglass argued, was to issue a blatant insult. If black men were denied the right of full participation in the government of their country, it would be "no less than a crime against manhood" that would assign blacks—even with their newly obtained freedom—to the status of a "degraded caste."

Although bluntly denying the "invented nonsensical theories about master-races and slave-races of men," Douglass argued that there was the danger of creating among blacks an isolation from mainstream society that would damage both the Union and blacks themselves. As Douglass put it, to say to a man that he shall not vote was "to deal his manhood a staggering blow, and to burn into his soul a bitter and goading sense of wrong, or else work in him a stupid indifference to all the elements of a manly character" (3).

The pleas by Douglass and other spokesmen for the freedmen did not fall on deaf congressional ears. In the Republican-controlled Congress, legislative strides were made to bring blacks (i.e., black males) into a position of political equality. During this era of Radical Reconstruction, blacks in the South seemed to be making significant gains. For the first time, they were involved in the political process. They held positions within the local, state, and federal government.[10] They served as police officers and magistrates. In Hampton (Village) in the 1870s, a black sheriff, Andrew Williams, and his deputies were coping with "a wide open town catering to the wants of soldiers and tourists." Gambling, drunkenness, and violence were among the crime problems with which Williams and his men had to deal (Eng, 1979: 164). In Danville, Virginia, a stopping place for Jefferson Davis as he fled Richmond, in 1883, black policemen and at least one black police court magistrate were serving (Bailey, 1986).[11]

However, the events that occurred in Danville that year illustrated the process by which blacks gained and lost political ground during the postbellum era. As Grantham (1988: 10) states, in Virginia in the 1880s and North Carolina in the 1890s, two of the "most spectacular Republican efforts to perfect coalition politics" occurred; in each state, "bitter conflict" followed. In Virginia, in 1883, the Readjuster party had achieved a statewide coalition of whites and blacks. To regain control of the state legislature, the white Democrats in Virginia needed to break the coalition. It was an election year in the state. As election day approached, the Democrats made speeches and issued circulars. They charged that the situation in Danville was illustrative of the corruption of the blacks and carpetbaggers who had taken control of the state. In the Danville Circular of 1883, signed by "merchants and manufacturers and mechanics of the town of Danville" (*Senate Report*, no. 579: ix), members of the white commercial–civic elite in Danville offered their allegations. They claimed that farmers were reluctant to take their tobacco to Danville to market it and instead were going to Durham, North Carolina. They alleged that white men now feared to walk the streets of Danville because they were arrested for the "most frivolous acts by negro policemen and borne along to the Mayor's office followed by swarms of jeering and hooting and mocking negroes" (*Senate Report*, no. 579, 1884: vi–ix). The signers of the circular also alleged that the Police Court had become "another scene of perpetual mockery and disgrace." One of the magistrates, a man named Jones, "first became famous by seducing a girl under promise of marriage" (*Senate Report*, vi–ix).

The Democrats also pointed to the criminal acts of blacks in the area. In the summer of 1883, a white farmer and his son returning home from the city had been attacked by three black highwaymen. The farmer was killed.

The highwaymen were only saved from mob violence by their removal from the city (Bailey, 1986: 90).

> This episode of black violence coupled with what many whites in the city perceived as the unconscionable arrogance and rudeness of former slaves contributed to the erosion of the racial situation in the community. The arrival of a prominent white Readjuster named William Sims for a round of speech-making on the Friday afternoon prior to the Tuesday election was the final insult. Sims' arrival set the stage for what was to happen. (Bailey, 1986: 90)

That Saturday afternoon as the Democrats held a mass meeting, a black man bumped into a white man on the sidewalk. The white man went to the Democratic rally. He then returned to the street, where he and a friend became involved in a brawl with the black man and his two friends. The brawl escalated into a riot as whites rushed into the street. The armed whites drove the unarmed blacks off the streets. That evening, the local militia patrolled. On the following Tuesday, election day, blacks stayed home from the polls. Whites "returned to the Democratic fold" (Bailey, 1986: 91).[12]

The Danville Riot of 1883 had broken the back of the Readjuster party in Virginia. The Democrats moved to solidify their power base. In the 1901–1902 Constitutional Convention, the black voter was presented as a "bug-aboo" who had to be disenfranchised in order to end political corruption in Virginia. The white–black alliance that had existed briefly in the 1870s and 1880s was no longer viable (Bailey, 1986). This same pattern of white violence aimed at destroying Reconstruction governments in which blacks played a significant role occurred throughout the South. The withdrawal of federal troops from the South in 1877 had marked the end of Radical Reconstruction. As several historians have observed, this withdrawal—the result of a political bargain—meant that the North had left the white South to resolve its own racial problems.[13]

In cities such as Richmond and Danville, a black middle class (a "commercial–civic elite") was developing on the other side of the color line. The members of this middle class found themselves in the position of having to walk cautiously. Like the free blacks in the South during the antebellum era, they were dependent on white goodwill and paternalism. Like the free blacks in the urban North, they had as their primary strategy in dealing with issues of crime and justice to establish their own respectability and then to engage in the uplift of the lower classes. Members of the middle class tended to structure their efforts on behalf of the race through participation in reform movements. As black progressives, they worked for causes such as temperance and prison reform. But they did so with an eye to the special problems faced by their communities.

During this period, beginning in the 1880s, black newspaper editors became active in protesting against white violence and the other injustices that blacks suffered. One of the more outspoken (and fearless) editors in the South was John Mitchell, Jr., of the *Richmond Planet*. Mitchell became involved in several criminal cases on behalf of the defendants. In 1904, he led a streetcar boycott in Richmond to protest segregated seating (Dabney, 1987). Black newspaper editors such as Mitchell were members of the expanding black middle class in the South and recognized by whites and by other blacks as community leaders.

However, there is some evidence that working class blacks were also active in efforts to bring about reforms in race relations. In Atlanta in 1881, washerwomen staged a boycott, which was squashed in what Katzman (1978: 196) describes as an illustration of "the relative powerlessness of servants." But a year later the incipient movement was revived as washerwomen, joined by cooks, servants, and children's nurses, demanded an increase in wages. In response, white landlords threatened to raise rents. The city council voted in a twenty-five dollar annual license fee for washerwomen. But in a letter to the mayor, the women asserted, "We mean business this week or no washing." The strike was ended when the police began making arrests. Eight leaders were convicted of "disorderly conduct and quarreling." Five were given fines of five dollars; three received twenty-five dollar fines (Katzman, 146).

This incident illustrates the fashion in which the criminal justice system was employed to control norm-violating behavior by blacks. As Litwack (1979) writes, "The laws discriminated against them, the courts upheld a double standard of justice, and the police acted as their enforcers" (284). Or, in the words of two African American proverbs: "Cockroach nebber get justice when chicken judge" and "When all the judges is foxes, ain't much justice for poor goose" (quoted in Dance, 1987: 122).

CONCLUSIONS

On the face of it, the end of the Civil War and the emancipation of African slaves began a new day in southern (and American) race relations. However, the smoke of battle had barely dissipated before white southerners moved to bring a free—and, therefore, to them, immensely threatening—black population under control. They did this with the "Black Codes" that were intended to replace the "slave codes." They also responded to signs of black assertiveness with violence. As early as 1865, race riots erupted in Charleston and Norfolk; 1866 brought rioting in New Orleans. These riots, "long a feature of Northern cities, were new to the South" (Ayers, 1984 : 161). But in the postwar South was an environment that was conducive to racial eruptions. Among the factors contributing to the riot atmosphere were (1) the release of blacks from restrictions, (2) the postwar economy, (3) the presence of immigrant whites, and (4) law enforcement officers who were "often unreconstructed Southerners" and who exercised their authority "with little tact and much force. To whites, blacks on street corners appeared lazy and insolent; to blacks, whites appeared belligerent and uncharitable" (Ayers, 161–162).

One of the most significant changes in race relations in the postwar years was that blacks were now willing and able to defend themselves against white mob violence. However, blacks still found themselves defenseless in courts of law. In 1866, a group of blacks petitioned the Georgia Freedmen's Bureau "to be relieved from outrages practised upon them by the Freedmen's Court and the civil authorities of the place" (Ayers, 1984: 154). The United States Congress would offer blacks some brief relief from legal oppression during the period of Radical Reconstruction. But, as the federal military departed from the South, the legal rights African Americans had acquired through the Civil Right Acts and with the passage of the Thirteenth, Fourteenth, and Fifteenth Amendments began to be repealed.

In fact, the 13th Amendment had abolished slavery and involuntary servitude, "except as punishment for crime whereof the party shall have been duly convicted." The condition of black freedmen would worsen as more of them found themselves in courts, in prisons, and on southern chain gangs.

NOTES

1. The riots reflected the anger of working class whites over conscription laws that allowed men who were well-to-do to hire substitutes to fight in their place. They also reflected growing white frustrations over the war and the existing enmities between blacks and whites, particularly Irish, who often contended for jobs (Dinnerstein et al., 1990: 102).

2. See Berry (1977) on the relationship between the claims by African Americans to citizenship and their participation in the Civil War. She points out that "military necessity" forced the federal government to yield ideological ground with regard to how black males who participated in the war effort were perceived.

3. Under a discriminatory pay scale, white privates received thirteen dollars per month, black privates only ten dollars per month. White chaplins received one hundred dollars per month; black chaplins received ten dollars per month. This inequity was not corrected until June 15, 1864 (Angell, 1992: 56–57).

4. Proclamation celebrations by black Americans included revival meetings, which were also an expression of their new freedom to practice their evangelical religion (Angell, 1992: 77).

5. In the Port Royal Experiment, Salmon P. Chase, the secretary of the Treasury, persuaded President Lincoln to send teachers and agricultural superintendents to the South Carolina Sea Islands to prepare the black population there for citizenship (Rose, 1976). For more on this experiment, see Rose (1976) and the volume of letters by white participants in the experiment, edited by Pearson (1969 [1906]). As Rose (1976) notes, the Port Royal Experiment was the subject of debate among abolitionists and others who were concerned about the "repercussions that might arise from large scale benevolence to the Negro." Rather than fearing the negative impact on the character of the former bondsmen, they were concerned about the "impact on

the public opinion of the North." Charity toward the bondsmen also smacked of a "paternalism and condescending benevolence" that "was antithetical to that equality of man upon which their ultimate arguments were laid" (Rose, 158). More attention has been given here to Union activities in Hampton because as Gerteis (1973: 50) asserts:

> The concentration of reform energies at Port Royal was important, but it was also misleading as an indication of federal policy. Elsewhere in the occupied South, programs for the freedmen's advancement were more frankly subordinate to purely military needs and considerations. In some cases, as on Virginia's Eastern Shore, the reform impulse never influenced federal policy.

6. The American Missionary Society, founded in 1846, had first focused on the eradication of slavery. During the war and in its aftermath, missionaries went south to work with the freed slaves. However, although they found the former slaves—both adults and children—eager to attend the schools they started, the Congregationalist missionaries found that the slaves resisted attempts at religious conversion. Both the tenets and the worship services of the Congregationalists were incompatible with the evangelical Baptist and Methodist leanings of many slaves. Writing about missionaries in Georgia, Zipf (1997: 112) states that when they left in the 1870s, it was for a combination of reasons—lack of funding, white hostility, and the fact that blacks were "seeking more control over administration and curriculum" in the schools to which they sent their children.

7. In some places, such as lowcountry South Carolina, blacks were able to retain some of the lands they had settled on and worked during the war. However, the hoped-for "forty acres and a mule" never materialized for many former slaves. Smitherman (1994: 2) explains that this particular expression came from the language in the 1866 congressional bill, which strengthened the Freedmen's Bureau and stipulated each household of ex-slaves could receive an allotment of forty acres and start-up resources. Smitherman asserts, "This payment for 246 years of free African labor not only would have provided reparations for enslavement but would have established a basis for self-sufficiency and initiated the economic development of the African American community." Unfortunately, this reparation never took place.

8. See Painter's recent biography (1996) of Sojourner Truth. Painter discusses Truth's re-creation of herself from the New York–born slave Isabella—who numbered among her other troubles sexual abuse by her master's wife—to the powerful preacher she became as Sojourner Truth. Concerning Truth's present status, Painter writes that she "has become American material culture's female equivalent of Malcolm X" (Painter, 273).

9. The white commander of the black Sixty-first Colored Infantry Regiment at Fort Pickering described the Negro women in the temporary camps near the fort as "for the most part, idle, lazy, vagrant . . . exercising a very pernicious influence over the colored soldiers of this post" (Hardwick, 112). One military strategy for dealing with Memphis vagrants was to pick them up and force them to accept labor contracts (Hardwick, 1993: 115).

10. See Foner's directory (1996) of African American officeholders during Reconstruction. For discussion of black leadership during Reconstruction in South Carolina see Holt (1977). Holt notes class differences among blacks in the postbellum era: "subtle but distinct differences in emphasis and outlook between the largely mulatto

bourgeoisie and the black peasantry, with the urban-based slaves and ex-slave domestics constituting something of a swing group," who attended a Colored People's convention at Zion Church on November 25, 1865 (Holt, 17).

With regard to black leadership, Angell (1992) asserts that ministers such as Bishop Henry McNeal Turner assumed the role of "minister–politician," which was acceptable to a congregation if the minister's actions were "firmly founded upon their shared method of interpreting the Bible." The congruence of Turner's values with those of his congregation gained their support for his "opposition to the Ku Klux Klan, his advocacy of civil and voting rights, and his efforts to improve higher education" (Angell, 98–99).

11. Blacks in Virginia were also making some gains as entrepreneurs. For an overview of black businesses see Kenzer (1993).

12. See also Dailey (1997), who applies the anthropologist James C. Scott's concept of the "hidden transcript" of resistance to the events in Danville. Dailey notes this approach has become the "central pursuit of scholars interested in domination and resistance" (554).

13. For discussion of postbellum crime and race relations in individual cities and states see Wright (1984), Crouch (1994a), Nieman (1989), Taylor (1991), Myers and Massey (1991), and Waldrep (1996).

CHAPTER 5

Lest We Forget

The honoring of fallen heroes is an important ritual that unites the people of a society and reminds them of their common past. On November 14, 1888, such a ceremony was held in Boston, Massachusetts. It was a "delightful" autumn day. At eleven o'clock that morning a procession made up of military and civic organizations paraded to the State House to provide escort to the governor and other guests. They then proceeded to City Hall to pick up the mayor and the city officials who were to be included in the ceremony. At shortly past noon, in front of a crowd of thousands, the Germania Band played "America." Then the Reverend Eli Smith of Springfield rose to offer a prayer, the invocation.

It was an occasion Smith felt deeply. On this day in 1888, the dignitaries and the crowd had gathered to dedicate a monument to Crispus Attucks and the four other men who had fallen in the Boston Massacre on March 5, 1770. The occasion was made especially joyful for Smith because Crispus Attucks, the first man to fall under the fire of British soldiers, had been a mulatto, a runaway slave. As Smith told his God and those gathered there on the Boston Common, his thoughts that day were not only of the conflict of 1776 but of the more recent Civil War:

> We thank Thee that through the one [struggle] the principle of no taxation without representation was vindicated, and that this country was severed from Great Britain; and that through the other the mistaken notions of the right of secession were settled by the sword, and human slavery forever abolished from our land. We thank Thee that in both these struggles there were engaged those of an oppressed race, who for centuries had been made to toil as bondsmen. We thank Thee for the exhibitions they gave of patriotism, of love of

country, when they themselves were without a country. We thank Thee that
the first blood of the revolutionary conflict was shed by a black man, a representative of the race with whom so many of us here are identified. We take
great pride in the fact that bravely he lost his life battling for the right. We
rejoice that it is our privilege—a grand one may we esteem it—to do honor
to-day to Crispus Attucks and his brave compatriots. (Boston City Council,
33)

However, as Mayor O'Brien observed in passing later that afternoon at
Faneuil Hall, "The monument to Crispus Attucks and his martyred associates has been the subject of more or less adverse criticism" (Boston City
Council, 46). At least some of the criticism reportedly came from "two historical societies who [had] their headquarters in Boston." Dr. Henry I. Bow-
ditch wrote that the committees of these societies had protested against "a
monument to commemorate a 'mob,' as they call the event in State street,
and the just (as the historicals gentlemen would say) death of 'rioters' " (Boston City Council, 95).

In Massachusetts the critics of the monument were apparently in the minority. When a petition was presented to the legislature in spring 1887 pro-
posing a monument to honor the "first Martyrs in the cause of American
liberty," the resolve had been adopted by both houses without opposition
and "promptly signed" by the governor. Up to ten thousand dollars had
been allocated for the project. The costs of the dedication ceremony on
Boston Common and in Fanueil Hall had been raised by a committee appointed by the mayor. As the poet who composed a piece for the occasion
wrote, Bostonians saw Attucks and the others as fallen heroes in the fight
against British tyranny.

As to that, John Adams, who had defended the British soldiers accused of
the murder of the "patriots," observed that in the minds of many of his
fellow countrymen, "On that Night the foundation of American Independence was laid." No matter whether the British soldiers had been acting in
self-defense: As the lawyers representing the colony had argued, the rioters
that night had been "provoked."

And Crispus Attucks, a mulatto of black and perhaps Indian heritage, had
been at the front of the crowd that had confronted the soldiers on guard at
the Custom House. If Attucks was indeed the slave whom William Browne
of Framingham had advertised for as a runaway back in 1750, when he died
he had been a fugitive for twenty years. Apparently he was not a native of
Boston, but a sailor about to ship out to North Carolina. He may have been
working his way back to his home in Nassau (Boston City Council, 83). As
John Fiske, the Cambridge historian who gave the address at Fanueil Hall
that afternoon, acknowledged, not a great deal was known about Attucks and
the four white men who had fallen that night. What was important was what
they had come to symbolize.

In a letter to Boston officials, Frederick Douglass wrote about what Crispus Attucks symbolized for him. Douglass had been invited by the planning committee to come to Boston and give a speech at the ceremony. In a letter penned from his home in Anacostia [Washington], D.C., Douglass explained that he would be unable to give a speech because he would not have time to prepare one worthy of the great occasion. Until November 6, he was fully committed to his work for the Republican National Committee. Afterward he anticipated the nervous exhaustion that had followed other such campaigns. But although he could not speak, he hoped to be there in the audience: "Happy is the thought that the Commonwealth of Massachusetts is about to commemorate an act of heroism on the part of one of a race seldom credited with heroic qualities" (Memorial, 94). Douglass went on to say, "I do not forget that it was Massachusetts, by her advanced sentiments, [that] made it comparatively safe for me to dwell within her borders when a fugitive, not from justice but from slavery, fifty years ago" (Memorial, 94).

By 1888, Frederick Douglass was an old warrior who had fought during his lifetime for the freedom of black slaves and for women's suffrage, and who now faced the challenges of an era in which the rights blacks had enjoyed so briefly during Reconstruction were melting away.[1] Douglass had lived to see slavery replaced by "Jim Crow" and the whip of the overseer by the rope and faggot of the lynch mob. In 1888, African Americans were still in many ways a people without a country.

But as the Reverend Eli Smith and perhaps other African Americans in the audience looked on, the monument to Crispus Attucks was dedicated that day on Boston Common. Above the bas-relief of the monument stood "Free America," personified as a woman in Roman drapes with one breast bared. In one hand she clasped a flag about to be unfurled. In the other she held aloft the "broken chain of oppression." On the face of the bas-relief of the pedestal was a representation of the Boston Massacre. An official description stated, "In the foreground lies Crispus Attucks, the first victim of British bullets" (Memorial, 27).

It was ironic that the image of a black male should be in such close proximity to a bare-breasted "Free America." In the South black males were being lynched for the lust they were reported to exhibit for white women.[2] But as both Smith and Frederick Douglass might have attested, in America ideas about race and gender and freedom and bondage were complex and contradictory.

The concept of "lynch law" had been known in America since the Revolutionary War, when it was used by Virginia patriots engaged in vigilante justice directed at Tories and horse thieves.[3] But by the era of the 1880s, "lynching" had taken on "a new and more sinister meaning: the execution of a criminal or an accused person, usually by hanging or burning, with the victim often suffering perverse torture and mutilation of body parts before succumbing to death" (Downey and Hyser, 1991: 3).

In the 1930s Billie Holiday would sing mournfully of "strange fruit" hanging from southern trees. By then African Americans would have been engaged for over six decades in a struggle to end lynching and other forms of terrorism in the South. But lynching was "a problem about which liberal politicians and reformers—the so-called progressives—were strangely mute" (Downey and Hyser, 1991: 3). In the postbellum period, during the Gilded Age, reformers had turned their attention to other issues. Or, it would be more accurate to say that many white reformers had turned their attention to other issues. For black reformers, North and South, lynching remained a powerful issue—symbolic of their "place" in American society. It was an issue they could not ignore.

"BUCKET" POLITICS

In his autobiography, *Up From Slavery* (1901: 75), the African American educator Booker T. Washington wrote, "The individual who can do something that the world wants done will, in the end, make his way regardless of his race."[4] In an afternoon in September 1895, Washington had delivered a well-received address at the opening of the Atlanta Cotton States and International Exposition. After being introduced by the governor of Georgia, Washington gave a speech in which he captured in one vivid phrase his perception of how African Americans should handle the challenge of racial politics. "Cast down your bucket where you are," he said.

Washington assured the whites in the audience that Negroes were not seeking "social equality." What they desired was to be allowed to work hard and provide for themselves and their families. As August Meier (1988: 100) states, Washington's solution to the race problem "lay essentially in an application of the gospel of wealth." It was the "Gilded Age," and Washington had faith in a Horatio Alger brand of upward mobility.

> Washington's emphasis upon economic prosperity was the hallmark of the age. The pledges of loyalty to the South and the identification of Negro uplift with the cause of the New South satisfied the "better class" of Southern whites and Northern investors. (Meier, 101)[5]

It was to the "better class" of whites that blacks directed their appeals. Middle class blacks sought to ally themselves with them in their mutual desire for peace and prosperity. Like the white "commercial–civic elite," the black middle class tended to locate the problems that divided the two races as originating among the lower classes.

In his speech at the Atlanta Exposition, Washington established himself as the "spokesperson" and "leader" of the well-intentioned of the Negro race. Not all African Americans agreed with Washington's position, but they did come to recognize his power to make or break other upwardly mobile blacks. They also recognized that there was something to be gained from a strategy that accommodated white fears about black ambitions rather than challenging them. As members of the black middle class knew, it was necessary to work within the restrictions of color and caste placed upon them.

Moreover, some blacks shared, if not Washington's philosophy about race relations, at least his belief in the possibility of black economic progress. Others questioned the consequences of linking racial progress to pursuit of wealth.

> The Gilded Age's gospel of progress and prosperity had found endorsements from Frederick Douglass until his death in 1895, and from Booker T. Washington . . . [but] some black American intellectuals had been voicing criticism of the Gilded Age, at least as early as 1892, with the publication of Frances Harper's *Iola Leroy*. (Warren, 1993: 109–110)

Frederick Douglass himself had learned from bitter experience the traps and pitfalls of economics when he had served as the (last) president of the Freedmen's Saving and Trust Company. The bank had been established as the first black bank in America, chartered in 1865, at the initiative of a missionary group and the Freedmen's Bureau. By 1871, there were thirty-four branches, thirty-two of them in cities across the South. The initial capital behind the bank had come from the unclaimed deposits of black soldiers who had been killed or had disappeared during the war. At its peak, the bank had over seventy thousand black depositors and over $19 million in assets (Birmingham, 1977: 89). Unfortunately, although the branch offices had black tellers and cashiers, the board of directors was made up of a mixture of "financially naive, though well-intentioned white missionaries, and financially unscrupulous white entrepreneurs" (Birmingham, 89). The entrepreneurs depleted the bank of its capital through illegal loans, over-capitalized ventures, and embezzlement. By the time Douglass was invited to serve as the bank's president, the institution was in serious trouble. In spite of Douglass's efforts, including investing some of his own money, the Panic of 1873 forced the bank to close its doors. As Douglass said, "I inherited a corpse" (Birmingham, 89–90; Fabian, 128–136).[6]

But still he shared with Washington faith in the possibility of economic progress.

THE LIMITS OF UPLIFT

In the case of *Plessy v. Ferguson* (1896), the Supreme Court reviewed the existence of racial segregation in public accommodations. In his argument on behalf of Homer Plessy, the attorney, Albion Tourgee, had posed an intriguing question to the court. He asked whether in an America where blacks were denied their basic rights, it was "possible to conclude that the reputation of being white is not property? Indeed, is it not the most valuable

sort of property, being the master-key that unlocks the golden door of opportunity?" (quoted in Warren, 100–111).

Being white was a property that African Americans did not possess.[7] This
lack of whiteness not only restricted them in their access to adequate public
accommodation on railroads and streetcars and in theaters and hotels, it also
meant that they were barred from certain jobs that were "color-coded." It
meant too that they continued to suffer from the social oppression that
extended into and was sustained by the criminal justice system. Like public
accommodations, the criminal justice system was "Jim Crow."

GENDER AND JUSTICE

For black women, their lack of whiteness and their gender served as in-
terlinking sites of oppression. In the 1890s, the symbol of white American
female grace and beauty was "the Gibson girl," the creation of the illustrator
Charles Dana Gibson (Gutman, 1989: 15). A creature of willowy grace, she
was the image of youth and refined exuberance. She represented for black
women their own place in the scheme of things. When a white man called
a black woman "girl" it was an insulting reminder of her place. The sexual
threat implicit in the white male gaze reminded black women of their vul-
nerability. Black women were also painfully aware of the sexual politics that
could get a black man lynched for the "reckless eyeballing" of a white
woman. In contrast, a white man who raped a black woman had almost
nothing to fear from the criminal justice system. He needed to fear extralegal
justice only if a black woman or her brother, husband, or father were brave
enough or reckless enough to seek vengeance.

Aware of their place in the scheme of things, middle class black women—
who enjoyed at least limited protection because of their status—organized
to work for the race. Black women's clubs had existed in northern free communities before the Civil War. In the 1890s, the participation of women in
reform movements gave added impetus to organizing in both the North and
the South. But, although black middle class women were committed to the
welfare of their race, their sense of noblesse oblige was linked to their own
self-interest as a class. In this regard, another factor that spurred black middle class women in their efforts were the snide remarks made about the
morality of black women in the press and by white public figures. Seizing
the opportunity to speak frankly when she found herself among the few
carefully selected black women allowed to speak at the World Columbian
Exposition in 1893, Fannie Barrier Williams observed, "I regret the necessity
of speaking of the moral question of our women [but] the morality of our
home life has been commented on so disparagingly and meanly that we are
placed in the unfortunate position of being defenders of our name" (Giddings, 1984: 86).[8]

Faced with such challenges, a strong network of women's clubs developed nationally. The National Association for Colored Women was organized in 1896. The motto of the association was "Lifting As We Climb" (Meier, 1988: 135). Many of the women who were active in the women's club movement were involved in the temperance crusade or in work on behalf of children. They were involved in raising funds for playgrounds and orphanages and in supporting cultural programs. Like white female reformers of the era, black middle class women involved themselves in helping their "fallen sisters"—the girls and women who had "gone astray." They shared the sense of obligation to the lower classes that white female reformers felt.

During this period, the settlement house, which was mainly northern and urban, began to penetrate the South. However, few of the houses in the South served blacks. Two exceptions were the L Street Settlement House in Washington, D.C., and Jane Porter Barrett's Locust Street Settlement House in Hampton, Virginia. These houses focused on the problems of poor black communities. At the Locust Street Settlement House, classes were offered in how to grow vegetables, and "[a] particular effort was made to get children out of jail who might have been incarcerated for very minor offenses and either return them to their families, or if that proved impossible, care for them in the institute's orphanage" (Levine, 1997: 71).

In Atlanta, Lugenia Burns Hope, the wife of the Morehouse College president, John Hope, started the Neighborhood Union. This organization was involved in community organizing but it also provided some welfare services. A particular focus was on children—providing them with playgrounds and the other resources they needed for their "moral, physical, and intellectual development" (D. Levine, 73).

Gordon (1991) notes that North and South, black women reformers tended to be "church-centered." However, this was probably more true of "locally active, less elite" women reformers than of those who were active on a national level. The black churches did, however, play an important role in the fund-raising activities of black female reformers (Gordon, 1991: 567).

For some black middle class women a deeper commitment to racial causes led them to engage in behavior that challenged gender expectations. Among such nineteenth century women, the journalist Ida B. Wells (later Wells-Barnett) comes first to mind. Wells became famous—or notorious—as a crusader against lynching. She had been forced to forsake her life in Memphis because of the anger she had aroused among whites with an editorial in her newspaper, *Free Speech*, about lynchings in the South.[9] Wells continued her antilynching crusade, writing in the pages of the *New York Age* and traveling from city to city to address personal appeals to others to join the campaign (Davis, 1983: 191–193).[10] Wells also made several trips abroad to organize foreign support. She traveled to England in March 1894 to present her case to the British. Wells's strategy was to turn the southern mythology of lynching on its head. Taking advantage of the images related to respectable womanhood, she presented herself as a cultured, educated woman. She depicted the white southern men who lynched black men not as the chivalrous defenders of white womanhood they claimed to be, but as sadistic savages who rejoiced in their victims' pain and mutilated their bodies.

Wells was well received in England. To the chagrin and ire of southerners—and some other white Americans—she managed to influence British public opinion, creating sympathy for the victims of lynching and distaste for the lynchers. Her efforts were "vilified" by the white press (Bederman, 1995). After she returned from a 1904 trip, the *New York Times* reported that the day after her return to the United States, a black man had assaulted a white woman in New York City "for the purposes of lust and plunder." The newspaper suggested:

> The circumstances of his fiendish crime may serve to convince the mulatress missionary that the promulgation in New York just now of her theory of Negro outrages is, to say the least, inopportune. (quoted in Davis, 1983: 192)[11]

Before Wells left on her first trip to England, she had been involved in another crusade. Joining Frederick Douglass, she had protested the lack of African American representation at the 1893 World's Columbian Exposition in Chicago. The fabulous "White City" showcased "the millennial advancement of white civilization" (Bedermen, 1995: 31); the people of color represented at the exposition were exotic representatives of an African tribe (the Dahomey village). And, unfortunately, "[t]he popular reaction to the lightly clad Dahomans was part amusement, part repulsion." The only official black exhibit from a foreign country was the Haitian Building, of only which Frederick Douglass was the superintendent (Levy, 1973: 39). There was little about African Americans or about their contributions (Bederman, 1995; Levy, 1973).[12] Wells and Douglass published a pamphlet, "The Reason Why the Colored American Is Not in the World's Columbian Exposition" (Bederman, 39).

LEAVING THE SOUTH

However, colored Americans were on the move. In the postbellum period, African Americans sometimes continued to live on the land where they had labored as slaves. Unable to afford land of their own, many freedmen became tenants and sharecroppers. In doing so, they found themselves locked into a debt system from which it was difficult to escape. At the same time, the convict lease system and the chain gang became mechanisms that were often used for the control of black labor (Oshinsky, 1996; Lichtenstein, 1993).

The leasing of convicts as laborers was not unknown in the antebellum era. In 1858, Virginia solved its problem of what to do with the free blacks (nonslaves) who were incarcerated by leasing them out "to work outside the prison walls on canals, roads, and bridges" (Ayers, 1984: 62). The experiment worked so well the governor suggested extending it to white prisoners (Ayers, 67). However, although upper seaboard areas such as Virginia and Maryland had experience with free black inmates in the antebellum era, states in the Lower South had "virtually no free black inmates" in their penal system in the 1850s. In Alabama and Mississippi, they represented only 1 percent of the prison population, 4 percent in Tennessee, and 8 percent in Kentucky. These rates differed dramatically from those of Virginia, where free blacks made up one-third of the prison population, and Maryland, where free blacks were half of the inmates (Ayers, 61).

In the postbellum era, all southern states experienced a marked influx of African Americans into their penal system. It was at this point that the use of convict leasing and the chain gang gained increasing favor. In the post–Civil War South, the control of black labor was a particularly pressing problem. The criminal justice system provided one mechanism for achieving that control. In the case of Virginia, Keve (1986: 75–76) finds:

> The postwar period brought to blacks not only the "privilege" of penitentiary service for crime but caused them to be grossly overrepresented in the prison population. In 1893 for every 5,000 white persons in the general Virginia population there was one white prisoner; but for every 5,000 blacks there was 7.5 black prisoners. There was no unwillingness to contract out some of the white prisoners, but the natural inclination was to think first of sending the black prisoners to the labor camps.

As Franklin (1978: 103) points out, there were three basic ways in which African Americans could find themselves "bound by the law into servitude." They could sign a labor contract that they could not read. They could get into debt. Or they could "commit a crime as defined by an all-white criminal justice system." As Adamson (1983: 562) observes, in the postbellum South, "Crime control and economic oppression were one and the same thing." Crime control efforts by southern states included increasing the seriousness of a number of crimes. The theft of chickens and pigs was made a felony offense in Mississippi, Georgia, and North Carolina, producing a significant increase in "the prison labor pool" (Adamson, 562).

On the chain gang, prisoners suffered physical abuse. In the convict lease system, they suffered not only physical abuse, but starvation, deprivation of clothing and shelter, and unsafe (to put it mildly) working conditions in mines and swamps and other undesirable locales. In general, once prisoners were leased out to private contractors, corrections officials did nothing to monitor their treatment. Each year, a significant number of leased prisoners died—and were replaced in the next year's contract by others (see Mancini, 1996).

Adding insult to injustice, the spokesmen for the southern justice system offered their own negative pronouncements about African American prisoners. A physician from Tennessee discussed the Negro problem in his 1890 address to the National Prison Congress:

> We have difficulties at the South, which you at the North have not. . . . We have a large alien population, an inferior race. Just what we are to do with them as prisoners is a great question as yet unsettled. The Negro's moral sense is lower than that of the white man. . . . The Negro regards it as no disgrace to be sent to the penitentiary. He never cares to conceal the fact that he has been there. How are we going to reform that race we do not know. (quoted in Sellin, 1976: 146)

Some African Americans opted not to stay and find out. The rural South was a place where black success was limited by white racism. Those who worked hard and prospered found that their achievements were perceived as a threat by their white neighbors or that other whites simply resented that a black man should live well. These blacks were harassed, sometimes beaten, sometimes run out of town or killed. The possibility of a better life in another place lured blacks who migrated to Kansas and Oklahoma.

> Between 1870 and 1880 more than 21,000 blacks migrated from the former Confederacy to Kansas. This "Exoduster Movement" was large enough to draw the attention of the U.S. Senate, which held hearings and issued a three volume report on the matter. (Frehill-Rowe, 1993: 77)

This westward migration was in part to escape the conditions of the South. It was also a response to "agricultural opportunity consistent with the dominant U.S. values of the late 1800s of owning land and farming one's own land." In the "all-black towns" that were founded in Oklahoma, the migrants were also able briefly to experience self-government (Katz, 1996: 248–261).[13]

Other blacks, not drawn to the West, migrated to urban centers. Often this migration was a two or even several step process that involved a move from a rural farm to a nearby town and then to a southern city and then sometimes north (Bethel, 1981). Often, as with European immigrants, "chain migration" occurred, as migrants followed relatives and friends to the same urban city and neighborhood. Blacks were beginning the process that would transform them from a predominantly rural to a predominantly urban population.

CONCLUSIONS

It is not an exaggeration to say that for African Americans during the postbellum era, there was a clear link between the servitude they had experienced as slaves and the servitude they now experienced as prisoners in the criminal justice system. As Franklin (1978: 99–100) notes in discussing prison work songs:

> Certainly the prisoners throughout the South who were literally chained together while they worked and while they ate and while they slept had an experience no less oppressive and no less collective than their ancestors in chattel slavery, and the work songs have been every bit as important to their survival.

In the postbellum era, some of the prisoners who served on chain gangs were former slaves. They were now experiencing a new type of bondage. This is not to dismiss the crimes committed by blacks during the period. It is instead to point out that for both groups of black prisoners—both those guilty of a criminal offense and those caught up in the system because of the corruption of a white landowner or law enforcement officer—the parallels between slavery and prison were clear. Those parallels were also clear for other African Americans. It was very difficult not to realize that even in what was supposed to be freedom, black Americans continued to be harassed, imprisoned, and abused by the criminal justice system. And then, of course, there were the lynch mobs who administered their own brand of extralegal justice.

As Ayers (1984: 231) observes, "A vast and ever-increasing knowledge of white injustice and white hypocrisy did exist among blacks." This knowledge created "a reservoir of toleration" among African Americans of other blacks who became entangled in the criminal justice system. Undoubtedly, there was a sense of "There but for the grace of God go I." It was unnecessary actually to experience the chain gang to understand its meaning. For black Americans, chain gangs and convict lease and prison farms symbolized both white oppression and legal injustice.

These experiences became a part of the African American collective memory. They continue to color African American responses to the criminal justice system, particularly to such late twentieth century "innovations" as the reinstatement of the chain gang in some southern states.

NOTES

1. See Factor (1970) for his assessment of Douglass as a leader in the period after the Civil War. Factor asserts Douglass was "disillusioned and bewildered" by the responses of whites whom he thought of as friends of the Negro to the problem of lynching (Factor, 99).

2. Hall (1993: xx) describes "rape and rumors of rape" as "the folk pornography of the Bible Belt" during the postbellum era.

3. On origins of lynch law in America see Richard Maxwell Brown (1975) *Strain of Violence: Historical Studies of American Violence and Vigilantism*. New York: Oxford University Press.

4. Gross (1971: 127) describes *Up from Slavery*, Washington's autobiography, as a "public document as well as a personal memoir," which "is, at all times, directed to its white audience." However, Crunden (1994: 172–173) writes, "The book functioned in the black community in the same manner as the *Autobiography* of Benjamin Franklin had long functioned in the white: It was a handbook of the upwardly mobile survivor."

5. In 1890, at the conference "The Negro Question" at Mohonk Hotel in upstate New York, General Armstrong, superintendent of Booker T. Washington's alma mater, Hampton Institute, offered his assessment of the postbellum Negro:

> The great trouble with the Negro was not ignorance; it was deficiency of character. You can feed and clothe the Negro, build his home, and give him knowledge; but that does not necessarily build up character. That has got to be *worked* out. (Barrows, 1969 [1890–1891])

6. See also Factor (1970), who discusses Douglass's postbellum position on help and self-help in two regions (North and South). Regarding African American leadership in the postbellum era, Factor observes:

> In many ways, the Negro public was harder to comprehend and more difficult to represent and prone to greater public relations problems than the white community. The Negro public was newly formed, its problems newly formulated, its leadership and organization barely established. (89)

7. Of course, this depends on what one means by possessing whiteness. Some people of mixed heritage who were visibly "white" were defined by law as black and therefore denied whiteness as a property. Some of these people could and sometimes did pass into the white race. But neither they nor African Americans who could not "pass" considered this the most desirable alternative to the possession of equal rights.

8. See Giddings (1984: 30) on the historian Philip Bruce's "diatribe" against the black race, including African American women, whom he described as "morally obtuse" and "openly licentious."

9. In *Southern Horrors* (1892), Wells indicted "a malicious and untruthful white press" for its role in inciting mob violence (Wells-Barnett, 1969). See Tindall (1966: 238) on the situation in South Carolina. He reports "a tendency in the white press to approve, or to deprecate only mildly, the application of lynch law to victims guilty or suspected, of murder or rape."

10. However, Wells also advocated self-defense by blacks. She suggested, "A Winchester rifle should have a place of honor in every black home, and it should be used for that protection which the law refuses to give" (Wells-Barnett, 1969: 23).

11. This focus on Wells is not intended to minimize the work by the other black women who crusaded against lynching. One of the more famous was Mary Church Terrell, the first president of the National Association of Colored Women. In 1904—in response to an article by Thomas Nelson Page—Terrell wrote an essay for the *North American Review*. She refuted the causes and justifications Nelson, a popularizer of the "Old South," had given for lynching. Other women, both black and white, took active stands against lynching. See Hall's *Revolt against Chivalry* (1993) for her account of the antilynching crusade led by Jessie Daniel Ames, a white southern reformer. As Hall points out in this revised edition of her book, it is only in the last several decades that the work of black female reformers has been brought to light by a new generation of female scholars. See Hall's discussion of the difficulties black middle class and white middle class female reformers encountered when they tried

to understand each other's perspectives and work together. Also see the work of scholars such as Deborah Gray White (black women's clubs) and Evelyn Brooks Higginbotham (the women's movement in the black church).

12. But at least two blacks who would later be important contributors to both African American and American culture were there. James Weldon Johnson, later of the NAACP, joined twenty-five of his classmates in serving as "chairboys," who pushed visitors in wheelchairs around the exhibits (Levy, 1973: 37). Scott Joplin, the ragtime musician, spent his time in the "sporting district" that sprung up near the fairground to provide entertainment for out-of-town visitors (Haskins and Benson, 1978).

13. See also Painter (1977) for her account of the "Exodusters" migration to Kansas.

CHAPTER 6

Life in the City

In *Blues People* (1963: 96), the playwright and literary scholar Amiri Baraka (formerly published under L. Jones) writes, "It was a decision Negroes made to leave the South, not an historical imperative." A decision, yes, but blacks were affected by their own variations on the "push–pull" factors that affected European immigrants who left their homes to come to America.[1] In a process of internal migration, African Americans left their homes in the South, a region in which they suffered poverty and oppression, for other regions—the North, Midwest, Far West—where they hoped to find more and better opportunities. In this they had something in common with the immigrants they would meet in the cities they moved to—they were all searching for a better place, for a place where they and their children could have better lives.

In 1890, the majority of blacks lived in rural areas. Only 19 percent lived in cities. By 1920, one-third lived in urban areas. Between 1915 and 1925 almost one million blacks migrated north (Morris, 1980: 5–6). As the twentieth century began, many African Americans were on the brink of an urban adventure. Others had long been established in the cities to which the migrants were moving. There were tension-producing differences between these new migrants and the seasoned urbanites. Even so, these two groups found themselves sharing the limited living spaces available to them in American cities. Within these spaces, they strove to sustain urban communities. However, the spaces allotted to them became increasingly less desirable.

This matter of undesirable living spaces was not a new one. Even before the Civil War, the living conditions encountered by poor black laborers in the city constituted a threat to their health and safety.[2] These conditions continued to be a problem in the postbellum era. For example, in Columbus,

Ohio, in 1881, the Visiting Committee for the Negro schools complained about the " 'unhealthy moral atmosphere [of] saloons and streetcorners' which surrounded the city's largest black public school. In the 1890s the neighborhood came to be known as the 'Bad Lands' for its pervasive crime, gambling, and prostitution" (Gerber, 1976: 107).

With regard to crime and vice, one of the questions was who was responsible for its existence in black neighborhoods. Did the migrants create the crime problem? Gerber (1976: 96–97) observes that in Columbus, the perspective of upper and middle class whites was that "poverty and crime were not simply deprivation and violence, but 'Negro crime' and 'Negro poverty.' " These conditions were attributed to "race, rather than social circumstances." This white tendency toward "racial determinism" was illustrated in most of Ohio's daily newspapers, which gave "ample coverage to crime and social disorganization in black neighborhoods." These newspaper articles were "often humorous in tone (except when the victims of crime were whites)." They "revealed a deep-seated belief that fighting, drinking, gambling, and prostitution were the peculiar characteristics of an undisciplined, irresponsible people" (Gerber, 107–108).

By the turn of the century, educated African Americans were beginning to offer their own analysis of the social problems in black communities. Perhaps the most prominent spokesperson was the Harvard-educated social scientist/historian W.E.B. Du Bois. Commenting on Du Bois's study, *The Philadelphia Negro* (1899), Gaines (1996: 153) observes, "Du Bois sought to promote more enlightened approaches to issues like crime, linking it to poverty and a low standard of social justice, within which 'selfishness and greed prevail[ed].'" However, at the time when he conducted his study, he was not yet the militant spokesperson for his race that he would become; his approach to his research was grounded in his own elite background and training (Gaines, 155). In fact, Du Bois would help to lay the groundwork for what Gaines describes as the "urban pathology" approach to research on blacks in the city. With *The Philadelphia Negro*, Du Bois "broke tentatively with the usual perception of the cultural and moral shortcomings of urban blacks and rejected prevailing hereditary explanations of poverty and crime." However, his "construction of class differences among blacks was predicated on cultural and moral distinctions measured by the degree of conformity to patriarchal family norms." In his focus on urban poverty, Du Bois "anticipated the work of subsequent studies, more notably those of E. Franklin Frazier, which characterized black poverty as an irregular preponderance of matriarchal authority." But what both Du Bois and Frazier had intended to do was "to demonstrate the harmful effects caused by discrimination" (Gaines: 157).

In the 1960s, this early work by these two black scholars on urban pathology would influence Daniel Patrick Moynihan as he prepared his report on the black urban family. But at the turn of the century, blacks were engaged in living the urban history that would later be the subject of scholarly analysis.

CLASS CONFLICTS

In his "people's history" of the 1920s, Page Smith (1987) describes the black upper class in the city as having something in common with the prosperous German Jews. Both groups were concerned about the new arrivals who moved into their neighborhoods in the early twentieth century. They were concerned about the boisterous ways of these newcomers and about the effect they would have on old established neighborhoods and how they would reinforce ethnic stereotypes.

Smith makes the interesting assertion that rural and small-town blacks were equally disturbed by what they found when they moved to urban centers. According to Smith, these migrants "felt threatened by the involvement of poor urban blacks in crime and drugs and, during prohibition, bootleg liquor" (Smith, 212). In the 1920s and 1930s, African American writers such as Rudolph Fisher would begin to focus on this "culture shock" experienced by the migrants.[3] But initially, it was the established residents who provided the most vocal commentary about the impact of migration on their communities. They commented on the loud and emotional religious practices of the migrants. They commented on their rambunctious children. They commented on the ignorance of the women and the uncouthness of the men. They wondered why these people persisted in dressing in outlandish fashion and why they conducted so much of their lives in full public view. They offered their negative opinions of the music the migrants had brought with them to the cities—the spirituals they sang in the storefront churches and the blues they sang in saloons and at "rent parties."

By the turn of the century the music of the southern juke joints and roadhouses had made its way to urban centers such as Chicago and St. Louis. The "sporting life" attracted musicians to the "waterfront saloons in New Orleans, to Chicago's Midway, and eventually to Harlem's side streets" (Peretti, 1997: 22–23). Their music, secular and "sinful," was not the kind of music approved of by respectable black people. But it was the music that captured the life experiences of the lower class black migrants. These blue songs were the songs of the prisoners on southern chain gangs.[4] These were the songs of love and betrayal and hard work and debts. The blues also told tales of unruly women and of black badmen (Griffin, 1995). The blue songs described such figures of African American folklore as Stagolee (Stackolee), the unrepentant outlaw. In the postbellum era, white newspapers carried stories about the "new Negro"—the black badman, the "bad nigger"—who challenged racial mores. This was the reckless black who gambled, stole, got drunk, and lived off willing black (and sometimes white) women. He fought both black men and white. He was the black man whom whites were finally forced to kill or send to jail.

Sometimes when he got out of jail, he went north. Leadbelly, the blues singer, had gone north when he got out of Angola Prison. He became a famous musician and toured in Europe and sang in Carnegie Hall. But Leadbelly was special. Some of the southern badmen just took their badness to the city, where they joined their northern counterparts to drink and brawl together. The blues captured in its lyrics the life-styles of these men and the women with whom they associated. But even more significantly, the blues captured the everyday struggles of blacks who were trying to cope with the "troubles" in their lives.[5]

STANDING ON THE CORNER

> Standin' on the corner, wern't doin no hahm,
> Up come a 'liceman an' he grab me by de ahm. (Franklin, 1978: 104)

For black migrants to the city, one of the basic issues they encountered had to do with the use of public space. In the city, public spaces such as street corners were subject to surveillance and monitoring. Standing on the corner could constitute "criminal behavior." As Gerber (1976: 284) states, "The villagers' custom of standing along the Main Street to talk and pass the time now brought arrests." The arrest of a lounging black man would not necessarily have been viewed as an injustice by everyone in the black community. In truth, "[t]he settled black northern population viewed with distaste the street-corner men and other newcomers who turned old respectable black neighborhoods into ghettos" (Henri, 1975: 196). Even the *Chicago Defender*, the black newspaper that had been so vigorous in its boosterism of black migration, had some complaints about the new arrivals, taking the migrants "to task for their appearance and behavior" (Henri, 96). The Chicago Urban League offered new arrivals a list of dos and don'ts, guidelines for appropriate behavior in their new environment (Henri, 96).

Class differences were at work. But, at the same time, the settled residents had legitimate concerns about the quality of life in their neighborhoods. What they saw was that as more newcomers arrived, the communities in which they lived suffered. In the early twentieth century, the arrival of migrants was linked to increased overcrowding, poverty, crime, and illiteracy. The migration of more blacks into urban centers marked the point at which black neighborhoods began to decline.

But the migrants were not responsible for creating the ghettos,[6] which were created by whites who placed boundaries on black settlement and enforced those boundaries with petitions, restrictive covenants, and sometimes violence.[7] Because of these racial boundaries, middle class blacks, with no place else to go because of a lack of available housing, found themselves living as neighbors with people who seemed not to share their concern with respectability or to be as law-abiding. Prominent among these annoying new neighbors were the men who loitered on street corners and in poolrooms and bars.

However, as gender historians would argue, such behavior by black males should be examined within the context of American manhood. As Kimmel (1996: 100) observes, by the turn of the twentieth century, "masculinity" in America "was increasingly an act, a form of public display . . . men felt themselves on display at virtually all times . . . the intensity of the need for such display was increasing." For middle class males this awareness of their masculinity was exhibited in the "massive nationwide health and athletics craze" and the efforts of men to develop "manly physiques as a way of demonstrating that they possessed the interior virtues of manhood" (120).

> Traditionally working-class institutions, like the billiard hall, the saloon, or the street corner, occupied an increasingly important place in working-class men's lives. (Kimmel, 124)

Like other males of their class, black males engaged in "masculine" activities in male gathering places. But street corners were public spaces. Activities in billiard rooms and saloons spilled out into the streets. To their respectable neighbors, these men constituted a real or potential threat to peace and safety. At the same time, police officers might well have perceived them as personal affronts, challenges to their dominance of turf.

These conflicts symbolized differing perspectives about the black male's use of space and his appropriate public behavior. As Ownby (1990: 2) states, "Recreation takes places within systems of oppositions. When they are enjoying themselves people express not only who they are, but, very often who they are not." When some of these black males who loitered on city streets had lived in the South, they had attracted negative attention there too. As they engaged in recreations that expressed who they were, they gave visible proof of who they were not. Even though white males and black males sometimes passed their leisure time together, there were other white citizens who were concerned about the presence of black men on city streets and in places of amusement.

> Town life was, for many whites in the postbellum period, more threatening than it had been before emancipation. In the antebellum years, whites had always complained that blacks lounged around town too much, but their complaints intensified into fear after emancipation. . . . Rural whites viewed these groups of blacks, who seemingly had nothing to do and were unsupervised by

whites as one of the more menacing features of a trip to town. (Ownby, 1990: 54–55)

When they migrated to northern cities, black men continued to pass their time on the street. They continued to make public space their own. In doing so, they were again perceived by some people—both black and white—as an annoying and sometimes menacing feature of the city landscape. One of the questions for respectable people was what able-bodied men were doing lounging on street corners and hanging out in billiard rooms. Why didn't they have jobs?[8] Many of their black middle class critics were aware of the difficulties these black men—often semiliterate or illiterate, unskilled, and competing with lower class whites—had in finding jobs. Even so, they found the public display of their lack of gainful employment both irritating and embarrassing.

Perhaps many of the men who spent their time on street corners felt some degree of frustration if not embarrassment. In the city, both black males and black females found the job market was not always what they had hoped for when they left home. They often found themselves either with no job, competing with white immigrants for jobs, or working in domestic service occupations.[9] The good news was that these service jobs often paid better than they had in the South. The bad news was that such jobs still placed the men and women who held them in a subservient relationship to whites—with all that implied.

WORKING IN THE CITY

In Richard Wright's collection of short stories *Eight Men* (1940) there is a fable of sorts titled "Man of All Work" about a man who puts on one of his wife's dresses in order to get a job as a domestic. He is almost killed when the white wife of the household finds her husband engaged in lustful pursuit of "the maid" and expresses her displeasure with a gun. The black man comes away from this adventure with a check for two hundred dollars in payment for his gunshot wound and his silence. When he gets home, he does not tell his wife exactly what happened. He does ask her, "How do you women learn it?" That is, how do black women learn to survive the pitfalls inherent in being required to function in white-dominated space. He assures his wife that he will not be "caught dead again in a dress."

In this fable, Wright captures the half comic, half tragic dilemmas faced by black female domestics. Black females were certainly not the only women who worked as domestic servants. In fact, they sometimes competed with women of other ethnic groups for positions. However, because of the difficulty black males sometimes had in finding jobs, the income of the black woman became "a large proportion of the household income in the black community" (Henri, 1975: 3). And she tended to spend much, if not all, of her married life in the labor force.

A variety of issues existed around this concentration of black women in domestic employment. These issues included the impact on the woman's own family when she was required to "live in" or to spend long hours at work. The low wages received by the "hired help" meant that a woman with a family was often required to swallow her pride and accept hand-me-downs from her white employers. It meant that she supplemented her family's diet with the leftovers from the white family's meal—or sometimes with food she "pilfered" from the kitchen. It meant that she was required to observe the rituals of subservience required by her employer, and to tolerate verbal abuse.

But the domestic in the city was not as powerless as she might have been in a rural setting. She could—if she "lived out"—go home at night to her own black neighborhood. She could acquire several employers for whom she did "day work"—which paid less, but gave her some control over her labor. She could, if worse came to worse, simply quit and never have to see her employer again. However, as Wright's fable indicates, in the end it always came back to the fact that the black domestic was entering the "intimate space" of a white household. There she found herself engaged in an ongoing psychological game of wits with her employer.

Sometimes the conflict between employer and employee became a matter of crime and justice. Sometimes black domestics were victims of crimes. The offenses against them ranged from having the wages they had been paid stolen from their purses to being slapped by white women or sexually harassed, even raped, by white males. Sometimes black domestics committed—or perhaps more often—were accusing of committing offenses. These offenses ranged from stealing food, jewelry, money, and clothing to destroying property or striking a child.

Domestics were also suspected of "snooping." This was a charge that many of them would not have denied. In oral history interviews,[10] black women who worked as domestics indicate that they, like the female house slaves before them, saw the wisdom of knowing the people with whom they were dealing. In the South and to some extent in the North, there was a grapevine among domestics about white employers—about the ones who were good to work for and the ones who were not, and in general about what white folks were up to. In the North, domestics shared such information on their customary days off when they met in restaurants and clubs and other gathering places.

For some women who migrated to the city, the process of acquiring a job and becoming a "professional" domestic was one in which they received instruction. Settlement houses and other agencies offered formal courses in "domestic science." Some women took such courses. But often the path that migrants followed was one in which they arrived, stayed with a relative or

friend, and were shown how to go about securing employment and instructed on how to handle employee–employer relations. Some single
women in their teens or younger went to the city or were sent there to care
for the children of a relative while she worked. Later they would find jobs
of their own.[11]

However, it was the young female migrants who arrived in the city alone
and friendless who were of particular concern to the reformers. Like the
immigrant women who arrived by ship, they were preyed upon by unscru-
pulous characters on the lookout for new arrivals. These predatory men—
and women—hung about in train stations. For this reason, middle class reformers decided that it was necessary that they have their own agents in the
stations to greet migrant women and to direct them to a settlement house
or other agency where they could stay or receive information about lodging
and help in finding a job. For example, the White Rose Working Girls'
Home in New York City sent its agents out to meet young women who
were arriving in the city. It also had agents in Norfolk, Virginia, a terminal
of departure to the North. The home provided young women with housing,
training, and lessons in "race history" (Henri, 1975: 126–127; Cash, 1991).

The reformers were also concerned about the "employment agents" who
went south to recruit young women, enticing them to the city with promises
of jobs as domestics. The jobs often turned out to be in a brothel. The
reformers attempted to counteract the recruitment efforts of these bogus
employment agents.

Black working women were also organizing to protect themselves. They
formed organizations that focused on the concerns of domestics, particularly
fair wages and acceptable working conditions. In several cities, black domestics attempted to force employers to the negotiating table by going out
on strike. These strikes were limited in their effectiveness. But they did
provide one model for activism by black working class women. These women
were also acquiring experience as community activists through their work in
churches and in community organizations. Although they were working
women, many of them were wives and mothers who shared with middle class
woman ideas about "respectability."

Among black males, some migrants were able to establish themselves in
service occupations as barbers, butlers, or caterers. Some were successful in
obtaining the coveted position of a Pullman sleeping car porter.[12] There
were also the black preachers. Some of these ministers migrated to the city,
following their congregations, where they established churches that reflected
the southern roots of minister and members. Unfortunately, these new
churches often provoked negative responses from established residents of
black urban communities. They found distasteful the practices of the worshippers, who shouted, sang, and occasionally "spoke in tongues." The ministers of the new churches were suspected of being not only uneducated but

perhaps con men who were fleecing their flocks. In these urban settings, as in the rural South, the exploits of the black preacher became legendary.

The black minister was also legendary for his command of the "word." The word had power. The ability of the black minister—like the black preachers of slavery time—to comfort and to scold, to challenge and to exhort, made him an important leader in the black community. The man who could command words and use them well was a man who could lead his people.

There was also the black undertaker, the solemn faced man in the black suit—so caustically satirized by Chester Himes[13]—who received the bodies of black migrants. He was the man who arranged for their burials or shipped them home to be buried in southern soil. The undertaker was both respected and avoided. He was above all essential to the black community because even if a white mortician had been willing to handle a black body, few African Americans would have trusted him with the care of a loved one. Death, like life, was segregated.[14]

The black businessman who came from the South and opened a business entered into direct competition with the established black middle class. He was also competing with the white-owned businesses in the community. It was becoming a bone of contention for blacks that whites owned businesses, profited from them, but returned little to black communities. In Harlem in 1915, only 12 percent of businesses were black-owned; in Chicago, in the black ghetto, less than one-third of the businesses were (Henri, 1975: 159). At the same time, by the 1920s, blacks from the Caribbean were also becoming a part of the competitive mix (Holder, 1980).

ORGANIZATION BUILDING

But even as African Americans were dealing with life inside their own segregated communities, there was a continuing awareness that white violence remained a potent factor in their lives. The National Urban League had been founded to deal with the economic problems of blacks. The National Association for the Advancement of Colored People (NAACP) came into being as a response to the issues of crime and justice.

It was Booker T. Washington who was in part responsible for providing the impetus to the movement that would culminate in the founding of the NAACP. One of Washington's ideological foes, William Monroe Trotter, publisher of *The Guardian*, had been aggressive in his opposition to Washington's positions on race relations. On July 30, 1903, Trotter confronted Washington during a speech that Washington was giving at the Columbus Avenue AMC Zion Church in Boston. The encounter—which became known as the "Boston riot"—ended in the arrest of Trotter and his sister Maude. Trotter served thirty days in Boston's Walnut Street Jail. This disturbed W.E.B. Du Bois, who felt Trotter had been treated unfairly. Du Bois decided the time had come to take a formal position on race relations.[15] and became the moving force behind the Niagara Movement. The first conference of the movement was held near Niagara Falls in July 1905; the second convened at Harper's Ferry (site of John Brown's martyrdom) (Fox, 1970).

The Niagara Movement was "neo-abolitionist in outlook." It advocated "federal school subsidies, economic reconstruction, and black suffrage, and repudiated racial subservience and religious hypocrisy" (Capeci and Knight, 1996: 736). The activism of the Niagara Movement led to the founding in 1909 of the NAACP, an organization for racial advancement founded by black and white intellectuals (Henri, 176–177; Bennett, 1968: 221–229). The NAACP would eventually wage many of the legal battles that paved the way for the Supreme Court decision in *Brown v. Board of Education* in 1954 and the black civil rights movement that followed.

CONCLUSIONS

Black migrants came to the city. As Griffin (1995: 98) observes, both migrants and the cities to which they fled were changed by this process. The impact was "multifaceted. . . . Individual migrants [we]re influenced by their confrontation with the urban landscape, and as a group they beg[a]n the process of changing the sights and sounds of the cities they inhabit[ed]." As we have discussed, the street corner was symbolic of the conflict over public space and its use that was played out within the community between those of different classes and backgrounds. This matter of "contested space" would continue to be an important issue in urban areas. The use of space, the control of space, is today a factor in encounters not only between community residents but between African Americans and law enforcement officers.

The transformation of black neighborhoods by migration was accompanied by an increased use of black urban communities as locations in which "public order offenses" or "vice offenses" flourished. The blame for the presence of these activities would continue to be disputed. However, what would become clear was that black urban communities such as Harlem were locations in which law enforcement was both too vigorous and too lax. Police brutality was accompanied by police corruption. And law-abiding black people—domestics, laborers, teachers, and undertakers—continued to go about their days, trying to make a living, trying to cope with the social structure that defined how and where and what they could do. At the same time, they engaged in institution building (creating black churches and civic and mutual aid organizations) and continued to seek self-determination and control over their own lives.

NOTES

1. See Trotter (1991: 1–2) on the "three distinct, but interrelated conceptual orientations in black urban history" that appear in the literature on black migration: (1) the race relations model (which emerged at the turn of the century and peaked through the 1950s), (2) the ghetto model (which emerged early in the 1960s and dominated scholarship through the late 1970s), and (3) the proletarian approach (building upon the ghetto model and focusing on class formation). Earlier scholars, focusing on the "push–pull" factors of black migration, sometimes stripped the process of its historical context or failed to acknowledge the agency of black migrants as decision makers.

2. For example, see Savitt (1978) on the disease-engendering conditions free black laborers and those slaves who hired themselves out and were allowed to arrange for their own board encountered in the housing that was available to them.

3. See Griffin (1995) for her discussion of the handling of migration themes by black writers and artists, including Fisher and Wright.

4. See Franklin (1978: 108) on the development of the blues form "with the prison experience at its core." Franklin also discusses the criminal as hero in these songs and ballads.

5. In his cultural theory of delinquency, Walter Miller describes the "focal concerns" of the lower class as *trouble, toughness, smartness, excitement, fate*, and *autonomy*. These concerns are expressed in the lyrics of blues songs. However, this observation is not offered in support of Miller's theory concerning lower class culture as a "generating milieu" for delinquency.

6. See Henri (1975:125) on sociological studies of ghetto life. Henri cites Du Bois's reference to the "submerged tenth" to be found in urban neighborhoods (Henri, 118).

7. See Bardolph (1970) and Davis and Graham (1995) regarding the Supreme Court on restrictive covenants.

8. For discussion of street corner men in the 1960s see Liebow (1967).

9. Between 1860 and 1890, "the largest world-wide population movement in human history brought 10 million immigrants, mostly from Europe, but from Asia as well, to the United States" (Gutman, 1989: 17). For more on immigration and its impact on American society, also see Daniels (1990).

10. For example, Clark-Lewis (1996), who interviewed eighty-two women who migrated to Washington, D.C., at the turn of the twentieth-century.

11. This discussion of female domestics is drawn from the works of Gray (1993), Clark-Lewis (1996), and Katzman (1978). Also see Harris (1982), on the evolving images of domestics in black American literature, and Bailey (1999).

12. Henri (1975:143) notes that among the jobs coveted by black women was that of maid in a theater lounge or on a "limited luxury train."

13. The African American novelist Chester Himes includes among the characters in his first mystery novel (*A Rage in Harlem*, 1957) an undertaker named Mr. H. Exodus Clay. However, it should be noted that Himes satirizes all of the denizens of his ghetto. His police officers are named "Coffin Ed" Johnson and "Grave Dig-

ger" Jones. Himes offers in his "domestic Harlem" series one of the most sustained literary visions of the "dangerous ghetto."

14. Concerning black cemeteries and burial rites see Crist et al. (1997) and Maish et al. (1997)

15. Capeci and Knight (1996) provide a generally insightful analysis of the impact of Du Bois's stay in Atlanta (1897–1910) on his thinking about racial justice. While he was in Atlanta, a brutal lynching (of Sam Hose in 1899) and the 1906 Atlanta race riot occurred. In his autobiography (1968: 222) Du Bois recalls:

> Two considerations thereafter broke in upon my work and eventually disrupted it: first, one could not be a calm, cool, and detached scientist while Negroes were lynched, murdered and starved; and secondly, there was no such definite demand for scientific work of the sort that I was doing.

However, Capeci and Knight suggest, "Had [Booker T.] Washington's Atlanta Compromise of 1895 been effective Du Bois might have continued to concentrate on a scientific approach to solving the nation's racial riddle" (735). See also Fox (1970) on Du Bois's relationship with Washington and Trotter.

CHAPTER 7

The Era of Wilson and Griffith

In 1913, Monroe Trotter led a group of African Americans in a meeting at the White House with President Woodrow Wilson. Trotter and his associates were there to express to Wilson their concern regarding the movement to segregate the federal civil service. During his campaign, Wilson, a Democrat, had courted the support of black Republicans; Trotter had been among those who voted for him. Now, he had come to the White House to indicate his misgivings because the Wilson administration showed signs of being retrogressive in the area of race relations. Wilson assured Trotter that he would investigate the situation.

A year later, in 1914, an angry Monroe Trotter returned to the White House. He told Wilson that the black leaders who had voted for him were being branded race traitors because of the actions taken by the Wilson administration. Wilson offered no words of comfort. Instead he asserted that by segregating the federal civil service, he had prevented conflict between blacks and whites and suggested that Trotter and his colleagues were stirring up the racial cauldron by their agitation on the subject. The next day, a *New York Times* article reported that the president had been annoyed by the criticism ("President Resents Negro's Criticism") (Link, 1978 and 1979, Wilson Papers, Vols. 28 and 31).[1]

The following year, 1915, Wilson had another visitor in the White House. The filmmaker D. W. Griffith provided the president with a private screening of his new historical epic, *The Birth of a Nation*. Wilson was reported to have enjoyed the film immensely. Later, in the midst of the controversy surrounding the film, Wilson backed away from any appearance of endorsing its favorable portrayal of the Ku Klux Klan. But Wilson's attitude toward

African Americans was now painfully clear. They had no friend in the White House.

In fact, by the second decade of the twentieth century, when Wilson, the first southerner to be elected president since the Civil War, assumed his duties, the country had already moved toward the philosophical reconciliation of North and South. The country as a whole had moved toward accepting the southern assessment of the place of African Americans. This reconciliation had been hastened not only by the popular literature of the era, but by the work of historians such as Woodrow Wilson.

The country had also shared the experience of viewing D. W. Griffith's 1915 blockbuster. *The Birth of a Nation* was about the post–Civil War era of Radical Reconstruction in the South. It was based on the novel *The Clansman*, by Thomas Dixon, a former minister. Both novel and film were in the tradition of the southern mythology that presented the South as the victim of an alliance of white Republican carpetbaggers and ignorant black freedmen. In this film, the lustful black mulatto also had his role to play. In one scene, he (a white actor in "blackface") pursues the innocent young sister of the white hero through the woods. Before her brother can arrive to rescue her, she is forced to jump from a cliff to avoid being ravaged by the mulatto savage. But in the climatic final scene, the hero avenges her death and the other wrongs done to the South as he leads the newly formed Ku Klux Klan against the intruders.

In theaters around the country, white audiences cheered the triumphant ride of the Klan. Of course, there were other whites who, even though they admired the technical achievements of Griffith's movie, questioned its ethics. They joined the NAACP in attempting to ban the showing of the film but met with only limited success. Griffith's movie was unlike anything the American public had seen—it had everything: action, adventure, romance, family values, the triumph of "good" over "evil." It was worth the premium price being charged for admission.[2]

When Griffith provided a special showing for the members of the Supreme Court, they were favorably impressed. So was Woodrow Wilson, the former Princeton historian. Wilson was reported to have said after seeing *The Birth of a Nation* that it was "like writing history with lightning . . . my only regret is that it is all so terribly true" (Bullard, 1991: 19). With those words, he undoubtedly raised even more questions in the minds of African Americans who remembered his promise of "fair dealing" (Aptheker, 1971).[3] It was now clear that the Wilson administration could not be depended upon to take vigorous action against the acts of violence against blacks that were still occurring in the South and elsewhere.

THE NEGRO AS BEAST

The continuation of racial violence in the twentieth century was rooted in the perceptions that dated back to the era of slavery about black inferiority and black savagery.[4] These perceptions had been given the color of social science in the postbellum era with the rise of social Darwinism. In books such as Charles Carroll's *The Negro as Beast* (1900), a popular bestseller, the Negro was rendered subhuman.[5] The focus of such works on the alleged emergence of savage characteristics in blacks that had been masked and controlled by the institution of slavery—black "regression"—provided justification for white "self-defense." The savage black must be controlled. He must be taught his place if he were to live among civilized whites. The ritual of lynching provided an object lesson for all blacks. It was an exercise in not only specific but general deterrence.

These acts of white assertion came at a time when white males as a group were feeling increasing concern about their own manhood and virility. The result was a white male celebration of the "vigorous life." White males were exploring their own "natural man"—the "primitivism" in themselves. But the natural white man was a superior creature. Nowhere was this better reflected than in the adventure novels published during this period. Perhaps the best-known and most enduring are the adventures of a white "Lord of the Jungle." Edgar Rice Burroughs began his series with *Tarzan of the Apes* (1911). Tarzan, the heir of Lord Greystoke, is orphaned when his parents die in West Africa. He is raised by a tribe of monkeys. In spite of his circumstances, he emerges as a natural aristocrat, lord of all he surveys. He dominates not only the wild animals, but the black natives. Tarzan was a literary product of the colonial imperialism that fueled the rise of the British Empire (Pieterse, 1992: 109). In America, that same spark had ignited the Spanish-American War.

American males, inspired by President Teddy Roosevelt's exploits in the wild West and in darkest Africa, had flexed their muscles and displayed their virility. But the assumption of many white males was that such displays were reserved for themselves. A black male who engaged in such behavior represented a social threat.

TWO LYNCHINGS

In May–December 1911, the houses in a densely populated section of Boston's Beacon Hill were demolished. The black Bostonians who had lived in the houses had been evicted to make way for an "elevated railway" (Boston University Art, 7–8). The elevated railway—and even the displacement of the residents of the neighborhood to make way for it—might be described as symbolic (or perhaps symptomatic) of twentieth-century progress.

The events that took place in Coatesville, Pennsylvania, during that same year were another barometer of American progress. In August 1911, a black man named Zachariah Walker was lynched and "burned alive as a large crowd looked on, fascinated by the spectacle" (Downey and Hyser, 1991: 1). At least seventy other lynchings happened that year, but what was significant about Walker's lynching was that it happened in "a growing steel town in the North, where people were thought to be more tolerant on matters of race" (Downey and Hyser, 1).

Walker was a migrant from Virginia who had gone north, enticed by the promises of labor agents that a job in the steel mills would be available. The absence of "Jim Crow" (segregation laws) was also an attraction for black men like Walker. But Walker's new life took a sudden and dramatic turn one evening when he got drunk and became involved in an altercation with a special policeman for the steel mill. In the struggle, witnessed only by the two men involved, Walker killed the policeman.

As Zachariah Walker was being thrown onto a burning pyre by the white mob who had taken him from jail, he pleaded with them, "I killed Rice in self-defense. Don't give me no crooked death because I'm not white" (Downey and Hyser, 35). His pleas had no effect. Each of the three times he tried to crawl from the fire he was tossed or beaten back. Walker's death was slow and painful.

His lynching became a "catalyst" for the fledgling NAACP (Downey and Hyser, 8), which mobilized to conduct its own investigation and monitor what was happening in Coatesville in the aftermath of the lynching. After forming a special Coatesville Committee, the NAACP hired the William Burns Detective Agency to gather information. The cost was "nearly $2,400, a substantial sum for the often financially strapped NAACP" (Downey and Hyser, 101).

In the pages of the NAACP journal, *Crisis*, the editor, W.E.B. Du Bois, expressed outrage about the lynching.

> Blackness must be punished. Blackness is the crime of crimes, as the opera-bouffe senator-elect from Mississippi has amply proven. Why is it a crime? Because it threatens white supremacy. A black might—why civilization might be black! It is therefore necessary, as every white scoundrel in the nation knows, to let slip no opportunity of punishing this crime of crimes.

He went on to add, "It must warm the hearts of every true son of the republic to read how the brawn and sinew of Coatesville rallied to the great and glorious deed." And, with sarcasm and irony, he repeated as his refrain, "Let the eagle [symbol of American civilization] scream!" (Walden, 1972: 118–119)

The editors of other black periodicals joined Du Bois in denouncing the actions of the white mob in Coatesville. When President Taft failed to take a stand on the lynching, Monroe Trotter, editor of the *Boston Guardian*, carried the president's picture "with the caption: 'Wm Howard Taft—Silent as Citizens are Burned Alive' " (Ziglar, 1992: 333). Over the following months, more than one dozen black newspapers carried "periodic updates" on Coatesville (Downey and Hyser, 46). In fact, there was something to report: the state of Pennsylvania took action in response to the lynching. Arrests were made. Trials were conducted. But after ten months and the expenditure of ten thousand dollars, no convictions had been obtained. The defendants had all been acquitted.

Throughout this episode, the black community in Coatesville was restrained in its actions. The only significant response was by a group of businessmen who signed a "memorial" protesting Walker's death. However, it was not an emotional expression of outrage. The businessmen "were careful to condemn both murders; and while criticizing the practice of lynching in general, they exercised caution in calling for the prosecution of the instigators" (Downey and Hyser, 48). This measured response of the black community reflected the class divisions between the established residents and newcomers such as Zachariah Walker. The "established black citizens held the newcomers at arms length . . . wary of the migrants' potential to undermine whatever social and economic advantage they had achieved" (Downey and Hyser, 142).

These class differences also existed in urban communities in the South. Following a 1917 lynching in the city of Danville, the *Richmond Planet*—the black newspaper that served the Danville black community—offered this summary of the events:

> Walter Clark, a colored ne'er-do-well killed a policeman, wounded six other men and himself was shot to death by armed citizens. (*Planet*, October 20, 1917, quoted in Bailey, 1986: 155)

Walter Clark had shot and killed one of the policemen who came to arrest him after he wounded his common-law wife. According to the *Planet*, from all reports, Clark had not been "worth his salt." But he had been sharp enough to ask the police officers who were to arrest him for a warrant. And even though he had obviously been crazed "by contraband liquor or insane emotion," Clark had decided that his life would be sacrificed "as dearly as possible" (Bailey, 1986: 156).

The black newspaper went on to praise the actions of the mayor and the police force who had acted to prevent further violence. In an aside, the newspaper suggested that black people might have been able to persuade Clark to surrender. But, all and all, "race feeling" had not predominated in Danville. It seemed that "everybody there except Clark and the lynchers were in favor of upholding the majesty of the law" (Bailey, 1986: 156).

These two lynchings, north and south, illustrate the complexity of the responses of black communities to episodes of racial violence. The established middle class tended to give a careful response to such events. While criticizing the practice of lynch law and mob rule, the black "commercial–civic elite" tended to take a conservative (in the sense of "conserving") position that also condemned any acts by blacks that had provoked mob fury. Actions by local and state officials to prevent, stop, or control the spread of violence were praised. These officials were described as belonging to the "better class" of white people, who, like the "better class" of black people, abhorred violence and respected the law. Given the potential for white backlash, it is understandable that the established black community would have been cautious in its response. However, such responses also reflected the black middle class's sense of being different from the lower class.

When events such as those in Coatesville and in Danville occurred, the NAACP as a national rather than a local organization (although there were local chapters) was in a better (safer) position to take a vigorous stand against mob violence. The organization dedicated itself to documenting episodes such as the lynchings of Zachariah Walker and Walter Clark. It sent its officials to the scene when a lynching occurred to mingle with the townspeople and gather information. Walter White—a blond, blue-eyed black man—became notorious for his bold mingling with whites who assumed he was one of them.[6]

But, as this racial violence continued, another black male would offer an overt assault on the social mores governing the behavior of black men. In doing so, he attracted the wrath of white Americans (and some blacks) and became the focus of criminal prosecution. In African American popular culture, his name would become synonymous with both foolhardiness and heroism.

JACK JOHNSON AND THE MANN ACT

In 1970, the Hollywood film *The Great White Hope*, based on the play by Howard Sackler, caused a stir. In this film based on the life of Jack Johnson, the first black heavyweight boxing champion, James Earl Jones gave a bold, compelling performance. In the film—and in the ads promoting it—Jones is seen bare-chested. In the film, he struts about wearing a bowler with his blond mistress (Jane Alexander) on his arm. As the heavyweight champion, Jones laughs and brags. He plays to the press and keeps up a continuous assault on the sensibilities of the white public. Eventually Jones is made to pay for both his triumphs in the ring and his violations of racial mores. Charged with a violation of the Mann Act, he flees the country, first to Europe—where he and Alexander perform in a "Tom" play in order to feed themselves—then to Mexico, where Alexander commits suicide. Jones is finally brought down. He is forced to throw a fight as the price for coming home again. The "White Hope" triumphs. The virile "black buck" has been put back in his place.

In real life, Jack Johnson's flamboyant life-style became one of the focal points for the American discourse about race. Of Johnson, Gilmore (1975: 5) writes:

> Privately and publicly many blacks applauded Johnson's exploits because he defied all of the degrading customs of America. He was rich when most blacks were poor; free to do as he chose when most blacks were circumscribed; and braggadocious when many blacks were forced to bear their oppression in silence.

Gilmore concludes, when Johnson, the prizefighter, "battered a white man to his knees, he was the symbolic black man taking out his revenge on all whites for a lifetime of indignities" (5).

Yet, at the same time, blacks were concerned about the consequences to the black community of Johnson's exploits. Johnson, in his celebrity, posed the risk of white hostility.[7] Johnson was too reckless in his displays of virility. He was, as some observers have suggested, the personification of the "bad nigger" of African American folklore. In fact, Gilmore called his book about Johnson's impact on the black community *Bad Nigger!* Gilmore contends that although historians "have given scant attention" to the historical importance of the "bad nigger," "the traditions, legends, and glory of this figure still flourish and definitely motivate the conduct of many blacks today" (12–13).

But whatever Johnson symbolized for African Americans then and later, the response of the criminal justice system to him was aimed at corralling and punishing his flamboyant behavior. In 1912, after Johnson became the first black heavyweight, Congress acted to ban the interstate distribution and transportation of films showing prizefights (Gilmore, 90). Shortly thereafter, Johnson was targeted for prosecution as a "white slaver." He was charged with violation of the Mann Act, the transportation of a female across state lines for immoral purposes. The young woman in question was a nineteen year old from Minnesota who worked at Johnson's nightclub in Chicago as his secretary (Gilmore, 95). The gossip was that she had traveled to Chicago on her own and had been a prostitute when Johnson met her. At any rate, inspite of her mother's urging, the young woman, Lucille Cameron, refused to cooperate in Johnson's prosecution. She denied the charges. However, Cameron was not the only white woman with whom Johnson had consorted. He was still vulnerable.

He was also vulnerable to extralegal violence—or at least some of the whites who observed the court proceeding wished that he were. According to the *Chicago Daily News*, as Johnson left the Criminal Court Building, there were cries from the gathered crowd of "Kill him, lynch him" (quoted in Gilmore, 97). Johnson was burned in effigy. After his marriage to Lucille Cameron, a group of white Louisianians made a public offer to raise funds for a posse to go up to Chicago and "take care" of Johnson southern-style (Gilmore, 106).

In the black community, as the Cameron case unfolded, there was ambivalence. There was some resentment among blacks because of Johnson's apparent preference for white women. The *Philadelphia Tribune*, a black newspaper, suggested Johnson had a bad case of "white fever" (Gilmore, 98–99). But many blacks also felt that Johnson was the victim of biased media coverage and of prosecution based on racial prejudice. When Booker T. Washington, speaking in Detroit, condemned Johnson and assured his listeners that Johnson's actions were "repudiated by the great majority of right-thinking people of the Negro race" (Gilmore, 102), Washington himself came in for criticism. His statements brought sharp responses from the local NAACP and from several black newspapers, one newspaper accused him of being jealous of Johnson's fame (Gilmore, 102).

In his autobiography, Johnson wrote, "I have matched my wits with the police and secret agents seeking to deprive me of one of the greatest blessings man can have—liberty." Of his own conduct, Johnson wrote that "it had been no worse than that of thousands of others." He felt he was persecuted because "of my color, perhaps, and because of prejudices and jealousies" (Johnson, 1992.)[8]

Johnson had trampled on sacred racial mores. Perhaps many whites thought of Jack Johnson as they watched *The Birth of a Nation*. However, the country's attention was about to be directed outward to the affairs of Europe.

WAR AND RACE RELATIONS

As the United States entered World War I, Woodrow Wilson appointed Emmett Scott, Booker T. Washington's former secretary, to the position of a special assistant to the secretary of war. The appointment of Scott was not universally applauded by black Americans. But black leaders such as Du Bois echoed the words of black leaders during other wars.[9] As fighting men, Africans Americans would have a chance to prove their patriotism and their worthiness of the full rights of citizens. Some blacks expressed their dissent, but African Americans in general joined the war effort.

Black mobilization for war included migration to those urban centers where workers were needed in the war industries. The migrants hoped for not only a chance to support the military effort, but an opportunity to improve their economic status and to escape the social conditions in the South that made their lives difficult. In the 1920 study of black migration that he undertook for the Carnegie Endowment for International Peace, Emmett Scott reported on the factors that had played a role in the decision by black Americans to migrate.[10] Scott commented on such oppressive criminal justice mechanisms as the "fee system." A sheriff, such as the one in Jefferson

County, Alabama, was paid for feeding the prisoners in his jail; thus encouraged, he had an incentive to arrest large numbers of African Americans for minor or no offenses.

Concerning the treatment of blacks in southern courts, Scott wrote:

> Negroes largely distrust the courts and have to depend on the influence of their aristocratic friends. . . . When a white man kills a negro he is usually freed without extended legal proceeding, but the rule laid down by the southern judge is usually that when a negro kills a white man, whether or not in self-defense, the negro must die. (19)

Scott also commented on the efforts that whites had made to prevent blacks from migrating—ranging from arresting them for loitering at the train station to printing newspaper stories about blacks in the North who were suffering greatly from the rigors of northern winters. In response, the African American newspaper the *Chicago Defender*, vigorous in its encouragement of migration, had replied, "To die from the bite of frost is more glorious than at the hands of a mob" (Scott, 1969 [1920]).[11]

The wartime migration by blacks had its parallel in the migration of rural whites. In cities, the two groups came into conflict. A riot in East St. Louis in 1917 reminded blacks that they were fighting the war on two fronts. At home, they were fighting white prejudice and racial violence. In the military, black soldiers experienced much of what they had in other wars—segregation, poor training, inadequate equipment, white officers. Racial tensions in the southern towns where they were stationed sometimes erupted into violence.

In 1917, in Houston, Texas, a riot involving soldiers of the black Twenty-Fourth Infantry took the form of "pitched street battles" with whites (Mullen, 1973: 42) that left some of them wounded, others dead. Sixty-four black soldiers were arrested.

> In a one day trial, the largest murder trial in American history, an all-white military tribunal sentenced thirteen of the convicted soldiers to death by hanging and the remaining fifty-one to life imprisonment. (Mullen, 42)[12]

Faced with simmering racial tensions in southern towns, the War Department hurriedly shipped several units abroad. But the black soldiers found they were being used as common laborers in support units rather than as fighting men. When they were allowed to fight, some black units displayed their lack of training. But several units performed so well that they received the highest military honors from the French.

These honors were awarded to black soldiers by the French in spite of the memo titled "Secret Information Concerning Black American Troops" issued from General Pershing's office on August 17, 1918, which warned of the dangers inherent in treating blacks as social equals. The French were requested to help their white American allies by keeping the black soldier in his place (Mullen, 1973: 44).

Back home in America, black men who were being drafted sometimes found themselves arrested because of chicanery by local draft boards. Black women faced attempts by local authorities to enhance the federal "work or fight order" by applying it to them. For example, in Bainbridge, Georgia, black women, married or single, were threatened with a fine unless they got jobs. In the summer 1918, the arrests of several women prompted a mass meeting by local blacks, who issued a warning to local officials that they intended to resist the enforcement of this law " 'to the last drop of blood in their bodies.' No further arrests were made" (Aptheker, 1971: 169).

The sense of oppression and injustice that led to black discontent also contributed to an upsurge in black membership in voluntary organizations. The NAACP, which had "80 branches and nine thousand two hundred members" in December 1917, grew by the next year to "165 branches and forty-five thousand members, twelve thousand of whom were in the South" (Aptheker, 170). In July 1918, under pressure from the NAACP and at the urging of his aides, President Wilson issued a statement condemning lynching (Aptheker, 1971: 171). However, he did not throw his support behind a federal antilynching bill. He did not provide significant aid to black communities that were under siege during the race riots of what James Weldon Johnson called the "Red Summer" of 1919 (Henri, 1975: 319). Approximately twenty-five race riots occurred from June to December 1919 (Mullen, 50).

The factors that contributed to this wave of riots were the same as those that had contributed to earlier riots in East St. Louis and Springfield and Atlanta.

> The harping of the press on black crime, especially sex crimes; the headlining of violence; the corrupt politicians and police; the mutual fear and suspicion between blacks and whites . . . the deliberate creation of labor friction; and the exacerbation of racial violence, once it was under way, by unequal law enforcement. (Henri, 1975: 318)

But there was one "striking common characteristic of the 1919 riots"—when attacked, black people fought back. This kind of assertiveness had "only begun to be discernible before the war" (Henri, 318). Now, it added a new element to race riots in American cities.

But racial violence was also occurring in rural areas of the South. In October 1919, in Elaine, Arkansas, a meeting of black tenant farmers was "attacked" by the local sheriff and his men. The farmers were suspected of plotting the massacre of whites. In the violence that ensued, two hundred blacks and forty whites were killed. Seventy-nine blacks were put on trial, charged with murder and insurrection. Twelve were sentenced to death. Through the intervention of the NAACP, their sentences were commuted to prison terms (Henri, 321).[13]

The role of the NAACP in chapters such as the one in Atlanta was important in the ongoing struggle being waged by blacks. In Atlanta in 1919, the local chapter had a membership of seventeen hundred. The chapter had been involved in the prosecution of cases of debt peonage and had come to the defense of two blacks who killed whites in self-defense. It was also involved in a voter registration drive that had brought blacks to the polls in record numbers. The response by white Georgia politicians was to propose in the state assembly the following year a bill to bar blacks from voting or holding any elected office. Such institutional responses to black challenges to the status quo were buttressed by the resurgence of the Ku Klux Klan. In the post–World War I era, the KKK experienced a new birth not only in the South but around the country (MacLean, 1994: 28). In 1921, the Dyer bill Antilynching legislation was again killed in committee as a part of a political deal.

However, there were some black Americans, such as A. Philip Randolph, who doubted the antilynching legislation would have been effective even if it had been enacted. In a March 1919 editorial in *The Messenger*, he said capitalism was the cause of lynching; socialism was its cure. He advised his readers, "Don't be deceived by any capitalist bill to abolish lynching; if it became law, it would never be enforced" (12). However, the December 1920 issue of *The Messenger* included "An Open Letter to America on the Ku Klux Klan." Urging all Americans to work together to destroy the Klan, the letter described the organization as "criminal" and as not only anti-Negro, but anti-Catholic, anti-Jew, and antilabor. The letter called on President-Elect Warren G. Harding to use his inaugural address as an opportunity to "make special mention of the anti-American and criminal nature" of the Klan (168).

Meanwhile, in Harlem, New York, a cultural awakening was about to occur that would be a significant aspect of the response of one group of African Americans to oppression. Art was about to become propaganda. At the end of the war, New York's Fighting 364th Battalion had returned to the United States as heroes. With their white officers, they had marched in a ticker tape parade from Wall Street to the heart of Harlem. They displayed their style in the close rank formation learned from the French. The military band that would later become famous provided the music. It was through music and art and literature that Harlem was about to become the site of a "Negro Renaissance."

CONCLUSIONS

The experience of participating in a world war had a profound effect on all Americans. For African Americans, the war gave impetus to urban migration. The war experience made young African American males who went to Europe aware of themselves as both Americans who were loyal to their country, ready to fight and die for it, and Americans who were always "outsiders" in the eyes of their white countrymen. Even in another country, they were subject to humiliation at the hands of white Americans who wanted to ensure blacks were kept in their place.

In the postwar years, the resurgence of the Klan, the new assertiveness of black Americans who fought back when attacked, and the indifference (or antipathy) of federal leadership to race matters contributed to an atmosphere in which the "Red Summer" of 1919 was inevitable. When blacks looked to the justice system, they found no relief, and certainly little comfort. Even as riots were occurring in the city, United States Attorney General A. Mitchell Palmer, in the midst of his "Red Scare" round-up of subversives, described *The Messenger*, edited by A. Philip Randolph and Chandler Owen, as "the most able and most dangerous of the Negro publications." Palmer added that *The Messenger* was "representative of the most educated thought among Negroes" (Henri, 1975: 156). Obviously, from the attorney general's point of view, it was a bad thing when educated Negroes thought about American society.

NOTES

1. In 1914, during their "dialogue," Trotter reminded Wilson that federal employees "have been going into [integrated] public toilets for fifty years. They were going into public toilets when your administration came in." Trotter asserted that segregation in the federal workplace amounted to "degradation." Wilson responded, "I don't think it's degradation. That is your interpretation of it" (*Wilson Papers*, Vol. 31: 308–309).

2. About the film and its impact see Campbell (1981: 47–54) and Lynes (1985: 265–266). See also Delany et al. (1993: 198–199) for Bessie Delany's account of the arrest of W.E.B. Du Bois, Walter White, and E. Franklin Frazier for protesting the rerelease of the film in 1925.

3. According to O'Reilly (1995: 83–85), African Americans found Wilson's desire to segregate the facilities used by federal civil service workers a matter for concern because of the symbolic message it would send. Wilson, however, saw segregation as a "rational scientific policy" that would protect white female workers.

4. See Henri (1975: ix) on theories "justifying the exploitation of darker races in the imperialist rush for colonies." Also see Pieterse (1992).

5. See Haller (1995) for his discussion of scientific attitudes regarding racial inferiority, 1859–1900.

6. White recalled as an adult that the Atlanta Riot of 1906 had a profound effect on his psyche. He was a young boy when the riot occurred. It was as he and his equally white-skinned father prepared to defend their home against white rioters who intended to get the "nigger" mail carrier that he recognized his racial identity (White, 1969: 9–12).

7. Johnson's defeat of Jeffries ("the White Hope") on July 4, 1910, was followed

by racial violence in cities around the country, including Pittsburgh; Uvalde, Texas; New York City; and Little Rock, Arkansas (Henri, 1975:197).

8. See also Langum (1994) on the Mann Act and Johnson.

9. In an editorial in *Crisis* (July 1918), Du Bois urged black Americans to "forget [their] special grievances and close ranks with white Americans for the duration of the war." This editorial proved embarrassing for Du Bois because he was being considered for a commission as a captain in the Military Intelligence Branch, and his editorial seemed self-serving (Ellis, 1992: 96).

10. Scott was secretary-treasurer at Howard University at the time. To assist him in the research, he employed Monroe W. Work and Charles S. Johnson (who was a graduate student at the University of Chicago). Robert E. Park (who was president of the Chicago Urban League) also provided input (Scott, 1969 [1920]).

11. See also Henri (1975: 62–63) on Robert Abbott, editor and publisher of the *Defender* regarding migration.

12. The socialist periodical *The Messenger* (1918) commented:

> We wish also to call the attention of this country to the bold misrepresentation of Negro leaders about the Negro's patriotism. Every ninety out of a hundred Negroes felt before the execution that it was very questionable whether they had any country to fight for. Since that execution, with large and extensive contact, we have not found a Negro man or woman whose position is not entirely passively against the country, or certainly indifferent to its appeals (7).

Also see Ellis (1992) on Du Bois's controversial July 1918 editorial in *Crisis* urging blacks to support the war effort.

13. As in other cases, there is some disagreement about the actual body count in the several days of violence that followed the initial incident in Phillips County. Shapiro (1988: 149) reports "According to official figures five whites and twenty-five blacks were killed in the conflict, but an investigator for the NAACP reported that whites had informed him that as many as 100 blacks had been killed." Kennedy (1997: 95) writes "approximately 10 whites were killed; the death toll for blacks ran from 200 to 250."

CHAPTER 8

The Harlem Renaissance: A Cultural War against Oppression

Harlem in the 1920s attracted fun seekers and intellectuals, slummers and serious artists. Harlem in myth was a glittering, jumping, exciting place to be. But some people in Harlem in the 1920s were just trying to get by.

> Still, it is a stereotype that everybody in Harlem did nothing but drink and play around and go to nightclubs. The poorest Negroes . . . probably never saw the inside of a nightclub, unless they were mopping the floor. (Bessie Delany in Delany and Delany, 1993: 188)

Among these "poorest Negroes" were the ones who had migrated to Harlem during the first two decades of the twentieth century—particularly those who had moved there as a part of the Great Migration during World War I.

In 1926, the radio series *Sam 'n Henry* debuted. It was about the experiences of two southern black men who migrated from Birmingham to Chicago. The first episodes followed Sam and Henry through their decision to leave home, their train journey northward, and their arrival in Chicago (Ely, 1991: 1–3). The creators of the series were, as it happened, two white men, Charles Correll and Freeman Gosden, who supplied the voices of Sam and Henry. Correll and Gosden seemed to have at least some empathy for the homesickness, the excitement, and the culture shock experienced by black rural migrants. They captured the tone of this experience well enough to be invited to be the guests of honor at a picnic sponsored by the black newspaper *Chicago Defender* (Ely, 3–4).

As the series continued, it attracted a wide following. It was so popular that it was "piped into restaurants and hotel lobbies, and into movie theaters between shows, to prevent a drastic loss of clientele." The show generated its own cottage industry of a candy bar, greeting cards, toys, and a daily comic strip (Ely, 4–5). By 1929, the series had moved to NBC radio and been redubbed *Amos 'n' Andy*. The setting of the series was now Harlem, New York. The series was in the tradition of other radio programs set in ethnic communities. It poked fun at the characters and their dilemmas. Whites laughed. But so did many black listeners.

In 1951 *Amos 'n' Andy* joined other network radio shows in the move to a new medium, television. This move required a color change in the cast of the series. An all black cast took over the roles of Kingfish, Sapphire, Amos, Andy, Lightning, and Lawyer Calhoun. In homes across America, families could now *watch* and laugh. Some blacks were happy just to see black people on television. True, Kingfish and Andy were buffoonish. Sapphire was a shrew, and Lightning was dim-witted. Lawyer Calhoun was without ethics. But the show featured other black professionals, including police officers and judges, who did their jobs effectively. And there was Amos, a solid, hard-working family man.

The black audience who liked the show must have had mixed emotions when the NAACP launched its campaign to get *Amos 'n' Andy* off the airways. The civil rights organization declared that it presented black people in the worst possible light. It was a step backward in race relations; it was negative propaganda. The show was eventually canceled, but it remained in syndication until the mid-1960s (Ely, 1991: 8).[1] This controversy over *Amos 'n' Andy*, the television show, occurred on the eve of the civil rights era. In 1929, the radio show, was still welcome in many black radio listeners' homes.

In 1929, Amos and Andy, the radio characters, were living in Harlem, and some people called Harlem the center of the African American universe.[2] As Langston Hughes said, "Harlem was in vogue." It was true that some blacks were more involved in this vogue than others. The black intelligentsia had been instrumental in creating it. They were the ones who hobnobbed with the white liberals, white slummers, and white musicians and artists who had discovered Harlem. They were the ones who were on a first name basis with white publishers, journalists, and politicians. They were the ones who were invited to Greenwich Village and to weekends in the country. They were the ones who traveled to Paris. They were the ones who had realized and were now making use of the propaganda possibilities of black culture.

THE NEW NEGRO

In the 1920s, Charles S. Johnson, a sociologist, was the editor of *Opportunity*, the journal of the National Urban League.[3] It was Johnson who in March 1924 sponsored a literary gathering at the Civic Club in Manhattan. Johnson thought that arts and letters could be used as a way of improving race relations. Among those who agreed with him were James Weldon Johnson, Walter White, W.E.B. Du Bois, and Jessie Faust, all of the NAACP (Lewis, 1997: xx). Also in agreement was Alain Locke, Rhodes scholar and Howard University professor. It was Locke who became identified with the phrase "the New Negro" when he used it as the title of a volume of poetry and prose that he edited. The concept of "the new Negro" had appeared from time to time among African Americans since the eighteenth century (Aptheker, 1971), referring generally to a new assertiveness among blacks. During the Harlem Renaissance, it came to be linked to the idea of a new generation of artists, poets, and writers involved in the creation of culture—asserting themselves through their work.

For W.E.B. Du Bois, sociologist and activist, the concept embraced his idea of "the Talented Tenth." This small group of university trained black men and women would become the leaders of their race.[4] They would lead the masses. They would influence white opinion. But, in the 1920s, the New Negro intellectual had something in common with the white literati of Greenwich Village. Both groups were without a place in American society. As Lewis (xvii) observes:

> The black Talented Tenth and the white Lost Generation shared the premise that arts and letters had the power to transform a society in which, until profoundly altered, there was no place for their likes except at the margins.

The members of the black intellectual elite set out to produce, market, and promote African American culture. They cultivated—and were cultivated by—the likes of H. L. Mencken, Carl Van Vechten, Heywood Broun, Fannie Hurst, and Dorothy Parker. In the midst of interracial literary evenings, publishers' parties, and "at homes," working relationships and friendships were forged. Patrons were acquired. For example, the novelist Fannie Hurst hired Zora Neale Hurston as her secretary, driver, and traveling companion. Hurston became Hurst's inspiration for *Imitation of Life* (Lewis, 129; Fishbein, 1982).[5]

The publication of Hurst's novel and the two films based on the book provide telling information about the state of American race relations. The novel was first made into a movie, a tear jerker about two widowed mothers, one black, one white, in 1934. In this movie Louise Beavers played the black woman who became the white woman's maid. The very light-skinned black actress Fredi Washington played Beavers's daughter. In the glossy 1959 movie based on Hurst's novel, the roles were assumed by Juanita Moore as the black maid and Susan Kohner as the rebellious daughter. After being beaten up by a white boyfriend who discovers she is black, the daughter leaves home. Her mother finds her dancing in a nightclub. She is again passing as white. She tells her mother that if she looks for her again, she will run away again. The mother goes home heartbroken and dies soon after. At her funeral, the white family sit in the black church to which their maid belonged. Mahalia Jackson, playing a soloist in the choir, sings a soulful spiritual. As the coffin is carried to the hearse, the prodigal daughter runs toward it. Shoving her way past the people who try to restrain her, she screams, "That's my mother!" She throws herself on the coffin, weeping. The white family lead her to the limousine. In the final scene, she sits between the white mother and daughter (Lana Turner and Sandra Dee, respectively), weeping on the white mother's shoulder.

This movie is interesting in several ways that make it worth considering here. For example, in one scene there is a brief conversation between the dying black woman and her white employer. The conversation reveals that the white woman knows nothing about the "other life" her maid leads when she is not there in the house. The maid belongs to a church. She has friends. But the white employer knows nothing about this until her maid begins to tell her about the arrangements she has made for her funeral. Another aspect of the movie is its exploration of the theme of "passing." When Fannie Hurst wrote her novel, passing was a much more common theme in popular literature than in 1959 when the second version of the movie was released. Yet the theme is one that has never completely disappeared from the discourse within the African American community and by extension American society in general.

The distress engendered in white society by a "black" person so "white" in appearance that he or she can pass into white society undetected harks back to the slavery era fear of the "pollution" of the white race by the products of miscegenation. It also raises the issue of the place of people who are "neither black nor white" in the black community and in American society. In popular literature by both blacks and whites, passing carries with it physical and psychic isolation from rich black "roots." There is the continuing risk of discovery—of being "unmasked" as an "impostor." This unmasking entails the danger of violent retaliation by whites who have been deceived (Berzon, 1978).

But in literary treatments, being an impostor may also provide an escape from violence. The first novel published in 1912 (anonymously) by James Weldon Johnson, who in the 1920s was executive director of the NAACP, was called *The Autobiography of an Ex-Colored Man* (1951). It is the story of a man who after witnessing a lynching made the decision to leave the South. He goes north and passes into the white race. In doing so, he leaves his black culture behind and adopts the materialistic values of a white businessman. The section of the novel devoted to the lynching was based on Johnson's own experiences in the South.[6] But Johnson was not advocating racial deception. What he did believe—in accord with other members of the Renaissance movement—was that (to quote Lewis, 1997: 148), "the assimilated, cultured Afro-Saxon was every whit the equal of his 'Nordic' counterpart."

The Harlem Renaissance was in many ways a class conscious movement. Those elite leaders of the movement who preferred that blacks be presented with their best foot forward found themselves in conflict with those cultural workers who were more concerned with getting to the heart of black culture. In 1926, *Crisis*, under Du Bois's editorship, sponsored a symposium, "The Negro in Art: How Shall He Be Portrayed." A series of questions were posed to well-known white and black writers about the moral obligations of the writer in depicting a people who were often the victims of stereotypes (Bailey, 1991). This matter of how the Negro should be portrayed was more than a philosophical question. The leaders of the Renaissance saw it as crucial to their campaign to use art as a way of improving race relations.

From the perspective of those who were concerned that the Negro be portrayed at his best—intelligent, hardworking, and responsible—a novel such as Carl Van Vechten's *Nigger Heaven* (1926) seemed to do little for the cause. Van Vechten, a wealthy white patron of the Renaissance, wrote a novel that dealt with the middle class, but that in the end plunged his protagonist into the Harlem underworld of speakeasies and gangsters. That underworld did exist. It was the other face of the Harlem vogue. But it was not a world that the many of the middle class participants in the Renaissance saw as particularly valuable in their crusade to improve the standing of the race.

However, the exotic aspects of black life appealed to whites on both sides of the Atlantic. In Paris the shockingly exotic Josephine Baker had in 1925 become the sensation of the French theater. In New York, on Broadway, revues featuring black dancers and black music attracted white theater audiences.[7] In Harlem, the blues and jazz, the "high yellow" black dancers, the laughter, and the booze drew white "slummers" uptown to the black community. Struggling with their postwar ennui, well-to-do young whites looked for new thrills. They found them in the clubs, speakeasies, and dives where interracial mixing was a part of the attraction.

Other more exclusive clubs such as the famous Cotton Club had a policy that limited such mixing. The Cotton Club featured black entertainers but it catered to white patrons. This was one of the peculiar aspects of this intrusion of whites into the black community. In the heart of a black community, segregation was being practiced.

There was another aspect of this intrusion—the takeover by white gangsters of lucrative organized crime activities in Harlem. Among the black gangsters doing a thriving business in Harlem at the beginning of the Renaissance was Caspar Holstein, who ran the numbers racket (Lewis, 1997). There was also Madam Stephanie St. Claire. Holstein and St. Claire were a part of the community—a questionable part, but still resident entrepreneurs.[8] In the 1920s, in the midst of the Prohibition escalation of syndicate takeovers, Harlem organized crime attracted the attention of "Dutch" Schultz. It was Schultz who took over Holstein's territory, employing more violence than Holstein was prepared to resist (Lewis, 220–221).

The nightclubs of Harlem were connected to white organized crime. The

mob owned the Cotton Club (Anderson, 1981: 176; Peretti, 1997: 43); black
musicians who played there were the recipients of mob largesse. The other
side of the coin was that they were sometimes the victims of mob pressure
tactics. Some, like Duke Ellington, are said to have played at the Cotton
Club after receiving an offer they couldn't refuse.[9]

Moreover, even as black jazz flourished in the clubs of Harlem, some
African Americans expressed their disapproval of the music. They saw it "as
a corrupter of youth and morals. . . . Ministers and others feared the white
ridicule and scorn that jazz might bring down upon the entire race" (Peretti,
1997: 52). Even if they were not particularly concerned about the corrupting
influence of jazz, the criminal underside of the Harlem vogue, along with
the elitist nature of the arts movement, must have led some working class
Harlem residents to shake their heads. They must have wondered how much
racial progress was actually being made. In 1929, on the eve of the Great
Depression, the majority of the residents of Harlem did not own property
or businesses. They were struggling to get by (Lewis, 219–221). The Renaissance had not had a trickle-down effect.

Yet there had been some effort to make racial uplift a part of the agenda.
The multifaceted W.E.B. Du Bois became a pioneer in the field of black
children's literature, when he and Jessie Faust published *The Brownies' Book*.
The magazine was the first for black young people and included poetry,
prose, and biography. It published only twenty-four issues (January 1920–
December 1921), but it was the only such magazine until *Ebony, Jr!* appeared
in 1973 (Cockett and Kleinberg, 1994: 118–120). In the first issue, Du Bois
stated that the magazine was a response to the special needs of the black
child. Stories and articles dealt with African heritage, "family loyalty, gender
roles, and racial unity" (Cockett and Kleinberg, 120). The magazine was
intended to refute for young people the stereotypical images of blacks present in the mainstream white media.

The Brownies' Book appeared at a time when black children were being
presented in mainstream popular culture as comic characters. In advertise-
ments, cartoons, comic strips, and films, they were lampooned. Often they
appeared as half-naked, hapless little pickaninnies. Sometimes they were being pursued by a crocodile. Images of black children, like those of black
adults, became a commodity in the American consumer market. "The Gold
Dust Twins"—along with Aunt Jemima[10] and Uncle Ben—were faces on
the products that millions of Americans took home from the supermarket.[11]
During this period, "Tom" shows, loosely based on Stowe's *Uncle Tom's
Cabin*, continued to find an audience in small towns and cities across the
country. These blackface shows often included "Topsy"—Stowe's black
pixie child. Given the prevalence of such images, Du Bois and others saw
the need to provide countereducation for black children.

With regard to education, black college students began speaking for themselves about the quality of the education they were receiving. In the 1920s,

they began to register their complaints about curriculums that reflected the legacy of the Washingtonian model of agricultural–industrial education for blacks. Sometimes joined by faculty, the students also protested faculty and administrative appointments. Strikes took place at Hampton Institute and other southern institutions (Aptheker, 1971). Such actions were indicative of increasing self-assertion by black Americans.

On a separate, but related front, African Americans were fighting for justice in the nation's courtroom. One case in particular riveted public attention. In September 1925, Dr. Ossian Sweet and his family moved into a new home in a white Detroit neighborhood. When a mob attacked the house, Sweet and two of his brothers shot into the mob, killing one white man. The NAACP and the lawyers Arthur Garfield Hays and Clarence Darrow came to the Sweets' defense. After two trials, the black men were acquitted (Lewis, 215). Five years later, in 1930, the NAACP was successful in the battle that it led to prevent the confirmation of Judge John H. Parker as a justice of the Supreme Court. Parker, a circuit court judge, was on record as having made antiblack statements. He was rejected in the Senate by two votes. The NAACP considered this an important victory.

However, President Hoover, as a part of his strategy to have Parker confirmed, had asked the FBI to gather information about the NAACP officials (O'Reilly: 105). In doing so, Hoover "established a troubling precedent here by turning to the Bureau of Investigation for assistance in dealing with the NAACP" (106). This precedent would have consequences during the civil rights era when J. Edgar Hoover, as the FBI chief, aligned himself against the NAACP and other black activist organizations.

Moreover, the news from the North about the Sweet case and the defeat of Judge Parker came as conditions were worsening in the South. From 1927 to 1932, floods ravaged the Mississippi Delta. Black tenants on the land were reduced to peonage.

CONCLUSIONS

In an essay in *Tulane Law Review* (1993), Sheri Lynn Johnson, looking at the racial imagery that sometimes finds its way into the courtroom in the testimony of witnesses and the arguments of attorneys, suggests that perhaps we should have the equivalent of rape shield laws with regard to race—that is, "a racial imagery statute" that would prevent negative images related to race from entering the trial process. As Johnson writes, both whites and people of color have been exposed to these negative images, "have seen the same films, heard the same metaphors" (1804).

These images have a long life, a long history in the collective memory of both black and white Americans. Looking back at the images of black children, such as the "Stage Topsys" that flourished in the popular culture earlier in the century, Turner (1994: 18) observes:

It is likely that the notion that black children are animallike and savage has influenced public policy. After all, leaders in the 1970s, 1980s, and 1990s grew up and absorbed the images discernible in the popular culture of the 1930s, 1940s, and 1950s.

The absorption of negative stereotypes of African Americans by whites is what concerned the leaders of the Harlem Renaissance. They knew that the negative depictions of blacks in popular culture—in films, books, and advertisments—were contributing to and perpetuating white perceptions of African Americans as an alien "other." Therefore, the Harlem Renaissance was not only a flowering of black arts and letters, but a culture war aimed at combatting the negative images of African Americans that had existed since the era of slavery. At the same time, the Renaissance created in the black participants a deeper awareness of their own culture and greater determination to control their own destiny.

The assertion of the right to control their own images—to substitute images that were more accurate depictions of who they were and how they lived for the white-crafted stereotypes—was an important aspect of the Renaissance that took place in Harlem. However, as Johnson and Turner assert, the war was not won. It would continue in the 1960s and is ongoing in the 1990s.

NOTES

1. Also see Turner (1994: 121–123). Most black newspapers stayed on the middle ground in this controversy between the NAACP and NBC (Cripps in O'Connor, 1983: 42). The controversy about the show occurred during the postwar era when Hollywood had moved to "message movies" and Truman's Civil Rights Commission had issued its report on social justice. In this atmosphere, *Amos 'n' Andy* was arguably "regressive" (Cripps, 35).

2. However, Chicago offered Harlem serious competition. See Haller (1991) on Chicago during the period 1900 to 1940:

> By the early 1920s, the nightclubs, dance halls, and theaters of Chicago's South Side ghetto were the major center for the development of jazz and other forms of black entertainment in the United States. In that same period, the rise of black-operated policy gambling syndicates gave black gambling entrepreneurs a critical place in the economy and politics of the ghetto. (719)

3. For more on Johnson and his work see Blackwell and Janowitz (1974). The authors also discuss E. Franklin Frazier and Du Bois.

4. Meier and Rudwick (1986: 8) state that interest in black history "flower[ed] during the New Negro movement of the 1920s." But in the 1920s the number of blacks with Ph.D.'s in history (or in any other field) was minuscule. In 1915–1916, Charles Godwin Woodson, the second African American after Du Bois to receive a Ph.D. in history, established the Association for the Study of Negro Life and History and the *Journal of Negro History*. In doing so, Woodson was attempting "to build

and popularize a serious interest in Negro history at the apogee of popular and scientific racism in Western thought" (Meier and Rudwick, 2). However, in 1931–1932, Woodson "aired his hostility" toward black liberal arts colleges and their curriculums. Du Bois invited him to summarize his views in *Crisis*. In 1933, Woodson published *The Mis-education of the Negro* (Meier and Rudwick, 55).

5. In contrast, "the house-rent party remained the staple entertainment of the majority of the black working class, and it became a favorite hangout for many of the writers" (Wintz, 1988: 91). As the phrase implied, a "house-rent party" was both entertainment and a way for the host to make extra money. The usual charge to the guest was twenty-five cents. Food (fried chicken, chittlings, and so on) and bootleg whiskey were available. As Wintz states, these parties were sometimes fronts for illegal activities (91), but they also provided an environment in which hardworking men and women could come together to laugh and dance.

6. In 1900, in Jacksonville, Florida, Johnson was walking with a female journalist who looked white. He was arrested by the military police. Luckily, he knew the provost marshal, and the matter was resolved when the woman identified herself as black. When he was seized by the police, Johnson cooperated fully, "thus calming the hostilities of the small mob who gathered as he and his friend were seized" (Sundquist, 1992: 42). But for months after the episode, Johnson had "recurrent nightmares of what could have happened" (Sundquist, 42).

7. In fact, black theatrical productions in New York City were not a new phenomenon. Peretti (1997: 15–16) notes that by the turn of the century blacks and whites were openly competing for New York theater audiences. White audiences came to see black stage shows such as *In Dahomey* (1902). But in 1900, a riot "erupted outside a New York theater presenting a Negro revue."

8. St. Claire was the wife of the political activist Sufi Abdul Hamid. Gray (1993: 24) describes her as "so influential that the New York Police Department and the syndicated mob made constant attempts to 'remove' her from the Harlem community." She was finally arrested in January 1930 for possession of policy slips. Although she accused the police of framing her and of taking payoffs, Madame St. Claire spent two years in prison. Gray asserts that St. Claire (whose name he identifies as "St. Clair") was considered "a positive influence in the community." He points out that she contributed weekly editorials to the *Amsterdam News* in which she spoke out about community concerns, including police brutality. She even wrote to President Franklin Roosevelt about the problem (Gray, 33).

9. However, Morris (1980: 131) states:

Salaries for black jazz artists, while not on a par with what whites received, nonetheless reflected the surging buoyancy of the period. Nightclub racketeering was one of the few growth industries in the 1920s generous enough to sharewindfall profits with blacks who helped create them.

Regarding the black musician during the 1920s and his cultural role, Sidran (1971: 56) writes:

The black musician became a symbol of the socially liberated America. This position was reinforced by the black musician's association in Chicago with gangsters who ruled the nightlife. . . . This underworld flavor of this life became subject to social myth, and the spirit of resistance in this music became all the more relevant to whites.

10. "Aunt Jemima" made her first public appearance at the 1893 World's Columbian Exposition in Chicago. A black woman named Nancy Green was hired to play the part (Turner, 1994: 49–50).

11. See Pescosolido et al. (1997) for discussion of portrayal of blacks in one form of popular literature, children's picture books.

CHAPTER 9

From Scottsboro to Chicago

The next day the front page of the papers was full of it: "5,000 Negroes and white sympathizers rioted yesterday when detectives used tear gas bombs to disperse an unauthorized meeting staged at Lenox Avenue and 126th St. to protest the Scottsboro case."

—Francie Coffin, heroine of *Daddy Was
a Number Runner* (Meriwether, 1989 [1970] 103)

In his memoir, *Coming through the Fire* (1996), C. Eric Lincoln remembers growing up in segregated Alabama. He remembers the "lessons" he learned about race relations, some of them in encounters with white people, others from his grandmother, who raised him. One such lesson came as Lincoln reached his teen years. His grandmother became reluctant to allow him to go to town, especially on Saturdays. When it was necessary that he go, she would tell him, "Go on down, tend to your business *and come on back directly!*" Finally, she revealed the source of her worry:

And as I grew older she began to conclude with "And, son, don't you go down there looking at them old country gals' legs. Just mind your business and come on home." It eventually dawned on me that she meant *white* country girls, and by extension, *all* white girls. (Lincoln, 27)

What Lincoln was learning from his grandmother were the rules that governed his place in southern (white) society:

To be a good nigger was to be blessed with the active goodwill of the white folks, an asset of extraordinary importance, though it might on occasion incur the febrile disdain of some blacks. . . . To be a good nigger meant that petty breaches of the law were overlooked or forgiven. It meant being looked after or provided for in sickness or distress. It meant having your credit or your credibility "stood for," and your funeral graced by the presence of white folks when you died. (Lincoln: 31)[1]

The Scottsboro Boys, natives of the South, surely understood this racial etiquette. But they had the misfortune to find themselves on a freight train with two white women. C. Eric Lincoln, a boy at the time, heard about the Scottsboro Boys, who were on trial for raping two white women. He also heard that the Communists were involved in their defense. He heard that in the opinion of the better class of white people, the two white girls who had accused the black youths were "trash." But the Communists—whom these white people linked to the NAACP ("a nigger front for communist Jews")—were up to no good and might even have put the boys up to committing the rapes (Lincoln, 60).

The Scottsboro Boys did not cause a great deal of disruption in young C. Eric Lincoln's life. They were a rumor, a whisper. They meant more to Arno Bontemps, who had been a promising young writer during the Harlem Renaissance. Bontemps had moved to Alabama because of the Depression. He was so disturbed by the trials of the Scottsboro Boys that he left Alabama. He went to Los Angeles and wrote the novel *Black Thunder*, about Gabriel's slave rebellion in Virginia in 1800. In the novel he gave Gabriel a courtroom scene—an opportunity to speak in a political voice about his oppression. The Scottsboro Boys had inspired this novel, this meditation on blacks and injustice (Sundquist, 1992: 93–94). Both then and later, the Scottsboro Boys would inspire many black Americans to meditate on the American criminal justice system.

JUSTICE AND THE AMERICAN DREAM

In 1931, James Truslow Adams, a historian, used the phrase "the American dream" to "describe his vision of a society open to individual achievement" (Messner and Rosenfeld, 1994: 6). But "[t]he American dream is a double-edged sword" (Messner and Rosenfeld, 2). In the pursuit of it, there are "winners" and "losers." After the stock market crash of 1929 and during the years of the Great Depression, many of the well-to-do became economic losers. For the poor, blacks and whites, who were already struggling, the "dream" slipped even further from their grasp. In both social and economic terms, the nine African American youths who became known as "the Scottsboro Boys" were among the losers. The two young white women, who had been on the train with them and who accused them of rape, occupied much the same place on the economic ladder. The Scottsboro Boys and the two women were "riding the rails" as they looked for work. They, like the white youths who had also been on the train and with whom the black boys had fought, were all members of the lower class. Their condition had been made worse by the Depression.[2]

Under other circumstances, the Scottsboro Boys might have encountered Victoria Price and Ruby Bates in one of those neighborhoods where whites and blacks in the South sometimes mixed. It came out during the trials that Price and Bates were known to frequent such neighborhoods. But instead the Scottsboro Boys and the two young women were found stealing a ride on a freight train. The two young women responded to the cues they received from the white men who discovered them by accusing the black youths of rape.

Twelve days after they had been arrested, in April 1931, the trials of the youths began in Scottsboro, Alabama, the Jackson County seat. The Boys, ranging in age from thirteen to twenty-one, were quickly convicted and sentenced to death.

> The Central Committee of the Communist Party of the United States assailed the verdicts, and the Party's legal affiliate, the International Labor Defense, announced that it would defend the boys. Countless people were outraged by the trials and the death sentences. Countless people were outraged by the outrage. Appeals led to seven retrials and two landmark Supreme Court decisions. The defendants spent no less than six, and as many as nineteen, years in jail. (Goodman, 1994: xi)

In the aftermath of the convictions in the first trials, both the NAACP and the Communist party–affiliated International Labor Defense (ILD) entered the picture. The two organizations became involved in a power struggle over who would represent the Boys in their appeals. The NAACP—which had sought to distance itself from organizations on the political Left—accused the ILD of using the case for propaganda purposes.[3] This accusation by the NAACP produced mixed reactions among black Americans. The families of the Boys after considering the arguments made by each organization decided to rely on the ILD to spearhead the appeals.

When the appeals reached the Supreme Court, the court ruled in *Powell v. Alabama*—by a vote of seven to two—that the defendants had been denied adequate counsel, in violation of the due process clause of the Fourteenth Amendment. It overturned the convictions and ordered new trials. For the second round of trials, the ILD brought in Samuel Liebowitz, a Jewish defense attorney from New York City. His reputation was somewhat mixed because he had defended such notorious clients as the gangster Vincent Coll, but he was known to win his cases, and he wanted to represent the Scottsboro Boys (Goodman, 101–102).

In the second trials, Ruby Bates retracted her story about having been raped. The prosecution charged that she had been bribed by the Communists with clothes and a trip to New York, but she stuck to her story. She even appeared with family members of the defendants at fund-raising events. However, this was not sufficient to prevent another round of convictions. On appeal, the Supreme Court discredited the jury selection process used by the state of Alabama. In *Norris v. Alabama*, the court said the black youths had not received due process because their cases had been heard before an all-white jury.

The state of Alabama reindicted and tried the case with a jury of one black man, a farmer and chairman of the board of trustees of the Negro schools in the town of Paint Rock (Goodman, 1994: 253). As might be expected, his presence had little effect on the outcome. However, the state dropped the charges against four of the Boys. The others received prison sentences instead of death sentences (Goodman, 1994).

The Scottsboro Boys case was perceived by many Americans both black and white as one of those outrageous examples of the South's ability to miscarry justice. Like the case of Leo Frank,[4] the case of the Scottsboro Boys was seen as reflecting the deep-rooted bigotry of the South.

THE NEW SOUTH

In truth, the regionalism that had divided North and South during the nineteenth century had begun to break down in the twentieth century as America acquired a national identity. In the South, mills and factories had drawn rural dwellers off the land and into the towns and cities. Throughout the South, mill towns had sprung up. But this industrial growth had limited impact on the economic status of blacks. They were relegated to the menial, dirty jobs in southern mills and factories. They were often concentrated in seasonal industries such as tobacco factories.

In the post–World War I era, greater distinctions began to be made between jobs that were suitable for whites and those that were suitable for blacks (P. Sullivan, 1996: 15). Blacks in the South had "dominated rural movement to Southern cities" during the early 1920s. Whites followed in their wake. Blacks found that "[a]s the economic squeeze tightened, white workers steadily took away what had been traditionally black jobs. Some towns passed municipal ordinances restricting black employment" (Sullivan, 20). These distinctions were enforced by white laborers and by white terrorist groups. In 1930, Black Shirts marched in Atlanta, Georgia, carrying banners that read, "Niggers back to the cotton fields—city jobs are for white folks" (Sullivan, 21). Under these conditions the rate of black male unemployment went up in southern cities such as Atlanta, New Orleans, and Birmingham (Sullivan, 21).

In this atmosphere of tense race relations, a group of white intellectuals at Vanderbilt University published a volume titled *I'll Take My Stand* (1930). In this volume, they stated their objections to the intrusion of the northern urban–industrial culture into the South. They spoke in praise of the organic sense of community that had characterized the the Old South. There were still racial remnants of the Old South to be found in the 1930s. The "good roads movement" of the 1920s had given impetus to the use of convict labor to create and maintain the infrastructure of the South. Blacks were prime candidates for the chain gangs that worked to build the roads of the South (Lichenstein, 1993). As Ayers (1984: 177–178) points out, the chain gang solved the problems of both crowded jails and poor roads. At the same time, black farmers were still caught up in a peonage system. For example, in 1939, the NAACP pressured the FBI to investigate a rather blatant case of peonage that the organization had discovered in Virginia (Aptheker, 1971).

In many ways, in the segregated South of the 1930s, little had changed for lower class blacks who labored on the land or worked at menial jobs. An exquisite system of racial etiquette still governed their relationships with whites. They were still at the bottom of the economic ladder. They were still subject to an oppressive dual system of justice.

NEW DEAL ECONOMICS

In 1933, President Roosevelt appointed a white Georgian, Clark Foreman, as his "special adviser on the economic status of Negroes." Foreman was to serve under Harold Ickes, the secretary of the interior. African American organizations and the black press protested Foreman's appointment not so much because they questioned his credentials as a liberal but because he was white. Foreman offered to resign. When his offer was declined, he hired Robert Weaver, a young black economist, as his assistant (P. Sullivan, 24–25).

Weaver and his close associate John Preston Davis, an attorney, had both been at Harvard at the time when William Hastie and Ralph Bunche were there. They were in regular contact with Charles Hamilton Huston, vice dean of the Howard University Law School. During the New Deal era, this group of men, in association with the NAACP and the labor movement, worked "to build an effective political movement to advance racial and economic justice" (Sullivan, 46). It was during this period that Charles Hamilton Huston became the mastermind behind the NAACP's legal strategies. His law school became "a laboratory for the development of civil rights law" (Sullivan, 85). But even as the NAACP and other black organizations pursued economic and legal strategies to improve the conditions of blacks, the South remained a dangerous place for some blacks—particularly black males—to be.

NATIVE SONS

In 1938, in *Uncle Tom's Children*, Richard Wright wrote about "The Ethics of Jim Crow." He had learned these ethics as a child in the South. Like his character "Big Boy," Wright eventually fled north. There he encountered the etiquette that governed race relations in the North. When he was employed at the South Side Boys' Club, Wright found himself engaged in what he viewed as the social control of black youths. By keeping them involved with sports and other activities, the workers were preventing the youths from engaging in acts that would disturb white society. In the preface to *Native Son*, Wright wrote:

> I am not condemning boys' clubs and ping-pong as such; but these little stop-gaps were utterly inadequate to fill up the centuries-long chasm of emptiness which American civilization had created in these Biggers. I felt that I was doing a kind of dressed-up police work, and I hated it. (Wright, 1940: xxvii)

In his short stories, such as "The Man Who Killed a Shadow,"[5] and later in *Native Son*, Wright pointed out the inherent flaw in this strategy of containment. Because black males performed much of the menial labor required by white society, it was impossible to keep them completely isolated in the ghetto. And when a black male, who had for years been taught lessons about the dangers of stepping out of his place, found himself in a situation in which he was about to be exposed as a violator of racial norms, his conditioned response would be one of panic. In Wright's *Native Son*, a black man's panic proves fatal for a young white woman.

In Part III of this novel of crime and punishment, Wright reveals his political leanings. In the North, he had become a member of the Communist party, convinced that collective action was needed to bring about change (Gross, 1971). But Wright became disillusioned with the Communist party agenda. He found that the Communist emphasis on class rather than race contradicted his own experiences. As he was questioning his own political views, Wright was enjoying the experience of having a best-selling novel. *Native Son* propelled him to prominence as an American writer. Still Wright turned his back on America and went to live in Europe. He left behind him as his legacy a vision of black urban life that became a mainstay of popular culture.[6]

In some respects, Wright's view of the black ghetto was not unlike the images that were being offered by social scientists. Wright depicted a black mother-headed household, in which the family lived crowded together in a rat-infested tenement apartment. The son, Bigger, escapes to the streets, where he spends time with his friends (his peers). In a theater, the young men watch the American dream as it is depicted in a Hollywood movie about rich white people enjoying themselves. Trapped in their ghetto, they dare each other to find the courage to commit a hold-up. The young men, living in the midst of social disorganization, contemplate turning to crime.

However, Wright goes a bold step further than the social scientists of the Chicago School.[7] He depicts a white slumlord who is known for his philanthropy to black causes. The slumlord, apparently ignorant of his offense, hires Bigger and brings him into his home. This is Wright's indictment of white capitalism and white moral blindness. In the novel, Wright presents an array of other images to symbolize the white oppression that sustains the black ghetto in which Bigger Thomas lives. A plane flies overhead—impossibly out of reach. The campaign posters for State's Attorney Buckley are everywhere. Underneath his picture are the words "IF YOU BREAK THE LAW, YOU CAN'T WIN!" (Wright, 16).

In this Chicago ghetto, there are none of the signs of vitality depicted by black writers and artists in the 1920s. It is in this ghetto that the residents are trapped by the social, political, and economic forces that determine the physical boundaries of their world.

BLACK RESPONSES TO GHETTO OPPRESSION

In the 1930s, a "Don't Buy Where You Can't Work" movement swept through the nation's cities. It began in Chicago during 1929–1930. From 1933 to 1934, there were major demonstrations in Baltimore, Washington, New York, and Richmond. In Harlem, in 1934, blacks carried picket signs to protest the hiring practices of stores in their community. By February 1935, the campaign "found itself helplessly crippled by court enforced injunctions forbidding picketing and bitter in-fighting between competing factions" (Crowder, 1991: 24). In March 1935, a major riot occurred in Harlem.

After the riot, Mayor Fiorello La Guardia appointed a biracial committee to investigate. The African American sociologist E. Franklin Frazier was among those appointed to serve on the committee. But when the committee had finished its investigation, its findings were suppressed. The report was leaked to the *Amsterdam News*; the black newspaper published it in July 1936. The committee had found the riot had its roots in the "deep seeded sense of wrongs and denials and the resentments of people of Harlem against racial discrimination and poverty in the midst of plenty" (Crowder, 1991: 27; see also Shapiro, 1988: 266–272; Steinberg, 1995: 26–29).

By 1935, when the Harlem riot occurred, the deterioration of black ghettos had been hurried along by the Depression.[8] What was becoming evident to many blacks was that there was little interest among white politicians in the fate of African Americans contained in these urban enclaves. As in the past, the question urban blacks asked themselves was whether there was some better place. They had come to the "Promised Land" and found they had been deceived. Where else could they go?

Some black Americans had gone to prison. In 1934, prisoners at Attica— far from the Promised Land—directed an appeal to Walter White of the NAACP. In a letter, Carl Bell, the spokesman for the African American prisoners, asked White to send a representative from the Buffalo branch to

Attica to "investigate the conditions there for colored inmates." There is no record of how or whether White responded (Williams, 1977).

"WHAT IS AFRICA TO ME?"

As the country moved toward the events that would culminate in American involvement in World War II, African Americans displayed an increasing awareness of themselves in relation to the rest of the world. In 1919 Du Bois had been involved in the first Pan African Congress, held in Paris. But for the urban masses, it was Marcus Garvey who served as their catalyst for Pan African awareness. His Back to Africa movement had been vital in reminding them of their links to the continent from which their ancestors had been kidnapped.

In *Cotton Comes to Harlem* (1965), Chester Himes satirizes a "Back to Africa" movement. In Himes's novel, the leader of the movement is a charismatic black minister who fleeces hundreds of poor people out of their life savings with his phony movement. In Garvey's case, his movement was real. It was his lack of business sense and of political savvy that limited its success. Garvey arrived in New York from Jamaica in 1918. He brought with him the Universal Negro Improvement Association (UNIA), which he had founded. In promoting his organization, Garvey was able to appeal to the black masses in ways the "Talented Tenth" did not. He framed his movement in pomp and ritual. He reminded African Americans of their heritage and their illustrious past. But for all his mass appeal, Garvey was not welcomed by the established leadership. He had received a cool reception when he visited NAACP headquarters soon after his arrival. Striking out on his own, he incorporated the UNIA in New York in 1918. By 1919, he had established the Black Star Line Steamship Corporation. The ships of this steamship line were supposed to transport the investors in the corporation back to Africa. Garvey had been able to raise almost $200,000 in four months from poor people in Jamaica and the United States. He purchased his first ship, the *S.S Yarmouth*, later renamed the *Frederick Douglass*. As a ship, it was less than seaworthy. Garvey had relied on the bad advice of his ship's captain, Joshua Cockburn who was working on commission (Lewis, 1997: 36–38; also see Stein, 1986).

From August 1 to September 1, 1920, Garvey held a huge rally in Madison Square Garden, which attracted thousands of people. It was the height of Garvey's triumph as a leader of the masses. But along the way he had also attracted the negative attention of both rival black leaders and federal law enforcement. Garvey's separatist philosophy did not sit well with integrationist black leaders. Some leaders believed Garvey's movement hindered their own efforts to organize the masses (Stein, 1986). For example, although A. Philip Randolph shared Garvey's race pride, Randolph was opposed to Garvey's movement. In the editorial pages of the *Messenger*, edited by Randolph and Chandler Owen, Garvey was described as "A Supreme Negro Jamaican Jackass" (Pfeffer, 1990: 16). Randolph was also involved in a "Garvey Must Go!" campaign (Pfeffer, 16).

As for law enforcement, the Federal Bureau of Investigation had sent an agent to infiltrate the UNIA. Then Garvey made himself more vulnerable by making a major misstep. In June 1922, he met in Atlanta with Edward Clarke second–in–command of the Ku Klux Klan (KKK). This was in keeping with Garvey's philosophy of black separatism.[9] The KKK shared his interest in racial separatism; however, it was not the kind of action calculated to reassure other black leaders. In an open letter to attorney general Harry Daugherty eight representatives of a "spectrum of official opinion" within the black community asked that the government vigorously pursue its investigation of Garvey. They wanted the government to use "full influences completely to disband and expirate this vicious movement" (Lewis, 44). A. Philip Randolph did not sign the letter. But Robert S. Abbott, owner and editor of the *Chicago Defender*, and Chandler Owen of *The Messenger* were among those who did (Stein, 1986: 166–167).

Garvey's problems with the law intensified. He had already served three months in prison on a mail fraud charge. In 1924, he held an international convention. Shortly thereafter, he was sentenced to the federal penitentiary in Atlanta, again on a mail fraud charge (Lewis, 111); in 1927, Garvey left prison after being pardoned by President Coolidge and was deported to Jamaica. But he, along with the much more intellectual W.E.B. Du Bois, played an important role in increasing African American identification with Africa. In 1935 when Italy invaded Ethiopia, the only independent country in Africa, African Americans viewed this as an act of imperialist aggression.

As American participation in the brewing world conflict became more likely, African American leaders expressed greater cynicism than they had in previous wars. This cynicism was probably shared by many African Americans, who had become less hopeful than in the past that their courage and patriotism would influence white opinion in their favor. But like other Americans, when the call to war came, they responded. This time their response was shaped by their determination to use this opportunity to forward their own fight for democracy.

CONCLUSIONS

"Scottsboro": One has only to say the word even now to conjure for many African Americans nightmares about southern justice. The Scottsboro defendants were lucky enough to have a trial—several trials. But these trials were conducted in a segregated courtroom before hostile white spectators. The Scottsboro defendants were accused of the worst crime a black man could commit in the South—the rape of a white woman. Black people at the time knew that even if the Scottsboro Boys were innocent, from the moment they were accused, they were guilty in the minds of many whites. Southern blacks, like the young C. Eric Lincoln, heard what white people said about the case: Communists were involved, white people said. That was bad. But what was worse was that the Scottsboro Boys violated the racial mores of the South. They would find little mercy in Alabama's courts. They did receive some relief from the Supreme Court, but they could not escape the tangle in which they found themselves. In the 1930s, the Scottsboro Boys stood trial in a segregated southern courtroom, and they went to prison.

But the 1930s were hard times for most black people. South or north, the Depression made everyday troubles worse. Adding to this burden was the questionable justice black people continued to receive. In October 1935, Walter White wrote in *Crisis* (309), "The Department of Justice in Washington may lay claim to a 100 percent performance in at least one branch of its activities—the evasion of cases involving burning questions of Negro rights." This was an opinion shared by many African Americans.

NOTES

1. As a child, Maya Angelou responded with silent contempt when the sheriff, who apparently considered her Uncle Willie a "good nigger," stopped by to warn her grandmother that her uncle should hide that night. A black man had "messed with" a white woman and the Klan was planning to come over to the black neighborhood to look for him (Angelou, 1969).

2. Sullivan (1996: 2) describes the South during this period as a region in transition that produced "an elastic labor supply of unskilled workers."

3. See Du Bois's essays in *Crisis* on the Scottsboro case and more generally on communism, socialism, and the Negro (Walden, 1972: 368–408).

4. In 1913, Leo Frank, a northern-born Jew, who was the manager of a factory in Atlanta, was convicted of the murder of Mary Phagan, a thirteen year old who worked in the factory. His death sentence was commuted by the governor, who was not convinced of his guilt, but Frank was kidnapped from the prison and lynched.

5. This story was based on an actual Washington, D.C., murder case.

6. See Pauly (1990) on black images in the dominant culture prior to the civil rights movement.

7. The Chicago School comprises the work of sociologists in the Department of Sociology at the University of Chicago. In the 1920s, Robert E. Park and his associate Ernest Burgess described the "human ecology" of Chicago neighborhoods with "natural areas" and "zones of transition." This work became the basis for an important school of social science theories about crime and juvenile delinquency in urban areas (see Vold et al. [1998] for their chapter on the Chicago School and the ecology of crime).

8. In 1935, Marvel Cooke, an investigative reporter for the *Amsterdam News*, did a series of articles about the street corner "slave market," in which white employers in New York City found their domestic servants (Gray, 1993: 57–58).

9. The bargain Garvey wanted to make with the KKK was that "he would remove

blacks from America and make the country safe for white supremacy if the KKK would help make Africa safe for black supremacy" (Pfeffer, 1990: 15). Stein (1986: 154) describes the meeting with Klan leaders as "a bold attempt to advance the UNIA in the South through political summitry." This bold move required Garvey to back away from his own earlier opposition to the Klan. He "fell back on the argument that the KKK could not be opposed because it was too powerful" (Stein, 159). In doing so, Garvey sought to make "the politics of accommodation" appear to be "the politics of triumph" (Stein, 154).

CHAPTER 10

Wartime

1940

- The United States Postal Service issued the first stamp in honor of a black American—Booker T. Washington.

- Benjamin O. Davis, Sr., was appointed a brigadier general, making him the highest ranking black soldier in the U.S. military.

- Hattie McDaniel won an Oscar for her supporting role in *Gone with the Wind*. She was the first black American to win the award.[1] (Harley, 1995: 246–248)

A good start to the decade? Racial progress in the form of recognition of black achievement? At least, symbolic progress? In 1939, Billie Holiday had introduced her song about lynching, "Strange Fruit," while performing at the Cafe Society in New York City (Griffin, 1995: 15). In 1939, the Daughters of the American Revolution had prohibited the singer Marian Anderson from performing in its Constitution Hall. Eleanor Roosevelt protested by resigning from the organization. The positive news was that, according to a Gallup Poll, 67 percent of the respondents supported the First Lady's action (Jaher, 1985: 159). And, in 1936, Jesse Owens had triumphed at the Olympic Games in Berlin:

> The games were staged in Berlin to provide a showcase of Nazism and Aryan supremacy. In this climate the medal-winning American blacks assumed, for the first time in our history, the status of patriotic symbol. . . . Adolf Hitler further enhanced the symbolism of their victories by leaving the stadium to avoid congratulating the black track stars. (Jaher, 160)

It was also during this period that Joe Louis, the second black heavyweight champion (1937–1949), emerged as a national hero. Defeating both Primo Carnera[2] and Max Schmeling, Louis became "the athletic emblem of America's struggle against the Axis countries" (Jaher, 160). Louis's image was the exact opposite of that of Jack Johnson. Johnson had been flamboyant; he had challenged racial and sexual mores. Louis was low-key.

> The Louis legend was born when his black managers . . . realized that they were handling a potential champion. Refusing to adopt Uncle Tom tactics, they successfully resisted white takeovers of their protégé and rejected demands that their fighter . . . pull punches or take "dives." (Jaher, 160)

However, Louis's managers groomed him to make him acceptable to whites. They taught him table manners and personal hygiene. They even hired a tutor to polish his grammar. Louis's managers made it clear to him that he was to do nothing to remind the white public of the notorious Jack Johnson. He was not to be seen with white women or go to night clubs. He was to be well-mannered and well-behaved at all times (Jaher, 160–161).

The state of prizefighting at the time worked in Louis's favor. It was "an age of nonfighting champions, fixed bouts, and gangster influences." Louis won fans by fighting "honestly and often" (Jaher, 161). When the war came, Louis garnered even more public approval by refusing to seek a draft deferment (Jaher, 165). As Sergeant Joe Louis, he participated in an exhibition tour of military posts overseas (Brandt, 1996: 179). In the postwar era, Louis was still popular. A 1947 Gallup Poll listed him among the fifty-eight most popular people in America (Jaher, 165). Louis, who began his life as the son of an Alabama sharecropper, had become an American success story. As in the past, the high visibility and public acclaim of a few black Americans such as Joe Louis obscured the general atmosphere of racial intolerance.

In 1941, in this era of intolerance, Ed Bradley was born. He would one day become a CBS news correspondent and later an anchorperson on the newsmagazine "60 Minutes" (Harley, 248). In 1941, an event occurred that Ed Bradley, as news correspondent, would probably have been sent to cover. In East St. Louis, Illinois, a race riot broke out. It continued for four days. This was not the first such riot to occur in East St. Louis. During World War I, the city was the site of "the bloodiest riot of the war." During that July 1917, forty blacks and three whites were murdered by mobs. It was this event that prompted the "Silent March" of fifteen thousand Harlem residents down Fifth Avenue (Brandt, 45).

World War II brought another round of violence in East St. Louis. In 1943, a riot in Detroit, Michigan, required federal troops to calm the situation. Thirty-four people were killed. In New York City, in August 1943, Harlem too experienced another riot. The Harlem riot began with a rumor that "a black soldier had been killed by a black policeman" (Brandt, 5).[3] At the time there were 155 black police officers on the New York City force of nearly 18,000. However, "[m]any Harlemites resented the black policemen as much as they did the white officers" (Brandt, 36).

The role of the black press in covering this riot and other racial episodes in the 1940s must be understood within the context of the readership served by African American newspapers. As critics of the black press argue, black newspapers could be partisan in their coverage and did at times engage in the same kind of inaccurate and careless reporting as did the white press. However, the black press was crucial in covering the stories to which the mainstream white press gave little attention or covered only from white perspectives. In 1943, there were about 164 "active" black newspapers. Most were published in large cities with populations of 50,000 or more. They were nearly all weeklies (published weekly). Together these newspapers had a total circulation of around 200,000 people (Birmingham, 1977: 174).

In 1942, the Justice Department threatened the editors of twenty black newspapers with sedition charges after the papers featured articles "exposing segregation and injustices in the U.S. military" (Harley, 250). From the beginning of his tenure with the General Intelligence Division of the Justice Department in 1919, J. Edgar Hoover had found the black press suspect. He had tried to indict many of the black newspapers, as well as the NAACP journal *Crisis* for subversive activities.

> To his mind [Hoover's], the preponderance of negative articles and editorials—whether stories dealing with instances of discrimination or editorials criticizing government policies—was proof that the black press was not just troublesome or radical, but un-American. He believed that the press between the two world wars had played into communist hands, or had been outright supporters of communism. (Brandt, 89–90)

During World War II, Hoover continued his surveillance of black publications. Their coverage of race and justice issues during the period was not calculated to please him. For black Americans, including the black press, the treatment of African American soldiers remained a sore point. The United States began this war as it had all wars—with a reluctance to recruit black soldiers. As in the Civil War, the Spanish-American War, and World War I, most of the black soldiers who were finally recruited served in segregated units led by white officers. In this war, there was some progress in that blacks were trained to serve in new positions—"as gunner's mates, petty officers, quartermasters, and coxswains, albeit at segregated bases" (Brandt, 111). The United States Marines opened their ranks to black recruits. Benjamin O. Davis, Jr., a black officer, commanded the all-black Ninety-Ninth Pursuit Squadron. A handful of other blacks—less than 2 percent of the total—served as officers (Brandt, 111). Black women joined the WACS and the WAVES (Harley, 1995: 250). Some progress was being made.

But black soldiers continued to experience episodes of verbal and physical abuse from white officers, white soldiers, and white civilians. Jackie Robinson, who in October 1945 would break the color barrier in Major League baseball, was court-martialed while he was serving in the military for his refusal to move to the back of a bus. Such mistreatment of black soldiers was perceived as an insult to all black Americans.

On the civilian home front, black Americans again migrated to urban centers to seek work in war industries.[4] However, in this war, black leaders were more insistent in their demand for integration of the war industries and the opening up of new jobs for black workers. Franklin D. Roosevelt found himself under increasing pressure to take executive action. Hoping to avert a proposed march on Washington, he summoned Walter White and A. Philip Randolph to the White House. Randolph, leader of the Brotherhood of Sleeping Car Porters, had formed the March on Washington Committee. Despite pleas from Eleanor Roosevelt and from his friend New York Mayor La Guardia, Randolph was adamant in his refusal to call off the march. He told Roosevelt he would have 100,000 marchers for the event—and the march would go on unless Roosevelt took action. When Randolph would not blink, Roosevelt did (Pfeffer, 48–49). Roosevelt issued Executive Order No. 8802, forbidding discrimination in war industries.

But even as they moved into this integrated work force, blacks were aware that the level of racial hostility in American society remained high. In 1942, representing the NAACP, Walter White met with Hollywood studio heads, hoping that the movie industry could be used as one mechanism for alleviating this hostility. He was able to obtain "a somewhat ambiguous agreement that the filmmakers would try both to employ more Afro-Americans and also to depict Afro-Americans more positively in their movies" (Scruggs, 1993: 10). In 1943, Twentieth-Century-Fox released the film *Stormy Weather*. It had been made by a nearly all-white production staff, but it did feature a black cast. Unfortunately, in spite of good intentions, the movie presented many of the old images of African America—"cakewalkers" and minstrels, a Harlem nightclub and a southern juke joint (Scruggs, 10–11). The final scene featured "zoot-suiters" and "zoot girls" dancing.

The same year the film premiered, the "Zoot-Suit Riots" erupted in several western cities including Los Angeles. In Los Angeles, the white rioters (off-duty military personnel) targeted Mexican American youths in zoot suits. African American youths were also victims of this white violence.

> The suits were seen as unpatriotic (they violated War Production Board standards of cloth rationing), but more importantly they were the "uniform" of the nonwhite population that was challenging the status quo within the context of the social disruption of World War II. (Scruggs, 11)

The riots generated protests from the Mexican government and threatened international embarrassment for the United States. Such racialized violence called into question the commitment of the United States to democracy.

Black soldiers also questioned the commitment of their country to the "Four Freedoms." When the war ended, they came home, sometimes reluctantly. Like their white counterparts, they faced the stresses of readjustment to civilian life. But for the black soldiers there was an additional stress. As in the aftermath of World War I, returning African American soldiers were again the targets of racial violence. But their wartime experiences had made them less willing to accept abuse passively.

Aside from the racial conflict of the postwar era, black men returning from combat found that another aspect of readjustment to civilian life was the impact of the war on the women they had left behind. For women, black and white, who had held war industry jobs, the return of their men meant that they too were demobilized. They were dismissed as men returned to claim their jobs. They were fired as war factories turned to the production of peacetime products. For the black women in the labor force, demobilization often signified not a return to their own kitchen but to someone else's. Many of them went back to domestic work[5] as their men began their search for jobs.

POSTWAR APPEALS TO JUSTICE

In 1947 W.E.B. Du Bois presented an appeal on behalf of the NAACP to the United Nations. It was an appeal against racism in the United States.

In the United States, the South was about to become the site for much of the postwar agitation by blacks against racial injustice and for equal rights. In 1942, three distinguished black Virginians—P. B. Young, publisher of the Norfolk *Journal and Guide*; Gordon Blaine Hancock of Virginia Union University; and Luther Porter Jackson, a close associate of Carter G. Woodson's (founder of the *Journal of Negro History*)—had convened in Durham, North Carolina, a meeting of black leaders, who "issued a public report that was for most of them unprecedently outspoken on matters of discrimination." The report was hailed by the leaders of the NAACP and by other black organizations as a "turning point" in southern black assertiveness (Meier and Rudwick, 1986: 69).[6]

In 1947, the Congress on Racial Equality (CORE) sent an interracial group on a bus trip through the South to test the Supreme Court decision in *Morgan v. Commonwealth of Virginia* (1946). In its ruling in this case, the court had banned segregation in interstate bus travel (Harley 256, 258). This trip sponsored by CORE (called "The Journey of Reconciliation") was "a precursor to the Freedom Rides of the 1960s" (Harley, 258).

On the criminal justice front, during the last years of the decade two cases involving black defendants began the journey that would lead to the United States Supreme Court. In each case, appeals were unsuccessful. In each case, black Americans felt that race had played a role in the outcome for the defendants. One occurred in the South. The other was on the other side of the world and was an example of military justice in action.

In January 1949, in the South, the case of the Martinsville Seven stirred echoes of the Scottsboro Boys case of 1931. In this Martinsville, Virginia, case the issue was less whether the youths involved were guilty than whether or not they had received due process. They had been convicted of the rape of a white woman.[7] The fundamental question in the case was whether or not they should receive the death penalty for rape. There was concern among those who protested the sentence about how the death penalty was administered. For the first time, social science data on discrimination in the application of the death penalty were presented during an appeal (Rise, 1995). But when the case reached the Supreme Court, the court declined to review it. No reason was given. The court was not required to give a reason.

A coalition of groups formed in efforts to prevent the executions. But in the end, their efforts were futile. In February 1951, the Martinsville Seven were executed. The executions occurred after "two years, six trials, five stays of execution, ten opportunities for judicial review, and two denials of executive clemency" (Rise, 148), after the best efforts by the NAACP, the Civil Rights Congress, and the Committee to Save the Martinsville Seven had failed.

In that same year, 1949, half a world away, another group of black males began the path that would lead to execution. These men were soldiers in the United States Air Force, stationed on Guam. The three, a sergeant and two privates, were arrested for the rape/murder of a white female clerk of an island gift shop. The handling of the case by the military raised serious due process issues for many black Americans and for white supporters of the men. Although all three claimed to be innocent, two of the men had confessed. One repudiated his confession in court, claiming it had been coerced. Later, the other did the same. All three men claimed that they had been subjected to beating, starvation, and prolonged bouts of questioning by the military investigators and the military's consultant, Inspector of Police Albert E. Reidel, from Berkeley, California.

The families of the men had become aware of what was going on only after an African American chaplin notified the uncle of one of the men. The uncle then appealed to the NAACP for help. The NAACP launched an investigation, which discovered that a white lieutenant colonel in the Judge Advocate's office on the island had been first removed from the case, arrested for misconduct, given a psychiatric exam, and finally forced to resign from the service. He claimed that papers had been stolen from his office. The officer believed he had uncovered evidence that suggested the men were not guilty.

In fact, two of the men had witnesses who swore that they were elsewhere at the time that the crime was committed. Also there was the matter of how the search for the missing woman had been conducted. When the owner of the shop reported she was missing, the military police had initiated a search. But it was a day and a half before the young woman was located, in a wooded area in the immediate vicinity of the gift shop. Medical evidence indicated that she had been alive when she was left there and had died during the prolonged period it took the searchers to find her. There was no conclusive medical evidence that she had been raped.

These and other factors suggested to some observers that perhaps some type of cover-up was taking place. They suspected the shop owner might have been a part of a drug or black market operation that involved members of the military, but there was no proof, and the crucial goal was to stop the executions. An appeal to the Supreme Court failed even though several of the justices believed the men had not received due process.

In a last ditch effort, black leaders sought a meeting with President Eisenhower. Eisenhower listened, but he did nothing to stop the executions. The sentence of one of the men, Calvin Dennis, had been commuted to life in prison. On January 27, 1954, Robert W. Burns and Herman P. Dennis (no relation to Calvin) were hanged by the military. In a last letter Burns had smuggled out to the black newspaper *The Pittsburgh Courier* a few days before his execution, he wrote, "Death hover over my door. . . . I have committed no murder." He urged the newspaper, "Let my people know we are yet in bondage" (Aptheker, 1971)[8]

CONCLUSIONS

In *An American Dilemma* (1944), the monumental study of "the Negro problem" funded by the Carnegie Corporation, the Swedish social scientist Gunnar Myrdal reported:

> Some of the "crimes" in the South may possibly be committed only by Negroes: only Negroes are arrested for violations of segregation laws, and sometimes they are even arrested for violation of the extra-legal racial etiquette (the formal charge is "disturbing the peace," "insolence to an officer," "violation of municipal ordinances," and so on). The beating of Negroes by whites in the South is seldom regarded as a crime, but should a Negro lay hands on a white man, he is almost certain to be apprehended and punished severely. (Myrdal, 969)

On July 31, 1943, an editorial in the black newspaper *Amsterdam News* called on the FBI to take some action in response to lynchings in Mississippi. Even as black soldiers fought for victory in the war, black civilians fought for justice on the home front—the "Double V" that African Americans hoped would come at the end of the war. Again, as in other wars, black soldiers fought not just to achieve an American victory but to prove themselves worthy of all of the rights of American citizens. Those rights included the right to equal justice under the law.

As in the past, the coming of peace did not bring the significant gains for which black Americans had hoped. But what they had learned by the 1940s was that it was possible to engage in sustained agitation—in the courts, in the halls of Congress, even in encounters with the president of the United States—and by sheer sustained effort win a series of victories. These victories were sometimes more symbolic than actual. But they represented the continued resistance by African Americans as individuals and as organizations to injustice.

Black servicemen in the 1940s returned home to a changing social climate. They and other black Americans in the postwar years would not be content with the legal status quo. They would challenge it. But, ironically, in 1951, when Thurgood Marshall went to Korea in response to a request for assistance that the NAACP had received from thirty-six black soldiers, not much had changed with regard to the way black servicemen were treated. The men he went to see had all been convicted in military court-martials. Marshall reported to the NAACP board members, "Justice in Korea may have been blind, but not color-blind" (Davis and Clark, 1992: 130).

NOTES

1. Hattie McDaniel once told a reporter, "It's much better to play a maid than to be one. The only choice permitted me is either to be a servant for $7.00 a week or portray one for $700.00 a week" (Pomerance, 1988: 189).

2. Angelou (1969) recalled the celebration in her grandmother's general store. Joe Louis was champion of the world. It was a night when a black man and his family should not "be caught on a lonely country road" by disgruntled whites. People who had come from a distance made arrangements to stay in town (Angelou, 114–115).

3. See Turner (1993: 43–45) for discussion of the role played by rumors in racial discord during World War II.

4. Between 1940 and 1970, about 5 million blacks would make the trek north and west (Mohl, 1993: 13).

5. For an overview of the economic status of black Americans at the end of the decade see the staff report prepared by the Subcommittee on Civil Rights (1954).

6. The report was written by Charles S. Johnson of Fisk University. During this era, Johnson was one of the most powerful black men in the South. Like Booker T. Washington, he was able to attract white philanthropy to his institution and had "succeeded in creating at Fisk a machine that almost came to dominate black sociology" (Meier and Rudwick, 1986: 71).

Regarding the "Durham Statement," see Hall (1993) on the role played by the white female antilynching activist Jesse Daniel Ames in suggesting the conference to Hancock, with whom she shared similar views about the need for interracial cooperation between the better class of whites and blacks. Hall states, "Although conference representatives declared themselves 'fundamentally opposed to the principle and practice of compulsory segregation in our American society,' they refrained from demanding the abolition of Jim Crow" (258).

7. The woman was a Jehovah's Witness who had been accustomed to entering the black neighborhood to do missionary work. According to her testimony, she was attacked by the young men, who had been lounging by a railroad track, when she passed and when she returned from her mission. Black residents of the neighborhood, who had given her directions and who helped her to get aid when she went to their home, verified key points of her story (Rise, 1995).

8. This account of the case by Aptheker originally appeared in *Masses and Mainstream*, February 1955. Aptheker was contacted during the course of the campaign to save the men. He asserts that the two men "were legally lynched by the government of the United States" (Aptheker, 243).

CHAPTER 11

"To Secure These Rights"

The brief for the petitioners to the Supreme Court in *McGhee v. Sipes* (1947) stated:

> Judicial enforcement of restrictive covenants has created a uniform pattern of unprecedented overcrowding and congestion in the housing of Negroes and an appalling deterioration of their dwelling conditions. The extension and aggravation of slum conditions have in turn resulted in a serious rise in disease, crime, vice, racial tension and mob violence.

The petitioners argued that restrictions with regard to where they were allowed to live forced black Americans into a physical environment that was hostile to their well-being. Such residential restrictions were a part of the continuing pattern of oppressive race relations that existed.[1] In 1946, at the request of a group headed by Walter White of the NAACP, President Harry S. Truman had agreed to create a commission to examine the state of race relations in the United States. On December 5, 1946, he issued an executive order establishing the President's Commission of Civil Rights (Goldman and Gallan, 1992: 73), the first presidential commission with that focus (Goldfield, 1990: 54). The committee was composed of fifteen prominent people, including two southerners.

On October 29, 1947, the committee issued its report, *To Secure These Rights*. The committee made forty recommendations; three were concerned with "restrictive covenants" that prevented blacks from purchasing houses in white neighborhoods. One of these recommendations was that the Department of Justice intervene in future litigation on the side of the petitioners. The next day, Attorney General Tom C. Clark announced that the solicitor general would submit an *amicus curiae* brief in the restrictive covenant cases that were then being litigated. Thurgood Marshall, one of the attorneys leading the legal battle for the petitioners, described this move by the Justice Department as "the first *amicus curiae* brief ever filed, by the United States in private civil rights litigation" (Goldman and Galan, 73).

Victory by the NAACP Legal Defense and Educational Fund in the "Restrictive Covenant Cases" gave impetus to its battle on other fronts. In 1954, in *Brown v. Board of Education*, the NAACP legal defense team would score its most decisive victory. But that was yet to come. In 1947 when Harry Truman received the report from his committee on civil rights, postwar violence was sweeping the South. In its report the committee

> included a sweeping agenda for transforming race relations not only in the South, but in the nation: an antilynching law; the abolition of the poll tax; laws to prevent voter-registration discrimination; desegregation of the armed forces; an end to segregation in Washington, D.C., and in interstate public transportation; the establishment of a permanent civil right section within the Justice Department; and the withdrawal of federal funds to institutions practicing segregation. (Goldfield, 54)

An election year was approaching and Truman was aware that the proposals would have little chance of passage in Congress. However, he did present the recommendations to Congress—in part perhaps because "an ideological war was escalating with the Soviets" (Goldfield, 54).[2]

In November 1947, his adviser Clark Clifford gave Truman his analysis of the upcoming election. Clifford—himself a southerner—told the president that he could win the election without carrying the Solid South. It seemed that the more than 1.7 million blacks who had moved to four major "swing states" made it feasible to win without total southern support. In fact, black leaders, recognizing their emerging political clout, were putting pressure on the president to act in response to his committee's recommendations.

In summer 1948, Truman issued two executive orders: One abolished segregation in the military; the other prohibited discrimination in federal employment and at facilities with federal contracts (Goldfield, 54–55). These events at the federal level gave black Americans hope that they had entered a new era of racial progress. This hope was reinforced when General Douglas MacArthur was removed from his command. He was replaced by General Matthew L. Ridgway, who carried out Truman's order to desegregate the armed forces. By July 1953, 90 percent of all soldiers in Korea were serving in integrated units (Harley, 264). Another political milestone was achieved when Congressman Adam Clayton Powell, Jr., persuaded the Democratic party to take a stand on civil rights in its party platform. This was another indication to black Americans of their emerging ability to exercise political clout.

But this clout was limited to those regions of the country in which blacks could vote. In the South, many remained disenfranchised, with little control over the institutions that affected their lives. Blacks who were tenant farmers and sharecroppers could not vote; they had no power to correct a situation in which their children received a substandard education. Their children walked to one room rural schoolhouses that were operated on shoestring budgets and opened for fewer months each year than the white schools. Their children were taught by poorly paid teachers from castoff textbooks. This Jim Crow policy extended beyond the schoolhouse to movie houses and hotels and restaurants. It extended into the courtrooms, jails, and prison farms. In the midtwentieth century, segregation and racial injustice still reigned in the South.

In 1954, Thurgood Marshall and the legal team of the NAACP argued the case of *Brown v. Board of Education* before the United States Supreme Court. Their strategy included testimony from social scientists. The psychologist Kenneth B. Clark was called to testify about the impact of segregation not only on the education of black children but on their self-esteem. He presented his now famous research indicating that when given a choice of a brown doll or a white doll, black children preferred the white doll. The children declared the brown doll—which looked like them—"bad." In the *Brown* case, Thurgood Marshall made strategic use of Clark's research.

> Marshall took a decidedly sociological tack in this brief, as he had done in *Sweatt* and *McLaurin*.[3] Relying heavily on the South Carolina testimony of Dr. Kenneth Clark and the published work of Clark and his wife, Mamie, Marshall tried to demonstrate the inherent evils of segregated education. (Davis and Clark, 1992: 156)

Clark, who had earned his doctorate in psychology from Columbia University, was "noted for his doll tests." This was a technique he and his wife, Mamie, also a psychologist, had developed in order to compare the attitudes of black children who attended segregated schools to those of black children who attended integrated schools. The testimony by Clark and the strategy used by Marshall were effective. When the court ruled in *Brown*, it overturned the decision in *Plessy v. Ferguson*, declaring that separate was "inherently unequal." The court extended its ruling not only to schools but to other public facilities. Jim Crow in the South was now under serious attack.

Later, in the 1960s, the strategies that should be employed to secure their rights would become a subject for debate among black Americans. But at the beginning of the modern civil rights movement, the strategy of choice was nonviolent civil disobedience. A major event in this movement occurred when in 1955, Rosa Parks, a black seamstress, refused to give up her seat on a city bus. In the lore about the modern civil rights movement, this act of disobedience has assumed the status of that moment at which black resistance was born. It was not.[4] Kelley (1994) points out that working class blacks had long been engaged in individual—often spontaneous—challenges to the Jim Crow system. However, their acts of disobedience were often less than civil and their resistance more than passive.[5]

In this sense, Rosa Parks's conscious use of nonviolent civil disobedience as a form of resistance marked a new era. Her defiance of the law came at a psychological moment when it could galvanize the black community: It was the right action at the right time. The local NAACP in Montgomery, Alabama, had been waiting for such an opportunity.[6] When Rosa Parks refused to give up her seat and move to the back of the bus, she was arrested. And the bus boycott in Montgomery began. For over a year, blacks walked and car pooled. In 1956, a federal court ruled that segregation on Montgomery buses was unconstitutional. The striking blacks in Montgomery had won.

But it was an early battle in an escalating war. The Reverend Martin Luther King, Jr., was emerging as a charismatic leader of the budding civil rights movement. But white southerners were also organizing for resistance—for massive "take no prisoners" resistance. In 1956, the "Southern Manifesto" was issued by 101 southern congressmen, who urged states to resist the *Brown* decision, (Harley, 1995: 272). The White Citizens Council was organized, the council was "a sort of white-collar Klan, for the specific purpose of making it difficult, if not impossible for any Negro who advocate[d] desegregation to find and hold a job, get credit, or renew a mortgage" (Davis and Clark, 1992: 185). As the civil rights movement continued, verbal resistance by white southerners would be accompanied by acts of terrorist violence.

In 1957, black religious leaders formed the Southern Christian Leadership Council (SCLC). Martin Luther King moved from Montgomery to Atlanta to head it. In 1960, the Student Non-Violent Coordinating Committee (SNCC) was founded at Shaw University in Raleigh, North Carolina. In the beginning, these two organizations were able to cooperate, but they would eventually diverge in their strategies. The SNCC would become the first civil rights organization to denounce the Vietnam War (Harley, 296). Stokely Carmichael, elected chairperson of SNCC in 1966, would also become one of the first leaders in the movement to advocate the concept of "Black Power," which would both unite black Americans in their struggle for self-determination and create disruptive ideological conflicts regarding acceptable strategies.

NORTHERN RESISTANCE

As the civil rights movement in the South moved from Freedom Rides to sit-ins at lunch counters, black leaders in the North were also organizing for resistance. There had always been some activism by leaders, for example, the "Don't buy where you can't work" boycotts of white-owned stores. In Harlem, the flamboyant minister Adam Clayton Powell, Jr., with the Abyssinian Baptist church as his power base, had worked with other community leaders to gain concessions from the white merchants of the stores on 125th Street and the bus company that served Harlem residents. In 1940, Powell spoke to reporters about crime in Harlem:

> The so-called recent crime wave is neither a crime wave nor is it recent. It is not a crime wave in the accepted sense because it is not being conducted by criminals. It is not recent because it dates to the beginning of the Depression. (Hickey and Edwin, 1965: 66)

Since 1901, there had been only three blacks in Congress. In 1944, Powell would join them as the representative from his district in Harlem (Hickey and Edwin, 85–86). In Congress, Powell served as a perpetual irritant to southern representatives; for example, he challenged John E. Rankin, of Mississippi, over Rankin's use of the world *nigger* on the floor of the House. As Hamilton (1991: 484) observes, Powell "certainly did not change Rankin's mind or behavior, but he gave solace to millions who longed for a little retaliatory defiance."

Powell was still in Congress in the 1960s when civil rights activism in the North (and in the West) became more sustained. In the 1960s, the Black Panthers claimed media and law enforcement attention. But this should not obscure the fact that since the 1950s, the Black Muslims had been engaged in their own brand of resistance. Like the Black Panthers of the 1960s, the Black Muslims challenged police actions. When, in 1957, a member of the Nation of Islam was beaten by the police while in jail, Malcolm X, one of the emerging leaders in the Nation, led a group of Muslim men to the police station. They were joined by curious onlookers. Malcolm X went in and asked to speak to the police. Concerned about the Muslims lined up outside the stationhouse and the excited crowd of other blacks who were gathering, the police commander complied with his request that the arrested man be taken to Harlem Hospital.[7]

In his autobiography, Malcolm X recalls:

> For New York City's millions of readers of the downtown papers, it was, at the time, another one of the periodic "Racial Unrest in Harlem" stories. . . . But the police department, to be sure, pulled out and carefully studied the files on the Nation of Islam, and appraised us with new eyes. Most important, in Harlem . . . the *Amsterdam News* made the whole story headline news, and for the first time the black man, woman, and child in the street was discussing "those Muslims." (Malcolm X and Haley, 1964: 235)

In 1959, Malcolm X received national attention when he was featured in a five-part ABC report anchored by Mike Wallace about the Nation of Islam. It was titled "The Hate That Hate Produced." Malcolm X's later assessment of the report was that it was decidedly slanted. He told Alex Haley, "Every phrase was edited to increase the shock mood. As the producers intended, I think people sat just about limp when the program went off" (Malcolm X and Haley, 238).

As Malcolm X knew well, he was not perceived as a positive force for racial harmony by most white people. He believed his image was deliberately distorted by the white-dominated mainstream media, by law enforcement, and to some extent by other black leaders. Placing this in the context of black history, he said, "Since slavery, the American white man has always kept some handpicked Negroes who fared much better than the black masses suffering and slaving out in the hot fields" (Malcolm X and Haley, 239). He added—speaking of the reactions to the ABC report—"why, he [the white man] didn't even need to instruct the trained black puppets. They had seen the television program; had read the newspapers. They were already composing their lines. They knew what to do" (Malcolm X and Haley, 239).[8]

Such comments made Malcolm X controversial both to whites and within the black community. But as he conversed with Mike Wallace, the cool, articulate Malcolm X seemed far removed from the zoot-suit-wearing, hustling Malcolm Little he had once been.[9] Little had gone to prison for burglary. In prison, he was introduced to the teachings of Elijah Muhammed and became a convert to Islam. He emerged from prison to assume a position as Elijah Muhammed's protégé.

For white Americans, Malcolm X emerged in the late 1950s as an elegant and well-spoken version of the "bad nigger." As a Black Muslim, he did not drink, gamble, or consort with white women. But he did challenge the racial status quo. He did not care whether whites were well disposed toward him. He did not try to be cooperative. He rejected both accommodation and assimilation. As an outspoken leader within the separatist Nation of Islam, in the late 1950s he represented a new and decidedly threatening element.

But other black public figures also attracted negative attention during this period. In 1956, Paul Robeson, the black actor and singer, was called before the House Committee on Un-American Activities. He was suspected of being a "Communist sympathizer" because of his trips to the Soviet Union. Even the elegant crooner Nat "King" Cole, a native of Alabama, was vulnerable. In Birmingham, Alabama, "six white men rushed on stage and brazenly tried to attack him." Cole canceled his concert, saying he "wouldn't sing in the South for a million dollars" (Pomerance, 1988: 155). Cole's show on network television was canceled soon after it premiered because the sponsors withdrew their support. His friendly exchanges with his white guests did not play well in the South.

Even so, the mass media—particularly television—were about to become major players in the civil rights movement.

ONE PICTURE . . .

"Sorry, Cable Trouble" was the graphic display used by television WLBT when it interrupted coverage of news events related to the civil rights movement (Montgomery, 1989: 23). In 1964, a coalition of civil rights groups filed a petition with the Federal Communications Commission (FCC) asking the commission to deny license renewal to station WLBT in Jackson, Mississippi. The coalition claimed the station blatantly discriminated against blacks in both its hiring practices and its programming. This was the first time such a petition had been filed by an interest group. The challenge to WLBT was a part of a nationwide strategy spearheaded by the Office of Communication of the United Church of Christ, based in New York (Montgomery, 23). When civil rights groups began their assault on the practices of the television and film industries, they employed "the same tactics which were gaining them access to other American institutions: Widespread publicity, appeals to the government, and direct confrontation when needed." That is, they employed economic boycotts, picket lines, and legal action (Montgomery, 23).

Civil rights activists were beginning to realize how important the media were in their struggle; in the modern movement, which began in the 1950s, television became the medium that transmitted to a national audience the images of black protest. As the movement continued, television cameras captured the violence that punctuated the white response. The presence of television cameras (and to a lesser extent radio and newspaper reporters) would be crucial to the civil rights leaders, who needed to get their message out to the American public. One picture was indeed worth a thousand verbal or written claims of injustice. In fact, the relationship between television (the new medium) and the civil rights movement was symbiotic, as the movement provided the networks with the raw material that they needed to build their news divisions. The sit-ins, the marches, the riots, and the speeches made for great television.

But civil rights groups were also concerned about the other images of blacks being broadcast on daily television programs that were produced as entertainment. In the 1950s, black groups were active in their efforts to control these images; organizations such as the NAACP pressured both local networks and the national networks for changes. As a result, in 1951, NBC began a campaign to improve its own image with the black community. This action by the network was a recognition of the growing power of blacks as consumers; by 1953, black Americans represented a $15 billion consumer market (MacDonald, 1983: 17). However, the networks were also faced with pressure from southern white groups. Actions calculated to please black

Americans tended to displease these groups. For example, in 1952, the governor of Georgia threatened to organize a boycott of television programs with integrated casts (MacDonald, 8–9). The efforts of black groups to control black images also had the effect of allowing networks to conclude it was easier simply not to use black actors (MacDonald, 1983).[10]

But real life was providing black Americans with increasing media exposure. In May 1954, the respected newsman Edward R. Murrow examined domestic racism in a broadcast eight days after the Supreme Court rendered its decision in *Brown* (MacDonald, 36). A year later, in the Mississippi Delta, where a kind of American apartheid existed, Emmett Till's mutilated body was pulled from the Tallahatchie River. The murder of Till in August 1955 mobilized black resistance to racial violence.

Till, a fourteen year old from Chicago, had been visiting relatives in Mississippi. He was alleged to have violated racial etiquette by whistling at a white woman. The woman, Carol Bryant, ran a rural store with her husband, Roy. Three days after the alleged event, Roy Bryant and his half brother, J. W. Milam, kidnapped Till. They brutally beat, shot, and mutilated the teenager before throwing him into the river (Burns, 1990; Feldstein, 1994). The two men were acquitted of murder by a jury of white males (Whitfield, 1991).

Many white southerners—even those who deplored the murder and questioned the verdicts—were sensitive to the brand of criticism they received over the Till case. In what became a "war of images," the NAACP offered its support to Emmett Till's grieving mother, Mamie Till Bradley. Mrs. Bradley insisted that her son's coffin be open at the funeral because as she said, she "wanted the whole world to see" his battered body. Till's mother was juxtaposed against the young white wife and mother whom Till was alleged to have insulted with his "wolf's whistle."[11] The NAACP sponsored Mrs. Bradley as she traveled around the country speaking to groups about the case.[12]

Because Mrs. Bradley was a single working mother, her status was questionable. Her claim to be "a good mother and respectable, feminine woman was as precarious as it was essential to a condemnation of the murder" (Feldstein, 1994: 270). By the 1950s, the idea of the "black pathology" of the urban ghetto had already entered the public domain. Therefore, if Emmett Till were to be seen as a good boy who did not deserve to die, his mother must be regarded as a good woman who had done her best for her family.

> For Till defenders, constructing Mamie Bradley as a respectable mother was a means through which African Americans could assert their right to the American credo of equal rights to all. The message was that if Till came from a family that loved him, that cried for him—a "good" family, then his murder, and racial discrimination generally violated these American values.... His

identity as an innocent victim depended on his position as a son in a stable family. (Feldstein, 269)

Emmett Till's murder happened four months before blacks in Montgomery began their bus boycott. He became another symbol of what it was black Americans were fighting for. It was not just a matter of being able to sit in the front of the bus. It was not just a matter of having the right to have a soda at the Woolworth's lunch counter. It was not just about having the right to go to a school that provided the same kind of education that white children received. It was about all of this and more. In the minds of black Americans, criminal justice was inextricably linked to social justice. They did not believe they could receive justice in the courtroom until they had justice on the buses, at lunch counters, and in the schools of America.

CONCLUSIONS

In the 1960s, Joyce Ladner of Mississippi, a SNCC worker, recalled that in 1954 when Emmett Till was murdered, she had been twelve years old. But Till's murder had made a profound impression on her and on other young people of her generation:

> I can name you ten SNCC workers who saw that picture [of Till in his casket] in *Jet* magazine, who remember it as the key thing about their youth that was emblazoned in their minds. . . . One of them told me how they saw it and thought that one day they would avenge his death. (Payne, 1995)

For many black Americans, the photograph of Till's multilated body in his coffin, and the contrasting image of the two smiling offenders walking out of the courthouse, represented all that was wrong with American justice. The two white men had not only gotten away with murder, they had told their story in an interview for *Look* magazine. The jury had returned a verdict in their murder trial in one hour and seven minutes. One of the jury members reported, "If we hadn't stopped to drink pop, it wouldn't have taken that long" (Oshinsky, 1996: 230).

As Michael Eric Dyson (1993: 196) writes:

> The unspeakable horror of Emmett's death caused shock to ripple through the entire nation. More importantly, his death galvanized a people perched on the fragile border between heroism and fear to courageously pursue meaningful and complete equality. In the curious mix of fortuity and destiny that infuse all events of epic meaning, Emmett's death gained a transcendent metaphoric value.

A few months later, Rosa Parks would break the law in the name of justice, by refusing to give up her seat on the bus.

NOTES

1. See Mohl (1993 in Hirsch and Mohl) on the reshaping of American cities that began in the 1940s. As Mohl (14–17) observes:

"White flight" to the suburbs would eventually leave many urban cities with a population that was predominantly black and other racial minority. These changes in urban cities were marked by ethnic transitions, relocations, and displacement of populations as changes in the urban economic and physical infrastruction occurred.

2. The reference is to the Cold War that was developing between the Soviet Union and the United States.

3. These two 1950 cases dealt with higher education. *Sweatt v. Painter* involved a lawsuit against the law school at the University of Texas; *McLaurin v. Oklahoma State Regents* was a suit against the graduate school of education at the University of Oklahoma. Marshall had won victories in both cases.

4. In the period from 1900 to 1906, blacks in at least twenty-six cities engaged in local boycotts aimed at resisting the new laws segregating streetcars (Sullivan, 1996: 14).

5. Kelley (1994) examines the many occasions in the 1940s when blacks were forcibly ejected from Birmingham, Alabama, buses after refusing to give up a seat or after getting into a heated exchange with a driver or a white passenger. In his analysis of these events, Kelley considers them as interactions that occurred in contested "public spaces."

6. In August 1955—the same month Emmett Till was murdered—Parks, an active member of the NAACP, had attended the Highlander Folk School in the Appalachian Mountains of Tennessee. There she had taken part in a workshop on racial integration (Burns, 1990: 3).

7. The outcome of the police brutality suit was that the victim, Brother Hinton, was awarded seventy thousand dollars, at the time "the largest police brutality judgment" ever won against the City of New York (Malcolm X and Haley, 234).

8. See Smitherman (1994: 109) for her discussion of Malcolm X's updating of the concept of "field nigga" and "house nigga."

9. Note that in his autobiography, Malcolm X displays disdain for himself during the period when he was a "hustler" in a zoot suit with "conked" hair. In retrospect, he did not see his dress or his life-style as a form of resistance. However, Kelley (1992) discusses Malcolm X's zoot suit period in terms of "black cultural politics."

10. See also Turner (1994: 123) regarding television producers' "damned if you do" dilemma in handling black male representations.

11. Meyerowitz (1994) notes the campaign by *Ebony* magazine in the 1940s and 1950s to elevate the status of black women. The magazine's focus, however, was not on motherhood. Its goal, as stated in a March 1956 editorial, was to offer alternative—black—standards of beauty to its readers:

Because we live in a society in which standards of physical beauty are most often circumscribed by a static concept of whiteness of skin and blondeness of hair, there is an aching need for someone to shout from the housetops that black women are beautiful. (quoted in Meyerowitz, 1994: 244)

12. Relations between Mrs. Bradley and the NAACP later deteriorated amid rumors about inappropriate fund-raising activities (Feldstein, 282–283).

CHAPTER 12

"Ain't Afraid of Your Jails"

In April 1963, the Reverend Martin Luther King, Jr., spent Easter weekend in a Birmingham, Alabama, jail. Sitting in his cell, he scribbled on the margins of a newspaper, a response to an open letter by white clergymen that had appeared in a newspaper. In the letter, the clergymen accused King of being an outside agitator. They said he was demanding too much too quickly. In his response, King wrote:

> Perhaps it is easy for those who have never felt the stinging darts of segregation to say, "Wait." But when you have seen vicious mobs lynch your mothers and fathers at will and drown your sisters and brothers at whim; when you have seen hate-filled policemen curse, kick, and even kill your black brothers and sisters . . . (quoted in Goldfield, 1990: 136)

King went on to express the pain of seeing "twenty million Negro brothers smothering in an airtight case of poverty." He wrote of the pain of trying to explain to a child why she could not go to an amusement park. He wrote of having to sleep in the car during a cross-country trip because motels did not accept blacks, and of knowing that to a white man, "your first name" was "nigger" and "your middle name" was "boy" (Goldfield, 136). For all these reasons, King told the clergymen, it was impossible for Negroes to wait for their freedom from oppression.

In this letter, King's power with words is evident. He conjures up racial images from the collective experiences of black Americans.[1] In presenting these images and his reasoning in this open letter, King was engaged in the "educative function of his work" as a civil rights leader (Goldfield, 136). But as King had already proved, he was prepared to engage in action as well as rhetoric. However, in presenting his case to the white clergymen, King denied that his actions made him an extremist. He described his position in the civil rights movement as that of the moderate middle. King described himself as engaged in a moral crusade against immoral laws. In doing so, he drew a distinction between "just" laws and "unjust" laws. An unjust law was "sinful," he told the white ministers (Goldfield, 136).

In protesting these unjust laws, civil rights demonstrators in Birmingham had faced Police Commissioner Eugene "Bull" Connors. Connors's police force had attacked with dogs and water hoses. The demonstrators had been arrested and placed in jail cells. But from the perspectives of many in the television audience who had watched the confrontation, it was a battle that the civil rights demonstrators had won. The demonstrators—attacked with water hoses and police dogs—had won the battle for the "moral high ground."

Later that year, as he addressed the more than 200,000 people who had joined the March on Washington (Harley, 288), King again took the high ground. Standing in front of the Lincoln Memorial, he shared with the marchers his vision of a color-blind society in which people would be judged by "the content of their character." In his speech, "I Have a Dream," King placed his dream within the context of the American creed, of the words of the Constitution and the Declaration of Independence. He said that "millions of slaves . . . had been seared in the flames of withering injustice." He said that "America has defaulted on this promissory note [the Constitution and the Declaration of Independence] insofar as her citizens of color are concerned." But, King, asserted, "There will be neither rest nor tranquility in America until the Negro is granted his citizenship rights." He expressed his dream that one day the state of Mississippi would be "an oasis of freedom and justice," and he called for a "biracial army" of blacks and whites who would together "storm the battlements of injustice." He cautioned his listeners that they must not allow "our creative protest to degenerate into physical violence" (King, 1963, in Washington, 1986: 215–220).

King's call for America to live up to her obligations to all her citizens was destined to be hailed as one of the great "American" speeches and to appear in dozens of anthologies. It is the speech that Americans still hear on every Martin Luther King Day. But King's speech did not capture the violence of the season. That year Medgar Evers, field secretary for the NAACP, was shot in the driveway of his home. That year a church was bombed in Birmingham, killing four little black girls. That year President John F. Kennedy, who was regarded by many blacks as an (albeit, sometimes reluctant) ally, was assassinated in Dallas. King's speech was about the dream, not the reality.

When John Kennedy was shot, Malcolm X made the observation that it was a case of "chickens coming home to roost." The remark was controversial.[2] Many said it was a hateful and disrespectful remark to make when a beloved young president had just been murdered. But Malcolm X believed it was a true statement about violence in America. In a speech delivered in April 1964, he said:

> If George Washington didn't get independence for this country nonviolently, and if Patrick Henry didn't come up with a nonviolent statement, and you taught me to look upon them as patriots and heroes, then it's time for you to realize that I have studied your books well. (in Hord and Lee, 1995)

To white Americans—and to many blacks—Malcolm X seemed to advocate violence if there was no other way to precipitate change. But when he returned from his pilgrimage to Mecca, where he had experienced brotherhood among white and black Muslims, Malcolm X indicated his willingness to work with other black leaders and with well-intentioned whites.

The next year, Malcolm X was assassinated in the Audubon Ballroom in New York City. In delivering his eulogy, the actor Ossie Davis said, *"Malcolm was a man!"* [italics in the original].

> Protocol and common sense require that Negroes stand back and let the white man speak up for us, defend us, and lead us from behind the scene in our fight. This is the essence of Negro politics. But Malcolm said to hell with that! Get up off your knees and fight your own battles. That's the way you win back your self-respect. That's the way to make the white man respect you. And if he won't let you live like a man, he certainly can't keep you from dying like one! (Davis, 457–458, in Malcolm X and Haley, 1992)

Davis admitted that he, like many others, had been "too chicken, too cautious" to be identified with Malcolm X when he was alive. But he had always known that Malcolm X, "even when he was wrong, was always that rarest thing in the world among us Negroes: a true man" (Davis, 459).[3]

In 1968, Martin Luther King too was assassinated. It happened in Memphis, Tennessee. He had gone there—gone back there—to finish the march he had started in support of the striking black sanitation workers. The first march had been interrupted by violence between whites and blacks. His return to Memphis was to be an attempt to lead a nonviolent march. He was shot on the balcony of his motel room.

Two of the most important symbolic leaders of the civil rights movement were now dead. Each before he died had began to broaden his ideological perspective. In 1967, King had announced his opposition to the Vietnam War. In a speech at the Overseas Press Club in New York City, he had suggested that those who "find the American course in Vietnam a dishonorable and unjust one" should avoid military service (Harley, 300). King's concerns about social justice had expanded to a more direct focus on poverty. In the aftermath of King's assassination, the Reverend Ralph Abernathy, one of King's closest associates, led "the Poor People's March" on Washington, D.C.

But other leaders were emerging. Within the civil rights movement, there had always been a "youth movement" of sorts. Now it moved to the forefront.

SITTING IN

Late Monday afternoon, 1 February 1960, four well-dressed young men, first year students at the mainly black North Carolina A & T College in Greensboro, bought some supplies at Woolworth's, then sat down at the lunch counter and ordered coffee. "I'm sorry," the waitress said, "We don't serve you here."(Burns, 1990: 11)

This was the start of the sit-in protests by college students at lunch counters and restaurants. By the end of that month, sit-ins had spread to seven states. By April the movement had "pervaded" the South (Burns, 11). Ella Baker of the SCLC heard about the sit-in protests and became interested in organizing the student activists. She believed that the student group should be autonomous, independent of the SCLC, "with the right to direct their own affairs and even make their own mistakes" (Burns, 12). With Baker's help, the Student Non-Violent Coordinating Committee (SNCC) was born.

From the beginning, SNCC differed from the SCLC in being less centralized in its leadership and more loosely structured. SNCC was also more oriented toward the development of grass-roots activism. The organization's slogan was "We are all leaders" (Burns, 13). With CORE sponsorship, SNCC members set out on "Freedom Rides." The "Freedom Riders," black and white, boarded buses together and headed for the Deep South. The buses were attacked by white mobs. Sometimes the riders were beaten up. In one incident, the governor of Alabama provided a National Guard escort to a bus. When the bus reached the station in Jackson, Mississippi, the riders were arrested by the police. The riders ended up serving time (almost two months) in the county jail or in the notorious Parchman State Prison (Burns, 16).[4]

To the annoyance of their guards, the Freedom Riders kept on singing. Like the demonstrators who marched with Martin Luther King, they had adopted song as a part of their movement. A traveling group known as the SNCC Freedom Singers had been organized, but much of the singing was impromptu, at rallies. Often songs were made up in response to a particular incident. The singing was an aspect of the movement that linked old and young, black and white, college student and dirt farmer. "Singing was the main language of the protest . . . and the vital tool to build solidarity and instill courage and deepen commitment" (Burns, 18).

These qualities were needed by the SNCC workers who ventured into Mississippi to organize local blacks to register to vote. In this registration drive, they were joined by local grass-roots workers such as Fannie Lou Hamer—who would later be prominent in the Mississippi Freedom Party.[5] With the help of local people like Hamer, the volunteers went from house to house talking to people about registering to vote.

During the Mississippi Freedom Summer of 1964 almost a thousand students from the North—most of them white—came to the state. They stayed in the homes of black families and taught in the "freedom schools" directed by the Yale historian Staughton Lynd (Burns, 1990). Three volunteers, Michael Schwerner and Andrew Goodman, both white, and James Chaney, a black Mississippi native, were killed that summer. Six weeks after they disappeared, their bodies were found in an earthen dam. In the movie *Mississippi Burning*, the FBI agents sent to investigate are made the heroes of the story. In real life, the FBI showed some reluctance to get involved.

However, the FBI responded more vigorously in its investigation of black groups suspected of being "domestic terrorists."

BLACK POWER

In June 1966, black leaders organized a special march after James Meredith[6] was shot from an ambush during his solitary "march against fear." The special march became the occasion for a debate about strategies. The key players in the debate were Stokely Carmichael, who had recently been elected chairperson of SNCC, and Martin Luther King, leader of the SCLC. During the planning stages, Whitney Young and Roy Wilkins had withdrawn from the march. However, King remained, and he eventually assented to Carmichael's insistence that white participation in the march be limited. He also reluctantly agreed to armed protection by the Deacons of Defense (Burns, 41–42).

At a night rally in Greenwood, Mississippi, Carmichael told the crowd, "We been saying freedom for six years and we ain't got nothin'! What we gonna start saying now is Black Power!" (Burns, 42). Members of SNCC were told that "Black Power was to be their rallying cry for the rest of the march" (Van Deburg, 1992: 32).[7] King did not approve of Carmichael's use of the slogan. When they met in Yazoo City, he told Carmichael that he did not object to the concept; what he was concerned about was that the phrase "Black Power" gave the wrong impression: It conjured up violent images that could be counterproductive for the movement (Burns, 42–43). But the slogan had immediate appeal for the young activists, who were becoming frustrated and impatient with the speed of change.

Historically, the concept of Black Power was linked to black nationalism— "the conception of African Americans as a colonized people with a rightful claim to nationhood (a perspective antedating the Civil War)" (Burns, 48).[8]

As the concept entered popular discourse, it was embraced by a new generation of African American writers and artists who were engaged in what they perceived as a cultural revolution. Cultural forms would become "weapons in the struggle for liberation" (Van Deburg, 1992: 9).[9]

But it was Stokely Carmichael who became the principal popularizer of the concept. Following SNCC, CORE also adopted the concept of Black Power. After SNCC and CORE expelled their white members, the two groups began to organize in northern cities (Burns, 48). However, the Black Power spokespersons had a problematic relationship with the media that lessened their effectiveness in publicizing their blueprints for social change. In 1969, Floyd McKissick of CORE complained to a national gathering of newspaper editors that newspapers were unwilling to give coverage to "an in-depth critique of the black condition." Indeed they punished those who offered such critiques with lack of coverage (Van Deburg, 13). Advocates of Black Power realized there were risks involved in dealing with media. There was the danger "the press would stigmatize them as part of a new and insidious criminal element, but they also recognized that this lawless macho image had its benefits" (Van Deburg, 12).

There was another group that also made use of a lawless image—the Black Panthers. The Black Panther Party for Self-Defense (BPP) had been founded in 1966 by Huey Newton and Bobby Seale in Oakland, California. The BPP developed a ten-point platform "centering on community control [and] freedom for all black prisoners." But the BPP considered the most important point to be the call for a United Nations plebiscite to determine "the will of their Black people for their national destiny" (Burns, 48–50). Chapters of the Panther party were formed in dozens of cities, including Chicago and New York. In black urban communities, the Panthers sponsored community "survival programs" such as free breakfast for children (Burns, 50). They also engaged in monitoring the police for acts of impropriety or brutality in their interactions with black citizens. The police response was to monitor the Panthers.

Much of the Panthers' early notoriety resulted from the group's sense of the theatrical. As a group, the Panthers had a kind of "urban guerrilla chic." They were immediately recognizable in their berets; sometimes they were photographed holding their loaded weapons. They said their display of weapons was symbolic of their constitutional right as American citizens "to bear arms." They pointed out that state law allowed them to possess and display rifles and shotguns (see Risbane, 1983). Aside from the theatrics, the Panthers were making a serious statement about their willingness to use arms in the defense of themselves and their community. However, the Black Panthers were identified by the FBI as a terrorist group. The agency used informants to infiltrate Panther chapters. By the end of the 1960s, most of the Panther leaders were "killed, imprisoned, or self-exiled" (Burns, 50).

PRISON RESISTANCE AND RESPONSE

While a prisoner in San Quentin, George Jackson, a former Panther field marshal, wrote *Soledad Brother* (1970), a collection of prison letters.[10] In 1971, Jackson was shot by a prison guard during an alleged escape attempt (Burns, 50). Jackson's death sent shock waves through the California prison system. On the other side of the country in New York State, the prisoners in Attica reacted to Jackson's death with shock, grief, and anger:

> Every Attica inmate who had ever received a visit in prison believed Jackson must certainly have been subjected to a thorough search before entering and immediately upon leaving the visiting room. Even if a gun could have been concealed in his hair, inmates reasoned, it would certainly not escape detection during such a search. Jackson had been murdered, they concluded, and if officials could get away with it at San Quentin, so could they at Attica. (*Attica* 1972: 139)

In Attica, as in many other state prisons, the demographics of the population had been changing. There were more black and Latino prisoners. Moreover, the prison population in 1971 was more politically aware than in the past. Many of the inmates characterized themselves as "political prisoners."[11] This reflected their perception of themselves as a colonized people engaged in acts of resistance against a dominant power structure.

A significant portion of the prisoners serving time in Attica and other state penal institutions in 1971 had been involved in one way or another with the social movements of the 1960s. For example, in Chicago at Stateville, gang members entering the prison had been exposed to Saul Alinsky's Woodlawn Project. In Stateville and in Attica, Black Muslims were influential in prison politics. In Stateville, the Muslim prisoners had engaged in hunger strikes to protest prison conditions. Members of the Black Panther party were also serving time in state prisons such as Stateville and Attica.

In some prisons the level of racial violence was on the increase. White prison gangs confronted black and Latino gangs. But at Attica in 1971, the prisoners shared a sense of oppression and injustice. On Thursday morning, September 9, 1971, they took control of the prison yard. On the morning of September 13, 1971, Commissioner of Correctional Services Russell Oswald gave the order to the New York State Police to storm the yard.

In his memoir, *Attica—My Story* (1972), Oswald wrote: "I have emphasized throughout this book that the militant revolutionaries at Attica found minimal support—I would be tempted to say no support—from the larger black community" (354). The support the prisoners received is debatable. But coming as it did at the end of a decade of massive resistance, the seizure of Attica by the prisoners became linked for some African Americans with the black struggle against oppression. The prisoners were largely black or Hispanic and poor. The storming of the yard and the shooting by the State Police of both prisoners and hostages created a perception among some African Americans that the men at Attica had been martyrs in the struggle for justice.

Moreover, the riot (or rebellion) at Attica spurred at least one group of black criminal justice professionals to activism. Gilbert Ware (1976) recalls that the black inmates at Attica asked the question "Where are you black lawyers?" In response, the National Conference of Black Lawyers (NCBL) became involved in the litigation that followed the rebellion. NCBL took on the defense of the sixty inmates who were indicted in December 1972 on charges associated with the rebellion (xxxiii). Ware notes, "From the outset, the NCBL stressed the necessity of black lawyers mounting a united, vigorous and sustained assault on inequality" (xxxv). NCBL was also involved in the defense of the revolutionary Angela Davis;[12] the lawsuit against Judge Hoffman, who had ordered Bobby Seale, chairman of the Black Panther party, chained and gagged during the 1969 Chicago Seven trial; and the representation of black students at Cornell University "who took up arms in self-defense." At the same time, the group provided services "to many of the more anonymous victims of the law" (xxxiii).

The original impetus to form NCBL arose from what Ware describes as a desire "to give black lawyers a means of helping people and themselves by fighting racism, including that within the legal profession" (xxxii). During the late 1960s and into the 1970s, black Americans were becoming more vocal in their critique of what they saw as racism within their own professions. In May 1972, the National Conference of Black Sociologists convened at the University of Chicago to examine their standing in the profession. One of the participants, Butler Jones, echoed his colleagues' complaints that historically black sociologists had not been recognized for their contributions to the discipline. Looking at the pioneers in the field, he concluded they had been relegated to positions at black universities, where they had been unfunded, underpaid, overworked, and largely invisible. Even when the profession came of age in the 1920s, "the black sociologist remained imprisoned in the black problem, and ... white academic sociologists were among his jailers" (1974: 134). In 1972, black sociologists were more assertive in demanding recognition and full participation.

CONCLUSIONS

The commission that investigated the riot at Attica found:

For the black inmates in Attica, the atmosphere on September 8, 1971, was not unlike that in cities before the holocausts of Harlem, Watts, Newark, and Detroit. Sit-ins, demonstrations, and petitions had been met with excuses, delays, and repression. Organized, peaceful efforts had been rebuffed or ignored. . . . No organizers were necessary; no plans were required; no leaders needed. As in the cities in 1967, the situation itself was explosive. (*Attica*, 1972: 141)

Both in the cities and at Attica, the riots ended in destruction of property and loss of life; what they represented was the growing frustration of those who had failed to obtain change.[13]

In the aftermath of the Attica riot, the rate of imprisonment of black and Latino men continued to increase. The "war on drugs" and other law enforcement efforts directed at inner city neighborhoods brought more young men of color into the system. More money was spent on supporting what Flateau (1996) describes as the "prison industrial complex." Less money was spent on providing social programs for inner city neighborhoods. In the years after Attica, going to prison would become a not unexpected "rite of passage" for many young black and Latino males.

But there are reminders of the activism that characterized some of the prisoners who went to Attica in the 1960s. At Green Haven Prison in New York State, a group of prisoners have been involved for almost twenty-five years in developing and analyzing the relationship between racial minority communities and the correctional system. In 1990, in a paper prepared for the Black History Month Legislative Conference, one Green Haven prisoner writes:

> The theoretical and analytical basis of our model for nontraditional solutions, arises from an Afro-Latino Historical Perspective that we have developed. This perspective offers us another way of viewing our history both as people of color and as prisoners. It opposes the view that the dominant society has given us. . . . It affords us an opportunity to create a "new consciousness," which is the first step in an act of empowerment that offers us identity, purpose and direction. (Ellis, 1990: 4)

The Green Haven prisoners recognize the need to accept the responsibility for their misdeeds. But, at the same time, they argue that it is important to make legislatures and community leaders aware of the link—the pipeline—that exists between prisons and black and Latino communities. They argue for the need not only to change themselves, but to change the system. This activism among the prisoners is in many ways a continuation of the struggle for change that was occurring at Attica in 1971.

NOTES

1. See Miller (1992) on the sources from which King drew in his speeches and writing.

2. Elijah Muhammad's response was to relieve his protégé of his duties and order his silence.

3. Thirty years later Malcolm X's daughter would be accused by the federal government of conspiring to kill the Black Muslim leader who she believed was responsible for her father's death. That case would take an unexpected turn when Louis Farrakhan, the man she was alleged to have been plotting against, stepped forward to defend her. The family would face another trauma when Malcolm X's grandson was charged with setting the fire that resulted in the death of his grandmother, Betty Shabazz (Malcolm X's widow).

4. See Oshinsky (1996) on the additional notoriety Parchman Farm gained because of the mistreatment of Natchez civil rights demonstrators imprisoned there. Civil rights attorneys later filed a damage suit in federal district court. Other suits against the prison on behalf of inmates would follow.

5. At the Democratic party convention in Atlanta City in 1964, delegates from the Freedom party asked to be seated. Hubert Humphrey's attempts (as Lyndon Johnson's liaison) to work out a compromise between the white regular party delegates and the Freedom party delegates were unsuccessful. Hamer and the other Freedom party delegates were not seated.

6. Meredith had been the first black to integrate the University of Mississippi in 1962. He was wounded by three shotgun rounds. Regarding Meredith's integration of Ole Miss, according to Birmingham (1977:165), a man named Harry Murphy was actually the first black man to attend the university. However, Murphy had passed as white, "and no one ever knew the difference."

7. "Black Power" was a shortened version of a phrase used by SNCC workers in Alabama: "Power for poor black people" (Van Deburg, 1992: 34).

8. Black leaders from Martin Delaney and Henry Highland Garnet to Marcus Garvey had employed some variation of the concept. In spring 1966, Adam Clayton Powell had used it in his baccalaureate address at Howard University (Van Deburg, 34).

9. See Peretti (1997: 141) on Black Power at the community level, creating "a context in which dispossessed urbanites could feel 'powerful,' politically and culturally." As participants in the movements, local activists organized to provide community services and to create African American businesses and schools.

10. See Cummins (1994) on Jackson's criminal career.

11. This idea of the "political prisoner" was one that had already gained "radical chic" in Berkeley. See Cummins's (1994) discussion of the interaction between the students and others of the radical Left and prisoners such as Eldridge Cleaver, who became a self-styled "outlaw."

12. Another black female prisoner gained notoriety in 1974. Joan Little was charged with stabbing to death the jailer she claimed came into her cell and tried to rape her. Reston (1977: xi–xii) notes, Little "became a symbol of women's groups, civil rights groups, prisoners' rights groups; and the opponents of capital punishment." See Harwell (1980: 114) on Angela Davis's activities in support of Joan Little. Ralph Abernathy, then president of the SCLC, also came to North Carolina to support Joan Little. He told reporters at an airport conference, "I'm a nonviolent minister, but I'm here in this white racist state to give the white man hell. When Joan Little comes to trial I'm going to bring reporters from all over the world to North Carolina" (Harwell, 144).

13. In an address delivered to the American Psychological Association in September 1967, Martin Luther King, Jr., said of the riots: "They are mainly intended to

shock the white community. They are a distorted form of social protest." He added, "The slums are the handiwork of a vicious system of the white society. Negroes live in them but do not make them any more than a prisoner makes a prison" (King, 1968: 4).

CHAPTER 13

Of Wars, Prisons, Politics, and Race Theory

In *The Wars We Took to Vietnam* (1996: 54), Milton Bates writes:

> During the early years of the Vietnam War, black soldiers were more satisfied with their lot than ever before. A high percentage served in elite combat units . . . and they were two to three times more likely than white soldiers to reenlist.

As Bates explains, this rate of reenlistment by black soldiers reflected a combination of satisfaction with military service and dissatisfaction with employment opportunities available to them as civilians. The high rate of unemployment in the black community made military service attractive even during a war. There was also the matter of black pride: "Pride in other areas of black accomplishment extended to military service. After centuries of being relegated to labor duty, the black soldier was now enjoying the prestige of the warrior" (Bates, 54).

But there was a downside to being a warrior. Black Americans were overrepresented as Vietnam War casualties. Between 1961 and 1967, they were 9 percent to 11 percent of the armed forces, and 14.1 percent of the fatalities. That rate peaked at approximately 25 percent in 1966–1967 (Bates, 54–55).[1] When black leaders expressed concern about the high rate of black casualties, "the Department of Defense moved to limit the participation of black soldiers in combat." Thereafter, black fatalities were "held to 13.1% of total fatalities for the war" (Bates, 55).

Black soldiers, like black civilians, continued to deal with the matter of race relations. Although the fighting force in Vietnam had been integrated, African American soldiers still perceived indications of white hostility. They responded with both self-segregation and assertions of black pride in their walk, in their ritual handshakes, in their Afro haircuts, and in the "shades" (sunglasses) that defied military dress codes (Bates, 55). These self-assertive responses were sometimes met by white soldiers with increased hostility. Racial incidents occurred. There were violent clashes between black and white seamen serving aboard the Navy aircraft carriers *Kitty Hawk* and *Constellation* (Mullen, 1973 : 83). There was also said to have been some concern on the part of white officers about "getting fragged" (having a fragmentation grenade thrown into a tent) by a black GI who had a grudge. Although the tales of "fragging" were "probably exaggerated" (Mullen, 80–81), such stories were an indication of underlying racial tension.

By the end of the war, however, many African Americans had something in common with their white comrades. Many soldiers, black and white, shared the sense that Vietnam had not been a "victory" for the United States. Still, Bates suggests, that black soldiers had won something in this war that they had never achieved in other American wars. They had won their "war for respect from white America" (84).

Perhaps they had won respect for their ability as warriors. But, like white soldiers, black soldiers came home to an American public that no longer supported the war they had been sent to fight. They also returned to increasing poverty and unemployment in black urban communities; black soldiers found their communities in the midst of an urban crisis that was receiving limited attention from policymakers. In retrospect, some African American scholars and leaders would suggest that it was during this era that a "retreat" from the social justice that had flowered in the 1960s began. Whatever was happening, something had changed. A "nadir" had begun that would stretch into the 1980s and beyond.

In *Gordon's War* (1973), a black Vietnam vet comes home to discover that his wife has died of a drug overdose. He declares war on the drug lords who have taken over the community. He brings to this war all of the skills he has acquired as a soldier fighting in Southeast Asia. In *Warrior Dreams* (1994), Gibson writes that in the aftermath of the Vietnam War, a "paramilitary culture" developed in America. Thus *Gordon's War* was only one of the many popular films made in the post-Vietnam era in which the returning soldier is drawn into a "war" on the home front. "Rambo" fought his war in a small town, "Gordon" fought his in an inner city ghetto. This militarism was reflected not only in the movies of the era, but in the tough talk by politicians who refocused their attention from the war in Vietnam to the "war on crime" and/or the "war on drugs."

The primary battlefields on which this new war would be fought were inner city neighborhoods. In these communities, illegal drugs were said to flow freely and gangs were reported to be engaging in increasingly violent behavior in defense of turf. When the new drug "crack" appeared on the streets in the early 1980s, the war escalated.[2]

As a part of this war, new prisons were built. The people who would occupy these spaces in penal institutions were drawn increasingly from impoverished black and Latino inner city communities. According to some observers, this was the beginning of the shift of state and federal funding from the "military–industrial complex" to the "prison–industrial complex." At the same time, a process was under way that deflected much of the blame for high rates of black imprisonment from the inequities of the social structure to the inadequacies of black Americans and their culture.

THE SOURCE OF THE PROBLEM

In a 1989 editorial in *Newsweek*, Patricia Raybon, a former *Denver Post* editor, lamented the "severe bias" of media coverage of black Americans. Raybon wrote, "In recent months . . . I have observed a steady offering of media reports on crack babies, gang warfare, violent youth, poverty and homelessness" (11). According to Raybon, the people featured in these stories and photographs were usually African Americans. As a middle class professional, one of the millions of blacks who are "ordinary, hardworking, law-abiding, tax-paying Americans," Raybon objected to such negative media stereotypes of black America. As she saw it, the media were focusing on the "urban underclass"—the "poor, criminal, and dysfunctional"—to the exclusion of other images of African Americans (Raybon, 11).

The media were not the only ones focusing on this underclass. Mohl (1993: 13) asserts that in the 1980s

> social scientists suddenly discovered the presence of an enormous urban underclass whose life prospects had been dangerously diminished by the failure of social policy and collapse of such urban institutions as the public school.

Important works such as Ken Aulette's *The Underclass* (1982) and William Julius Wilson's *The Truly Disadvantaged: The Inner City, the Underclass, and Social Policy* (1987) provided the foundation for scholarly debate about the underclass. What was becoming increasingly clear by the late 1980s, was that the "underclass" in many discussions by social scientists and by laypersons had become synonymous with a "dangerous class," which inhabited what came to be described in the popular media as the "war zones" of urban cities. The public spaces in these war zones were unsafe for noncombatants. In these urban battlefields, mothers—single and often inept at parenting—lost their sons to "the streets."[3]

Since the 1960s, the existence of large numbers of single mother–headed households in black inner city communities had been described as one important source of the problems plaguing black America.

THE MOYNIHAN REPORT AND THE BLACK RESPONSE

In 1965, Daniel Patrick Moynihan, in his role as assistant secretary of labor, prepared a report for President Lyndon Johnson on the state of the Negro family, *The Negro Family: The Case for National Action*. It became known simply as *The Moynihan Report*. In preparing his report, Moynihan turned to the works of historians and social scientists, citing well-known black scholars such as E. Franklin Frazier and Charles Johnson. In his report, Moynihan urged President Johnson to take vigorous action in the form of social programs that would improve the life chances of poor urban black families.

The controversy surrounding the report centered on the language Moynihan used in describing the state of the urban black family, which angered many black Americans. Moynihan described "a tangle of pathology" that had its origin in the "matriarchal" family structure of the urban poor. Describing this family structure as a legacy of slavery, he said that children who grew up in poor single mother–headed households were ill equipped to compete or to achieve success.[4]

The Moynihan Report produced immediate responses from critics, who challenged Moynihan's research and his conclusions. The *Report* became the catalyst for research and writing by both historians and family scholars who challenged Moynihan's description of the black family. By the 1980s, these scholars had moved from a reactive stance to efforts to develop new perspectives.[5] By the 1980s, African Americans were even more conscious of the negative images of the black family that were being presented to white Americans. In the wake of the *Moynihan Report* controversy, it seemed even more likely that those negative images would affect not only white attitudes but public policy.

In the popular culture of the period, there had been the positive, good feelings (with even a little guilt in white America) generated by the 1977 miniseries based on Alex Haley's *Roots* (Tucker and Shah, 1992). This saga, that began with the capture of young Kunte Kinte in Africa and ended with the triumph of his descendants over white treachery in the postbellum period, was about black people who were strong, fearless, and resilient. This was the "ideal" slave family who looked nothing like the broken family who had appeared in the pages of the Moynihan Report. This family looked much more like the family that the new generation of both black and white "revisionist" historians who had begun to publish in the 1960s said might have existed.[6] *Roots* informed many Americans about slavery, inspired some conversations about race relations, even sent some people to the library to check out history books or to find out how to do genealogical research on their own families. The miniseries was both critically acclaimed and highly rated.[7]

However, it was what Americans were seeing on their television sets on other nights that was of concern to some black activists.

In the 1970s, the white producer Norman Lear was the king of television situation comedies. Beginning with the controversial "All in the Family," he had generated "spin-offs" that were equally successful—"The Jeffersons," "Maude," "Good Times." He was also responsible for "Sanford and Son" and "That's My Mama." It was the four situation comedies about blacks ("The Jeffersons," "Good Times," "Sanford and Son," and "That's My Mama") that his African American critics found troubling. Many praised his policy of hiring black writers and black actors. But they were concerned about the images being presented. One particularly outspoken critic, Pluria Marshall, head of the National Black Media Coalition, said bluntly, "[The shows] are produced by white folks for white folks. . . . [The] men always have trouble finding jobs or keeping jobs . . . not a very positive image for my son to watch and try to emulate" (Montgomery, 1989: 72).

Those African American media watchers who were not as global in their complaints did agree that Lear (and other producers) should be aware of what was being projected to America about black families. For example, when John Amos, the actor who played the strong, loving father on "Good Times," left the series in 1976, black groups were particularly concerned that the sitcom would now be about a family headed by a single mother of three children. In the plot line, Florida Evans had been widowed when her husband was killed in a car accident. But the point was, whatever had happened, the father was no longer there. The family lived in an urban inner city ghetto (Chicago) and it was now headed by a black mother. Black groups feared that this would reinforce the stereotype of the "matriarchy" (Montgomery, 72).[8]

In 1972, "activist groups" had succeeded in having Benjamin Hooks appointed as the first black commissioner of the FCC (Montgomery, 25). However, the proposed broadcast of "Beulah Land" (1980) brought a new wave of protest. The made for television movie (miniseries) was a melodramatic story of the Old South. According to those who objected to its content, there were too many familiar black stereotypes in the movie.[9]

This offensive against the depiction of Old South stereotypes, including "Mammy," came as black women were engaged in a process Omolade (1994) describes as "demammification." In 1970, for the first time African American women were no longer predominantly employed as domestics or farm laborers and were beginning to move into other types of jobs. At the same time, they were forming more grass-roots self-help groups. For example, in 1972, the Sisterhood of Black Single Mothers was founded in New York City. The organization's purpose was to counteract slanderous stereotypes about black single mothers and to advocate for single mother families. Omolade describes this group as "perhaps the first Black feminist grassroots group of the post–civil rights era not to be connected to any black male organization" (Omolade, 1994: 168).

In the 1970s, black feminists, like their white "sisters," were reassessing their relationships with men. For black women, gender issues were confounded by race issues. In the introduction to her 1970 anthology, Toni Cade writes:

> Throughout the country in recent years, Black women have been forming work-study groups, discussion clubs, cooperative nurseries, cooperative businesses, consumer education groups, women's workshops on the campuses, women's caucuses within existing organizations, Afro-American women's magazines. From time to time they have organized seminars on the Role of the Black Woman, conferences on the Crisis Facing the Black Woman. (Cade, 1970: 9)

In 1973, Gladys Knight and the Pips recorded "Midnight Train to Georgia." Concerned with black migration narratives, Griffin describes the song as "the first post–Civil Rights Movement song to accompany the growing number of blacks and to document possible reasons for their return to the South" (Griffin, 1995: 142). The reason the man in the song was going back to Georgia was that he "couldn't make it" in L.A. The town proved too much for him. His dreams of someday being a star were shattered, and he was going back home to Georgia—to a "simpler place and time." The woman in this song had decided to go with him. She would give up everything she knew and follow him because she loved him. This was not a feminist statement. It was a statement about race and place. It was a statement about how one woman resolved a dilemma. But other black women continued to be caught in the cross-fire between gender and race.

During the civil rights era, black women had sometimes found their efforts unappreciated by the black male "leaders" of the movement.[10] In the 1970s and thereafter, one of the questions for the black woman—as it always had been—was how much she would sacrifice for a man. Would she give up a job? Sacrifice a career? Leave a place? Would she hold her tongue? Would black women take beatings? Not report rapes? Would they put up with sexual harassment? Would they sacrifice themselves to protect black men?

These questions would form the embedded text of the Clarence Thomas–Anita Hill debate in the black community. When Hill reluctantly came forward to accuse Thomas of sexual harassment, she had according to one perspective "aired dirty laundry" on television in front of millions of avidly watching white viewers. According to another related perspective, whatever Clarence Thomas might have done, Anita Hill, a black woman, should never have done something that might threaten a black man's nomination to the Supreme Court. It was hard for a black man to come as far as Thomas had come. There were enough white people out there ready to pull him down.

There was no excuse for a black woman to do it too. The other perspective was that whatever Thomas might have said, it was nothing Anita Hill, growing up black and poor, hadn't heard before.

And some people didn't believe her—or asked why if the harassment had happened and she was so upset about it, why she didn't report it when it happened. Of course, these two questions were the kind the Republicans on the committee of white males who were conducting the confirmation hearing were also asking Anita Hill. Feminists—black and white—had answers. White feminists were all over the news explaining the psychology of sexual harassment. Black feminists were less visible. They were not invited to respond as often.

> Aside from a few one-line quotes in lengthy news stories or articles in the alternative press, a Black feminist/Womanist viewpoint was sorely absent from the national debate. Voices of black women who for decades had struggled to address the concerns of Black women and to redress the injustice of racial and sexual oppression highlighted so graphically by the mistreatment of Hill were wholly ignored. (Ransby, 1995)

Excluded from the discussion, one group of black women began a "grassroots mobilization" that they called "African American Women in Defense of Ourselves." They prepared a statement and placed it in the *New York Times* and in seven black newspapers across the country. In the statement they objected both to the negative stereotyping of black women that had occurred during the hearings and to what they perceived as manipulation by Clarence Thomas of "the legacy of lynching" (Ransby, 44).

These African American women spoke out. But others felt silenced—caught once again between the responsibilities of race and the emotions of gender. Some of them believed Anita Hill, but they understood the feelings of support for Clarence Thomas in the black community.[11]

But the Thomas–Hill debate was atypical of the times. More black men were standing in front of a judge than aspiring to be a Supreme Court justice. In fact, some commentators were suggesting that prison had become a "rite of passage" for young black (and Latino) men. Links between the prison and the black community were becoming more explicit.

PRISONS AND PRISONERS

"In Richmond [VA] . . . 1772, slave prisoners did burn the gaol and escape" (Hoffer, 1984: xlviii). On May 31, 1984, six condemned prisoners at the Mecklenburg Correctional Center in Boydton, Virginia, escaped from death row. They did not burn down the prison or shoot their way out; however, Dance (1987: xv) describes their escape as "the most daring, the most ingenious, and the most spectacular Death Row escape ever attempted."[12] Since the escapees were condemned men[13] who had committed violent crimes, their escape "creat[ed] a situation in many ways reminiscent of the situation in Virginia following Nat Turner's revolt" (Dance, 71). The citizens of Virginia, informed by the media about the gruesome crimes the prisoners had committed, were both fearful and angry that the men had been able to escape. The escape caused a "major upheaval" in the state correctional system and created reverberations that reached the governor's mansion. Everyone was blamed, from prison guards to the governor (Dance, 92).[14]

However, the escape of the Mecklenburg Six might also be examined from another perspective:

> For any individual who is enslaved, incarcerated, constrained, the major goal is freedom. Escape from his or her present entrapment has been the major theme in the Black American's folklore and literature from its beginnings. (Dance, 2)

As Dance observes, there is a continuity of this theme from the narratives of runaway slaves such as Frederick Douglass to the migration narratives of blacks escaping the postbellum South. This theme is also to be found in the twentieth-century songs, novels, and poetry of African American prisoners.[15] An analysis of the role this theme plays in the collective memory of African Americans is an important step in understanding African American perspectives on crime and justice issues.

Equally relevant for African Americans is examining the hostility and contempt that continue to be directed at blacks as both offenders and victims of crime. Black offenders are rendered as "beasts" or "savages." Black victims are presented as people of little value. In *Ceramic Uncles and Celluloid Mammies* (1994), a survey of "contemptible collectibles," Turner comments on these images:

> The initial success with which white retailer Charles Stuart convinced everyone that a black assailant had brutally killed his wife and the infant she was carrying in her womb—the potency that the Willie Horton image developed during the 1988 presidential campaign . . . (Turner, xvi)

Turner goes on to mention the Rodney King beating and the refusal of the police to take the white serial killer Jeffrey Dahmer's black neighbors seriously. She concludes: "These and other recent confrontations reflect the tenacity of negative stereotypes about black men and women" (xvi). We should now add the Susan Smith case to this list. Some people would also add Tawana Brawley and the youths who were involved in the rape of the Central Park jogger.[16]

In any case, the point Turner is making is that these cases become flashpoints illuminating the stereotypes of African American men and women and white responses to those stereotypes. They also illustrate perceptions of white innocence based on assumptions regarding gender, class, and certainly race. One assumption has to do with the savage nature of some black offenders. "Wilding"—in effect, running wild—is what the youths in the Central Park rape case were said to have been doing.

"WILDING IN AMERICA"

Derber (1996) argues that the term *wilding* should actually be used to describe "a vast spectrum of self-centered and self-aggrandizing behavior that harms other" (6). Therefore, wilding would encompass economic, political, and social behavior (8). Derber asserts that an examination of American history over the last hundred years reveals "a succession of wilding periods alternating with eras of civility" (14). Thus the age of the nineteenth-century "robber barons" was followed by the progressive movement. The economic wilding of the 1920s was followed by the New Deal social programs. The civil rights movement of the 1960s has been followed by an era of all three types of wilding (social, political, and economic). The present era of wilding has produced a Charles Stuart. It has also led to a "triage" approach to social policy that involves "the sacrifice of the socially weakest sector of society" (14).

We summarize Derber's thesis here because we find it intriguing. It offers another point of departure for unraveling racial interactions around crime and justice issues. Hacker (1995: 48) makes another intriguing assertion:

So "black crime" is not mainly about taking money or articles of value, or even about demands at gun point. For white Americans, it represents racial revenge, as if each robbery—or rape—is part of an ongoing insurrection. It is the same fear slaveowners had of being slaughtered in their beds. (Hacker, 1995: 48)

African Americans have sometimes deliberately encouraged whites in these images of racial revenge. Eldridge Cleaver did so in *Soul on Ice* (1968), in which he wrote of his assault on white society through, among other means, his rape of white women.[17] In the "blaxploitation" films of late 1960s and 1970s, revenge against villainous whites was expected of the black protagonists. That was what black audiences came to the theaters to see. Admittedly few white adults might have ever seen these movies. However, the "gangsta rap" of the 1980s and 1990s has received much broader exposure. Threatening images of violent black men—"bad niggers"—are one hallmark of this subgenre of rap music. The life-styles and sometimes violent deaths of the rap artists (e.g., Tupac Shakur) reinforce these images.

"DOING THE RIGHT THING"[18]

Actually, the discussion of black images by African Americans is often two-pronged. On the one hand, there is the matter of images presented to whites and the ways in which they respond to those images. On the other hand, there is the matter of the impact of images on other blacks within the community. African American reformers who object to gangsta rap might well be concerned about the violent black personas presented to white America. But they are equally—perhaps more—concerned about the violent (and misogynistic) images presented to black youth.

Such reformers sometimes call on the purveyors of these negative images to "do the right thing" with regard to the black community.[19] At the same time, young people are encouraged to identify with more acceptable alternative role models who make a habit of "doing the right thing." Michael Jordan and Tiger Woods come to mind.[20] Obviously, although middle class black reformers no longer speak of "uplift," they sometimes still engage in much the same type of task in their relations with the residents of poor black communities. But, at the same time, some members of the middle class (no longer restricted to black ghettos) find it increasingly difficult to relate to or understand the perspectives of those on whom they seek to have an impact.

KNOWING THE TERRAIN

Recalling his experiences as a social scientist doing research in poor black neighborhoods in Philadelphia, W.E.B. Du Bois confessed that he had been "painfully aware" of the social distance between him and the people he was there to study:

> With my bride of three months, I settled in one room in the city over a cafeteria run by a college settlement in the worst part of the Seventh Ward. We lived there a year, in the midst of an atmosphere of dirt, drunkenness, poverty, and crime. Murder sat on our doorsteps, police were our government, and philanthropy dropped in with periodic advice. (Du Bois, 198)

This same kind of social distance can trouble present day African American social scientists who are concerned with problems experienced by people who live in neighborhoods into which they are reluctant to venture. Since the 1960s, there has been an "insider/outsider" debate in the social sciences about who is better qualified to do research on certain groups (Merton, 1972). Should only black men study black men or only white women study white women? Is sameness more important than other qualities such as empathy and integrity? This controversy is an element in the discussions among African American scholars and their nonblack colleagues about the nature of their disciplines and how research and teaching should be done.

We would like to look briefly at the impetus for the development of new academic perspectives on race, crime, and justice in three academic areas.

CRIMINAL JUSTICE/CRIMINOLOGY AND DIVERSITY

African Americans are overrepresented (by their proportion of the population) as criminal offenders and victims of crime. African Americans are underrepresented among the social scientists who study crime. These two facts have consequences:

- Historically, non-African Americans (usually European American males) have theorized about and studied black crime.
- Historically, European American males have also controlled the process by which candidates are recruited into the ranks of the graduate students who eventually become professors.
- Historically, many African American men and women have perceived a predominantly white academic environment as threatening and/or frustrating.
- Historically, African American scholars have not been encouraged to challenge traditional theories or ways of thinking about race and crime.

In the past decade interest has grown in considering race and crime from new perspectives. This interest may be attributed in part to an increase (albeit slight) in the number of African American scholars.[21] It is also attributable to the multicultural perspectives of some white male and female scholars.[22] However, exploration of race and crime issues, particularly with regard to African Americans, has been complicated by a historical taboo surrounding the discussion of race. Both African American professors and students and their non–African American colleagues often find it difficult to speak candidly about the issues. But as LaFree and Russell (1993) argue, "Our failure to study the connection between race and crime has not made race-related crime problems go away" (279).

We would add that there is a need not only to study race and crime but to conceptualize in new ways issues such as police–community relations, court processing, and prison reform. There is also the urgent need to rethink our responses to black on black crime, particularly the violence between young black men. In the disciplines of criminal justice and criminology, scholars such as Cora Mae Richey Mann, Anne Sulton, and Darnell Hawkins have been instrumental through their research, writing, and editing activities in helping to provide a foundation for further discussion of race and crime perspectives.[23] In this regard, *The Journal of Criminal Justice Education*, a journal of the Academy of Criminal Justice Sciences, has also provided a location in which scholars can explore issues of diversity and explore issues of curriculum and scholarship.

However, one of the more controversial perspectives concerning crime and its impact on African Americans has come not from those of us trained as social scientists but instead from African American legal scholars.

CRITICAL RACE THEORY

Critical race theory traces its roots to a course the African American legal scholar Derrick Bell taught when he was at Harvard. Bell, who had been a civil rights litigator, created his own materials for this course. He "developed and taught legal doctrine from a race-conscious view point." In his teaching, Bell rejected the idea of "the color-blindness of law, pedagogy, and scholarship" (Crenshaw et al., 1995, xiii). This rejection of the concept of color-blind justice is the starting point for those scholars who are participants in this movement. Not all are black, but they share in common a commitment to "challenge the ways in which race and racial power are constructed and presented in American legal culture and more generally in American society as a whole" (Crenshaw et al., xiii). There is no set of doctrines or canon governing the explorations of the legal scholars (Crenshaw, xiii).

However, critical race theorists sometimes dismay other scholars by their postmodernist assertion that there is no objective reality. Instead they sometimes employ the tool of "storytelling"—the sharing of experiences or parables—in order to understand an event. As Anthony E. Cook, a professor at Georgetown University Law School, explains, "Critical race theory wants to bring race to the very center of the analysis of most situations" (Lewis, 1997, B9). Critical race theorists argue that race does matter and cannot be ignored.[24]

It is the application of critical race theory to situations such as the Tawana Brawley case that tends to raise the ire of critics. The insistence by critical race theorists that the Brawley case must be examined in the historical context of the rape and devaluation of black women seems to be both meaningless and obstructionistic to those who would argue that the important issue is whether or not the teenager lied and whether she caused the resultant harm done to the law enforcement officers, to race relations, and even to herself. Viewed in this light, the critical race theorists seem obsessed with race to the exclusion of the search for truth. However, they would argue that racism in America is a truth that cannot be ignored, and, therefore, an awareness of America's racial history must inform any discussion about crime and justice. Race is not a pretext. It is the context and the subtext.

In this sense, especially in the aftermath of the O. J. Simpson trial, the concept of jury nullification has been under scrutiny. Paul Butler, one of the leading spokesmen for the jury's right to nullify, has argued in a recent issue of *Yale Law Journal* (1995) that with regard to nonviolent offenses the black community benefits when black jurors weigh the costs and benefits to the community of certain sanctions for criminal behavior.[25] Butler and other proponents of jury nullification argue this is not a new concept—in fact, white jurors in the South and elsewhere have always exercised this right. Actually, jury nullification has also sometimes worked to the benefit of those involved in social movements, such as the nineteenth-century abolitionist movement. However, the use of nullification—particularly in the aftermath of cases such as those of O. J. Simpson and Marion Barry—remains controversial when advocated by black legal scholars for use by black jurors.

Perhaps less controversial is the argument that we should develop new ways of conceptualizing social identity and social relationships.

BLACK MASCULINIST THEORY

Although not directly related to the disciplines of criminal justice and criminology, the developing scholarship on black masculinity seems to offer promise for increased understanding of the roles and adjustments required of black men. Lemelle (1995: vii) asserts, "Few studies of black men have highlighted the essential conflict between black and white values, despite the fact that this conflict has had historical significance." In a similar vein, Jackson (1997) argues that there are inherent problems in simply applying whole cloth to black males the theories developed about white manhood. He argues that historically, European American males have been in positions of cultural dominance that were not available to African American males. Traditionally African American males have been required to engage in "code switching," that is, to shift from one "cultural identity position to another" (735), as they moved from one situation to another. Jackson argues this has not been necessary for white males. Therefore, because of their position in American society, African American males should be the subject of "black masculinist research." This research should both draw upon and refine existing theories about manhood while also developing unique perspectives.

Black masculinist research focuses on black males within the context of their historical experience. Such research seems particularly relevant in light of such recent events as the "Million Man March."[26] With regard to crime and justice, there are a number of issues concerning black manhood that need to be addressed, such as how definitions of manhood structure male–male and male–female relationships. For example, Nisbett and Cohen (1996) argue that defense of "honor" is a powerful motivating force in encounters between black urban males.

CONCLUSIONS

What is clear is that in black masculinist theory, critical race theory, and the evolving theoretical perspectives of black criminologists, the basic demand being made is that scholarship no longer be ahistorical or Eurocentric. These scholars argue that to understand African American responses to criminal justice issues it is critical to theorize from perspectives informed by knowledge of and sensitivity to the collective experiences of black Americans. These scholars have turned their attention and their commentary to recent events in American history that have been particularly polarizing.

Unfortunately, in the years since the end of the war in Vietnam, too many events in this country have polarized whites and blacks, haves and have-nots. The ghettos that black Vietnam veterans returned to are now locations that many white Americans—and some blacks—view with fear, dismay, and sometimes loathing. The criminal justice system seems inadequate to the demands made upon it. It is the inability of that system to function in an unbiased manner in a society in which there are so many people with racial biases that makes events such as the cases of Charles Stuart, Susan Smith, Rodney King, and O. J. Simpson such symbolic exercises in not only American justice but American race relations.

NOTES

1. Bates indicates that there is variation in casualty figures depending on the sources consulted.

2. See Belenko (1993) for his discussion of the emergence of crack into public awareness and antidrug policy that developed in response.

3. The African American novelist Ann Petry's *The Street* (1946) deals with the problems of a mother who finds herself raising her young son alone when her marriage ends. It is not Lutie Johnson's ineptness or her lack of caring that led to her son's arrest and her desperate response. In the ghetto (Harlem) where she lives with her son, there are predators. Petry offered her book as an indictment of the struggle that black women like the protagonist face to protect themselves and their children in an environment in which social structure and racism create incredible odds against success. Lutie thinks of children like her son: "They should have been playing in wide stretches of green park and instead they were in the street. And the street reached out and sucked them up." (See also Morton [1991] for discussion of the "pathology thesis.")

4. The report had been intended for internal circulation within the Johnson administration; the controversy began when it was made public. For an account of the events and the controversy see the excellent study by Rainwater and Yancey (1967).

5. See Bailey (1996) for an analysis of scholarship on the black family in the post–*Moynihan Report* period. Also see Morton's discussion of the stereotyping of black women in history and in the social sciences in her book *Disfigured Images: The Historical Assault on Afro-American Women* (1991).

6. For an introduction to the scholarship on the black family see W. W. Nobles and L. L. Goddard (1984), *Understanding the Black Family: A Guide for Scholarship and Research*. (Oakland, CA: The Institute for the Advanced Study of Black Family Life and Culture) and R. Staples (1991), *The Black Family*, (Belmont, CA: Wadsworth), 4th ed.

7. For a discussion of the questions raised about Haley's claim that *Roots* was a "true story" about his ancestors and the charges of plagiarism and hoax, see Taylor (1995). But Taylor notes, "Haley constructed himself as both epic hero and African-American griot, whose 'quest' . . . came to symbolize that of all black America, indeed the whole of multi-racial America at Bicentennial time."

8. Since the early days of the show, African American commentators had also voiced concern about the character "J.J."—the elder Evans son. J.J. (as played by the stand-up comedian Jimmie Walker) was tall and skinny, always wore a hat, and at least once each show yelled, "DY-NO-MITE!" J. J. seemed always in danger of slipping over the line into the demeaning racial stereotype of the black comic buffoon. Only his love for his family and his talent as an artist redeemed the character. Interestingly, with the death of his sitcom father, J.J.—now the "man of the house"—became mature and responsible.

9. Some negotiation went on between the producers and the activists. A black historian was brought in as a consultant, but no significant changes were made in the script. When activists objected to the overrepresentation of minorities as perpetrators on "Hill Street Blues," NBC was more accommodating. The network also hired a consultant, who was more successful in dealing with the problem. The criminals passing through the inner city station house became more ethnically diverse (Montgomery, 1989).

10. For example, see Burns (1990: 12), who asserts that Ella Baker was never "accepted as an equal by King and his male associates [in the SCLC] despite her genius as an organizer."

11. See two volumes on Anita Hill–Clarence Thomas, Hill and Jordan (1995) and Morrison (1992).

12. The prisoners made their escape by a carefully orchestrated scheme that involved incapacitating the guards and two nurses by binding and gagging them. The guards were forced to disrobe. The prisoners escaped in a prison van. "Great Escape" T-shirts appeared. Cartoons lampooned the Virginia correctional system. But one of the prisoners, who had the embarrassing experience of being recaptured in a shower cap, was also the target of humor.

13. Regarding capital punishment in Virginia, Dance asserts: "Capital punishment from its early days in Virginia had been a tool for repressing slave rebellion and had always fallen disproportionately on the heads of Black men" (115–116). In July 1985, Roy West, the black mayor of Richmond, created an uproar when he "proclaimed his support for capital punishment as a deterrent to crime" (Dance, 140).

14. All of the prisoners were recaptured—but not immediately.

15. Also see Franklin (1978) on prison narratives.

16. See Helen Benedict's *Virgin or Vamp: How the Media Covers Sex Crimes* (1992) for her chapter on the Central Park rape case. Benedict compares coverage by white media to that by the black press. She also contrasts the depiction of the victim to that of the youths.

17. Cleaver describes rape as "an insurrectionary act" (in Atkins and Glick, 1972: 108).

18. This is, of course, a reference to the Spike Lee film. In Lee's depiction of a black community, the pizza parlor owned by an Italian becomes the space in which racial conflict is acted out. The riot at the end of the film begins when "Mookie" (played by Spike Lee) breaks the window of the pizza parlor.

19. Some rappers have been involved in the "Stop the Violence" movement with antiviolence television spots aimed at young people.

20. However, there might be a downside to telling kids to "be like Mike." Lee and Browne (1995: 523) report:

> Nike advertisements that feature basketball player Michael Jordan and film director Spike Lee have recently been the target of negative press. Critics have noted that shoes

have become so important that young urban African Americans are willing to kill for them.

21. See C. A. Heard and R. L. Bing III (1993), African-American Faculty and Students on Predominantly White University Campuses, *Journal of Criminal Justice Education*, Vol. 4, No. 1 (Spring): 1–13. They report that in 1987 "about 40 African-Americans had earned doctorates in criminology, criminal justice, or a closely related field."

22. See for example G. Barak (1991), Cultural Literacy and a Multicultural Inquiry into the Study of Crime and Justice, *Journal of Criminal Justice Education*, 2: 173–192.

23. See D. F. Hawkins, ed. (1995), *Ethnicity, Race, and Crime: Perspectives across Time and Place* (Albany: State University of New York Press); C. R. Mann (1993), *Unequal Justice: A Question of Color* (Bloomington: Indiana University Press); C. R. Mann and M. S. Zatz, eds. (1998), *Images of Color, Images of Crime* (Los Angeles: Roxbury Publishing); and A. T. Sulton, ed. (1994), *African American Perspectives on Crime Causation, Criminal Justice Administration, and Crime Prevention* (Englewood, CO: Sulton Books). Also see the special issue of *Justice Quarterly* (1992), Symposium: Minority Scholarship in Color and Justice, Vol. 9, No. 4 (Dec.).

24. For an example of a critique of critical race theory as it is applied to specific legal situations see Simon (1997) concerning the issues raised by the application of critical race theory to hate speech regulation. But also see Gates et al. (1994), an edited volume dealing with hate speech, civil rights, and the First Amendment. This volume includes an essay by Henry Louis Gates, Jr., on the "war of words."

25. Butler was a special assistant United States attorney in the District of Columbia at the time when Mayor Marion Barry was prosecuted for drug possession and perjury. Butler marks that as the point when he begin to think about the issue of jury nullification:

> My thesis is that, for pragmatic and political reasons, the black community is better off when some nonviolent lawbreakers remain in the community rather than go the prison. The decision as to what kind of conduct by African- Americans ought to be punished is better made by African-Americans themselves, based on the costs and benefits to their community than by the traditional criminal justice process, which is controlled by white law enforcers (1995: 679).

26. See Marable's opinion piece (1995), in which he discusses the issues raised by the March.

CHAPTER 14

In the Streets of L.A.

On April 24, 1992, California experienced an earthquake that registered 6.1 on the Richter scale. The quake happened out in the desert, 110 miles east of Los Angeles in Riverside County. Little damage was done to people or property, but it made Californians nervous. The quake had occurred only 5 miles from the San Andreas fault—the fault that Californians fear may some-day produce the "Big One." But California had experienced earthquakes before and life went on. Or it did for most people. On April 22, Robert Alton Harris, convicted of the 1978 slaying of two teenage boys, had become the first person to die in California's gas chamber in twenty-five years. *The New York Times* reported this was the 169th execution to take place since the Supreme Court had "restored capital punishment" in 1976. In prisons across the country about twenty-five hundred prisoners were on death row.

In California the controversy surrounding the execution was matched by the controversy surrounding the Los Angeles Police Department. In that month of April, residents of Los Angeles were keeping at least one eye on the trial that was going on in Simi Valley.

But for Californians, as for other Americans, life went on. The playoff games between the Knicks and the Pistons were coming up. As the two basketball teams prepared for their match-off in Madison Square Garden, New York City theatergoers were selecting from a smorgasbord of Broadway plays including *Jelly's Last Jam* and revivals of *A Streetcar Named Desire* and *Guys and Dolls*. For those Americans who didn't happen to live in New York City, there was always television. Or the movies. April marked the fiftieth anniversary of *Casablanca*. That month the actor Sidney Poitier received a Life Achievement Award from the American Film Institute. The actor Danny Glover praised him as "the first African American man to be accepted as a universal figure on screens around the world."

The ex-mayor of Washington, D.C., Marion Barry, was also in the news. Barry emerged from the federal prison in Pennsylvania where he had been serving six months for cocaine possession. He was greeted by over two hundred well-wishers, a church group who came from D.C. in a six-bus caravan. He told them, "I come out of prison better, not bitter." As Barry left prison, the "self-styled hotel queen" Leona Helmsley was going in. Her attorney, Alan Dershowitz, told reporters that she had offered to turn her hotel holdings over to the city of New York to use as housing for the poor. Later Mrs. Helmsley's spokesperson said the offer had been "more of a 'metaphor' used in bargaining for her freedom than a concrete proposal." But as Stephen Gillens, a law professor at New York University, observed: "You can't buy your way out of prison. It's something the courts simply cannot accept." So Leona Helmsley had gone off to a federal facility to serve her time for income tax fraud.

Thousands of miles away, in Seville, Spain, the organizers of the World's Fair to celebrate the quincentenary of Columbus's voyage to the "New World" opted to avoid controversy by downplaying the reason for the celebration. A reporter at the scene noted that King Juan Carlos "did not mention the great navigator by name when he inaugurated the last—and largest—universal exhibition of the twentieth century. Columbus, it seems, has become too controversial of late. Instead, the stars of the show are Seville, Spain, and humanity." The United States budget for its pavilion at the World's Fair had been cut back from $45 to $28 million, $4 million of which had come from the private sector. Back home in the U.S.A., the budget pinch was being felt by Nebraska farmers who were being forced to give up farming, and by New York City school administrators who were trying to cope with the influx of "120,000 immigrants from 167 countries [who] had enrolled in the schools over the past three years."

In a presidential election year, "the economy" was on politicians' tongues. In early April the Labor Department had reported only a slight improvement in the job market since March; Unemployment was at 7.3 percent. But times were tough all over. The Europeans' economy was "sluggish." In Japan, the economy was "hitting the wall and corporate profits were dropping."

At least Americans had the blessing of living in a country at peace. But some observers warned it was a fragile accord. In 1944, Gunnar Myrdal had called race "an American dilemma." In 1968, the Kerner Commission, after investigating the riots, had warned that blacks and whites inhabited two societies, "separate and unequal." That was the theme that Andrew Hacker advanced that April in his book *Two Nations*. Race in America was also the topic of Studs Terkel's new oral history, *Race: How Blacks and Whites Think and Feel about the American Obsession*. Both writers concluded that the "chasm" between blacks and whites was widening. On the campaign trail, the presidential candidate Bill Clinton echoed this sentiment: "We're divided by race and region, by income, by age, by gender. We are all cut up.

And I'm telling you, we can't fake it." He added, "We have got to say we want to be one nation again."

Based on any number of indicators, the gap between rich and poor, black and white, was widening. On April 21, the *New York Times* reported a "drop in black Ph.D.s." Educators said there were "complex reasons" for this, "having to do with crumbling inner city schools, a lack of role models," and a growing number of financially more rewarding alternatives. There was also the matter of the competition with foreign students for financial aid. But if black students were not becoming Ph.D.s., equally few were going on to medical school. Another story reported that there had been a "backward drift" of blacks in the field of medicine. This came at a time when acquired immunodeficiency syndrome (AIDS) was the "sixth-leading cause of death among people 15 to 24 years old." Black teenagers represented 37 percent of the AIDS cases among American teenagers.

The AIDS epidemic was only one of the problems troubling black communities. A feature story in the *New York Times* was about a book written by an African American social scientist, Richard Majors, a psychologist at the University of Wisconsin at Eau Claire, and Dr. Janet Manconi Billson, an executive officer of the American Sociological Association. The title of the book was *Cool Pose: The Dilemmas of Black Manhood in America.* In an interview, Majors said that "cool pose" was "a tactic for psychological survival" used by black inner city males. But, Majors explained, "What black males see as cool, as being suave and debonair, can be read by whites as signifying irresponsibility, shiftlessness, or unconcern."

In this same article, Dr. Robert Staples, a professor of sociology at the University of California medical school in San Francisco, and Dr. Alvin Poussaint, a psychiatrist at Harvard Medical School, both African Americans, observed that life for young black males in urban cities was problematic. Staples pointed to the decrease in the life expectancy of black men over the last decade. Poussaint said: "The picture is not as bad if you include all black males, but if you focus on inner city youth, the problems are overwhelming. For example, in 1965, about 25 percent of black families nationally were headed by women, while now the figure is at 50 percent. But it's more like 90 percent in many projects."

As Poussaint suggested, some African American males were not doing badly. Some were doctors and lawyers and businessmen. Some lived in comfortable suburban communities with their families. But few were in that "richest 1 percent" who owned much of the country's wealth. A report that month from researchers at the Federal Reserve and Internal Revenue concluded that the most significant gains in wealth during the 1980s had been by the richest Americans. The richest 1 percent "accounted for 37 percent of private net worth in 1989, up from 31 percent in 1983."

It was the perception of employment inequities that had led three hundred African American agents who worked for the Federal Bureau of Investigation

(FBI) to present a list of grievances to Director William S. Sessions the year before. They had threatened a class action lawsuit. That April the FBI, without admitting bias, had announced that an agreement had been reached with the agents "to promote some of them and provide dozens of others with new jobs and special training."

But the majority of young black lower class males had their encounters with law enforcement agents on urban streets. That was what had happened with Rodney King. That April in Los Angeles, the four white LAPD officers accused of brutally beating King were on trial in Simi Valley. Terry White, the African American deputy district attorney who was trying the case, urged jurors to rely on the evidence of their eyes. Referring to the videotape that a bystander had made of the encounter between King and the police officers, White said: "What more could you ask for? You have the videotape that shows objectively, without bias, impartially, what happened that night. The videotape shows conclusively what happened that night. It can't be rebutted."

On Wednesday, April 29, 1992, the Simi Valley jurors voted to acquit three of the police officers of all charges stemming from King's arrest on March 3, 1991. A fourth officer was acquitted on all but one charge; on that one count the jurors were deadlocked (*Los Angeles Times*, 1992: 6).

The verdicts were flashed across the country and around the world. In South Central Los Angeles, the residents heard the verdicts—and a tremor shook the city.[1] CBS News would later title a documentary about the riots that followed the verdicts "L.A. Ground Zero."

L.A.

> California was like heaven for the southern Negro. People told stories of how you could eat fruit right off the trees and enough work to retire one day. The stories were true for the most part but the truth wasn't like the dream. Life was still hard in L.A. and if you worked every day you still found yourself on the bottom.
> —Easy Rawlins, *Devil in a Blue Dress* (Mosley, 1990: 27)

African Americans came to California with the Spanish explorers. In 1790, according to a Spanish census, 18 percent of the population was of African descent. When Los Angeles was founded by an interracial group of whites, blacks, and Indians, twenty-six of the forty-four persons who settled there were black.[2] During this period, the areas that would later become Beverly Hills and the San Fernando Valley were held by black settlers. In the 1790s, one of them served as the mayor of Los Angeles (Katz, 1987: 117).

During the next century, more blacks would come; some came as "Forty-Niners" during the California Gold Rush. An estimated two thousand free blacks had arrived in California by 1852 (Katz, 1987: 122). The response from some white Californians was an attempt to block black migration. At the 1849 state constitutional convention in Monterey, the delegates debated the matter.

> Delegate McCarver, who introduced the exclusion resolution, insisted "an evil so enormous" as migrating blacks would see "idle, thriftless, free Negroes thrown into the state." Another delegate warned that . . . [this was] "the greatest calamity that would befall California." (Katz, 124)

The delegates did not approve the exclusion resolution, but they did decide black men should not be allowed to vote or to serve in the militia or to testify in court (Katz, 124). This last stipulation was one that seemed to the black community particularly cruel because it meant they could not speak for themselves in civil or criminal cases. They had no defense against victimization by whites.

The black community lodged its protests. The black Franchise League organized a petition campaign to persuade the legislature to reconsider. The legislators were brutal in their dismissal of the petitions (Katz, 135–136); however, the black convention movement that had been born of this denial of rights continued to pursue support for their petitions from not only blacks but whites as well. As one delegate to the 1856 convention pointed out, the antitestimony act also worked against whites if a black person happened to be the only witness to a crime. But in spite of the support they were able to rally from whites, including white attorneys, the antitestimony provision as well as the other black laws remained in place until the Civil War.

This response to blacks by the legislature paralleled the hostility that existed toward the Chinese. Both groups were resented in part because of race, but also because of economic competition. With regard to blacks, Katz (124) notes, "White resentments were further heightened by the widely held belief that blacks had some mysterious power to detect gold."

There was also the question of what position California was to take on the slavery issue. Slaveholders—to the distress of some white laborers—were arriving with their slaves. In spite of the objections raised by those whites who favored free labor, the legislature moved to extend the power of slaveholders. In 1852, a fugitive slave law was passed. Not only did the law give slaveholders the right to obtain a warrant for the arrest and return of fugitive slaves, it allowed the slaveholders themselves to seize such slaves. It also opened the way for abuses such as those that occurred when slaves who had made agreements with their owners to work for their freedom were "forcibly seized after satisfying their obligations and reenslaved by their masters" (Almaguer, 1994: 39).

The status of blacks in California remained precarious until the Civil War came and slaves were emancipated. Even then California's black laws were abolished over the protests of some whites. By 1910, almost 22,000 blacks lived in California. The two largest communities were in San Francisco to the north and Los Angeles to the south. In the last decade of the twentieth century, many black Californians still lived in urban centers. In L.A., in 1990, 278,213 non-Hispanic blacks and 12,363 Hispanic blacks lived in South Central Los Angeles. They shared this space with 218,941 other Hispanics, and with 6,147 whites, 4,889 Asian-Pacific Islanders, and 2,656 "others" (American Indians, etc.). In all, 523,209 persons—over half a million people—lived in South Central L.A. (Morrison and Lowry, 1994: 30).[3]

During the 1980s, some of the blacks—often those who were faring better economically than their neighbors—had moved out of South Central and into other L.A. neighborhoods. In the ethnic succession common in American cities, "as blacks moved out, Hispanics moved in" (Morrison and Lowry, 29). The Hispanics included both natives of California and recent immigrants from Mexico and Central America. They settled in areas that became Hispanic enclaves. This same pattern was followed by the Asians—many of whom were immigrants from China, the Philippines, Korea, or Japan (Morrison and Lowry, 29). Among these groups, there was racial tension as they jockeyed for urban space. There was also tension between the Los Angeles Police Department and these communities.

For blacks who lived in South Central L.A., the California dream was indeed different from the reality. By 1992, there were many black teenagers in South Central whose grandparents had come to L.A. from rural Georgia or Texas or Mississippi. But the world these teenagers knew was that of the streets of L.A. They were growing to adulthood in an inner city ghetto that the West Coast "gangsta rappers" had made famous, the ghetto depicted in the African American filmmaker John Singletons's 1991 film *Boyz 'n the Hood* with gang bangers, brutal cops, and murdered friends.

In the real South Central L.A., teenagers sometimes died. More found it hard to find a job. Between 1975 and 1985, the deindustrialization of urban centers had devastated South Central. More than seventy-five thousand jobs had been lost (Derber, 1996: 127; Gibbs, 1996: 19). According to some estimates, between 1990 and 1992, unemployment in South Central more than doubled (Derber, 127).

This was the historical context and the contemporary setting on April 29, 1992, when the Simi Valley jurors delivered their verdict in the Rodney King beating case. In this verdict, the jury acquitted the police officers[4] accused of brutally beating King. Like people around the country, the residents of South Central L.A. reacted with shock, distress, anger. In South Central, some of the residents took their anger and frustration out into the streets— "violent self-help."

This was not the first time a riot had happened in L.A. The August 1965 Watts riot (rebellion, uprising) had been devastating.

At least 34 people died . . . 1,000 more were injured, and 4,000 arrested. Property damage was estimated at $200 million in the 46.5–square-mile zone (larger than Manhattan or San Francisco) where approximately 35,000 adults "active as rioters" and 72,000 "close spectators" swarmed. On hand to oppose them were 16,000 National Guard, Los Angeles Police Department, highway patrol, and other law enforcement officers; fewer personnel were used by the United States that year to subdue the Dominican Republic. (Horne, 1995: 3)

One of the problems in South Central on April 29 was that the police had been ordered to fall back to regroup when the crowds began to gather and the first rocks were thrown and the first windows smashed. While Reginald Denny was being dragged from his truck and beaten at the intersection of Normandie and Florence—a scene that became almost as infamous as the Rodney King beating—the police were in a state of confusion. In fact, Denny was saved by black citizens who came to his rescue.

And so the riot—the unrest—continued from April 29 until May 4, when it was declared officially over. When it ended, much of South Central L.A. had been destroyed. Lives had been lost. Mass arrests had been made.

In many respects, the unrest was almost a textbook case, the prototypical big-city riot, resembling episodes of collective violence that occurred in Washington, D.C., Detroit, Newark, and scores of other U.S. cities during the 1960s. Like many of these earlier disturbances, including the 1965 Watts riot, the 1992 unrest was triggered by an event that highlighted the conflicts between a minority community and the law enforcement/justice system. (Tierney, 1994: 149)

In 1968, the Kerner Commission (the National Advisory Commission on Civil Disorders) appointed by President Johnson in July 1967 issued its report. The commission had studied the twenty-four disorders that had happened in twenty-three cities. It found that "specific grievances varied from city to city, [but] at least 12 deeply held grievances can be identified and ranked into three levels of relative intensity" (7). The three grievances the commission gave top ranking were police practices, unemployment and underemployment, and inadequate housing (7).

In South Central L.A., police practices had included "Operation Hammer," Chief Daryl Gates's military-style units that began their crackdown on crime in February 1988. On weekend evenings, sweeps were made in the projects and large numbers of young black males arrested. There had also been frequent reports of harassment of male motorists by the LAPD. There were also deaths—"sixteen blacks had died from police choke holds" (Gibbs, 1996: 260–261). These and other activities, including those directed at gangs, made the residents of South Central L.A. distrustful of the police.

That distrust made it easier for black residents of the inner city to believe

O. J. Simpson's lawyers that he had been framed by Mark Fuhrman and other members of the LAPD (Gibbs, 257–263). As Gibbs points out, Rodney King and O. J. Simpson were symbolic of the "social, political, and cultural conflicts dominating American society" (Gibbs, xx). One led the police on a "high speed chase" in his white Hyundai. The other led the police on a "low speed chase" in his white Bronco. Both ended up in an American courtroom where race, class, and gender were at the heart of the discourse.

In the Rodney King beating trial, white jurors in Simi Valley acquitted white police officers, and blacks and Latinos rioted. In the O. J. Simpson case, Johnnie Cochran was accused of "playing the race card," and O. J. Simpson went free. Many whites were outraged. Many blacks cheered. Even those blacks who didn't cheer when O. J. Simpson was acquitted—because they believed he might be guilty or because they were wearied by the carnival the trial had become or because two people were still dead—could understand why other blacks cheered. They could understand that for those other blacks, the issue wasn't O. J. Simpson. The issue was justice—or, rather, the justice system and how it worked.

Many African Americans wondered, often out loud, what whites were so upset about. They had set up the rules of the game. They had created a system that was often unjust. The emphasis in this system was not on guilt or innocence. The emphasis was on winning. So why did whites express such moral outrage when Johnnie Cochran and O. J. Simpson played the game by the established rules and won? The rules said, the state had to prove its case beyond a "reasonable doubt." The state hadn't. The state had produced a lying witness. The state had a problem with its chain of evidence. The state had problems with a black glove that didn't fit. The jurors could legitimately have reasonable doubt. As reasonable people, they had doubt. They didn't convict. The state had lost the game. Johnnie Cochran had won.

In her Introduction to an edited volume about the O. J. Simpson case, Toni Morrison (1997: xviii–xix) observes that in this case a theme of "racial incompetence" was present all along. The jury was attacked "as incapable of making an intelligent decision, as being (unlike other juries) grossly uneducated." Their decision was described as reflecting "ethnic bias"—"a sort of lunatic, vaguely illegal 'sympathy.'" In an essay in the volume, Higginbotham et al. examine the case as a "symbol of America's racial anxiety." They write, "In America, the 'race card' is usually played as part of a zero-sum game in which any gain by African Americans—real or imagined—is considered to be a loss by whites. The Simpson case was no different" (33). Higginbotham et al. conclude, "The uncomfortable reality is that neither our society nor our criminal justice system is color-blind" (49).[5]

This awareness of the lack of color-blindness in the criminal justice system is why those blacks we saw on television were cheering. They were not cheering *for* O. J. Simpson but for a black man who was rich enough and another who was smart enough to win the game.[6] Those cheers were born of anger and frustration and joy that this time—so rare—the "black side" had won.

Those cheers and the laughter must have seemed heartless to whites who watched and listened. Two people had been brutally murdered, and blacks were cheering. But, if asked, an African American might have responded, "If O. J. Simpson had been convicted, you [white Americans] would be cheering even louder."

And therein lies the racial chasm.

CONCLUSIONS

Recalling the symbolism inherent in segregated courtrooms, Higginbotham (1996: 130) writes:

> In the United States, segregated courthouse restrooms, cafeterias, and spectator seating also acted as signals. In these cases all participants, particularly juries in criminal or civil trials involving an African-American defendant or litigant, were constantly reminded that African Americans were to be accorded inferior status in this society. Every time jurors and spectators walked into a courtroom, they were presented with a ringing affirmation of the assumptions, myths, and attitudes that compose the ideology of racism in the United States.

Today courtrooms are no longer segregated. Blacks and whites share the public spaces in these rooms. But does the sharing of physical space reflect the dispensation of equal justice? Many African Americans—including those who rioted in the streets of Los Angeles and cheered O. J. Simpson's victory—would argue that the space might be shared but the justice is not equal.

NOTES

1. Except for the one exception indicated, this section is based on these articles appearing in the *New York Times*, April 1–27, 1992: P. L. Brown, "Ghost Houses Reflect Fading of Farm Life" (Apr. 2, A1); J. J. O'Connor, "Film Institute Honors Sidney Poitier" (Apr. 3, B15); "As Economy Drops in Japan, Chiefs Vie for Top Cut in Pay" (Apr. 11, A1); "U.S. Response to Youth and AIDS Is Criticized" (Apr. 12, L27); J. Berger, "Schools Cope with Influx of Immigrants" (Apr. 15, B3); R. Sullivan, "Helmsley's Last Legal Bid to Elude Prison Fails" (Apr. 15, B3); D. Goleman, "Black Scientists Study the 'Pose' of the Inner City" (Apr. 21, B20); A. De Palma, "Drop in Black Ph.D.s Brings Debate on Aid for Foreigners" (Apr. 21, A1); S. Mydans, "Prosecutor in Beating Case Urges Jury to Rely on Tape" (Apr. 21, A14); S. Nasar, "Fed Gives New Evidence of 80's Gain by Richest" (Apr. 21, A1); A. Riding, "The World's Fair Opens, but Where's Columbus?" (Apr. 21, A4); D. Johnston, "F.B.I. Promises Gains to Blacks in a Settlement" (Apr. 22 A1); K. Bishop, "After Night of Court Battles, A California Execution" (Apr. 22, A1); R. Reinhold,

"Quake in California Desert Put Authorities on Guard" (Apr. 24, A12); "Cheers As Ex-Mayor of Washington Leaves Prison" (Apr. 24, A12); C. Brown, "Playoff Question for the Knicks? Can Ewing Stand the Pressure?" (Apr. 24, B12); O. Ifill, "Clinton's Standard Campaign Speech: A Call for Responsibility" (Apr. 27, 24L).

2. See also Gibbs (1996), who gives the total number of "official founders" of L.A. as thirty-two. A reduction in number occurred sometime between the arrival of the eleven settlers and their families on September 4, 1781, and the compiling of the list on March 21, 1782 (xix–xx). She notes that although the settlers bore Spanish surnames, the group was " 'mainly of Indian and African blood, with only a moderate admixture of Spanish' " (xix).

3. The authors report these figures were calculated from the 1990 Census of Population (Bureau of the Census).

4. Fukurai et al. (1994: 97) identify some of the legal and extralegal factors that contributed to the acquittals and the subsequent riots.

These factors include: (1) the change of venue to a jurisdiction of a predominantly white community, (2) inherent biases in the jury selection system, ensuring the underrepresentation of minority jurors in the jury box, (3) elimination of a black judge on unsubstantiated information and overruling his decision that the trial be held in Los Angeles County where the alleged crime had taken place, and (4) racism within the Los Angeles Police Department, cojoined to a rising incidence of police abuse against racial and economic minorities.

5. For additional discussion of the Simpson case by criminologists and other scholars see G. Barak, ed. (1996), *Representing O. J.: Murder, Criminal Justice, and Mass Culture* (Guilderland, NY: Harrow & Heston); and J. Abramson, ed. (1996), *Postmortem: The O. J. Simpson Case* (New York: HarperCollins).

6. We realize there were other talented attorneys on the O. J. Simpson "dream team." We refer only to Johnnie Cochran because in the end much of the attention and the negative criticism focused on his summation to the jury.

Conclusions

In a recent essay, Sullivan (1996: 6–7) examines the decline of black "civic society." Referring to the *Newsweek* cover story that reported the generation gap between young blacks of "Generation X" and their elders, she writes, "A wide and deep gulf exists between a generation of 17 million African Americans born since the passage of 1964 and 1965 civil rights legislation and their elders born before the 1954 Brown Decision." But, Sullivan argues, it is not rap music or hip-hop culture that is responsible for this generation gap.

> [It] has much more to do with the institutional collapse of the inner city and the failure of traditional Black social and civic organizations to mobilize, organize and empower the most isolated and abandoned among the urban poor. (7)

As a result of this failure, she believes young people have lost faith in the leaders of civil rights organizations They have become "profoundly disconnected from Black civic action and civil rights activism" (7).

We would argue that historically it has been commitment to the values inherent in the resistance to oppression that has provided an important element of cohesion in the African American community. Even in those times and places where active resistance was impossible except at the risk of life, images of freedom and self-determination (captured in songs and folklore) provided the basis of psychological survival.

Some cultural theorists have argued that the members of the "hip-hop generation" have found alternative models for urban survival in their music and in their youth culture. But what seems to have weakened is the ability of the community to create an environment in which young people can move safely from youthful exploration (and rebellion) to responsible adulthood. This is not a problem that is unique to the African American community. However, it does seem to us that the African American philosopher Cornell West (1993) might be correct in suggesting that "nihilism" (or at least cynicism) has become an emotion to be reckoned with in the black community. The prolonged experience of "blocked opportunity" might finally have had its effect. Disbelief that race relations will improve might have become endemic.

As Randall Kennedy (1997) asserts, lies and deceptions have always been a part of race relations in America. Responses to the newspaper story about alleged evidence of CIA involvement in funneling drugs into the inner city indicate that African American distrust of the federal government runs deep; it is not confined to those who are poor and live in the inner city. As Gibbs (1996) touches on and as Turner (1993) explores more fully in her study of rumor in African American culture, "conspiracy theories" about government duplicity have been sustained by revelations of actual wrongdoing. Such revelations include the "Tuskegee Study," in which treatment was deliberately withheld from black men diagnosed with syphilis so that Public Health Service physicians could study the progress of the disease in blacks. This study, which began in 1932, went on for forty years before it was finally revealed.[1] Such revelations make more credible to some African Americans the theory that AIDS—human immunodeficiency virus (HIV)—was manufactured in a government laboratory and then deliberately introduced into communities of "expendable" people (gays, black, the poor). The people in these communities are, according to the theory, either serving as guinea pigs for research or being exterminated.[2]

Then there is the revelation of the FBI's intelligence gathering and surveillance activities (COINTELPRO) that included the use of wiretaps and tactics to discredit and harass prominent African American leaders. These revelations have involved not only the opening of "secret files" but "confessions" by blacks who served as "snitches" or "informants."[3] Therefore, the theory that Marcus Garvey's Back to Africa Movement was deliberately destroyed by the government is given support. Therefore, conspiracy theories about the government's involvement in the assassinations of Martin Luther King and Malcolm X seem less far-fetched.

Gibbs (1996: 237) finds that conspiracy theories in the black community fall into four basic categories: theories about (1) contamination and disease, (2) criminalization and drugs, (3) destruction of black leaders and civil rights organizations, and (4) racial and cultural genocide. Taken together these theories reflect the African American collective memory of official conspiracy and betrayal—of lies told and evil done by white folks.[4] It has as its antithesis the African American collective memory of the help and support rendered by other blacks.

THE DEMISE OF THE "HELPING IDEAL"

"Self-help" has always been an important value in the African American community. Neither federal nor local governments could be depended upon to provide African Americans with what they needed to survive. In fact, it was often the government that by its actions—or failures to act—created a hostile environment for African Americans (Hutchinson, 1996). Therefore, African Americans found self-help crucial to community survival.

Martin and Martin (1985) describe the "helping ideal" that they argue has traditionally existed in the black community. This ideal has been based on sharing and caring, it has been rooted in commitment to communal rather than individualistic values. However, Martin and Martin argue, the helping ideal has eroded during the twentieth century, losing ground to "street ideology,"[5] which is both individualistic and materialistic. The erosion of the helping ideal seems to be linked to the substitution of government aid for the mutual aid once common in the black community. In the twentieth century, in urban settings, the financial aid and social services provided by government have been both necessary and welcome in communities that lacked the resources to provide for their residents.

But this creation of a relationship of dependence with an impersonal bureaucracy has helped to erode the interpersonal bonds that were once cultivated by relatives, friends, and neighbors. Moreover, the development of agency–client relationships meant that the government became an even more intrusive presence into black communities. Informal mechanisms of social control that had been nurtured in rural communities were replaced in urban communities by the formal mechanisms of criminal justice appropriate among strangers.

We are not making an antigovernment argument here. We are not arguing against government aid to those who are in need of it. Nor are we suggesting that African American communities were once upon a time utopian enclaves in which everyone was loving, caring, and supportive. We are simply suggesting that once upon a time the ideal was mutual aid and support. By the midtwentieth century, in urban ghettos that ideal had become more difficult to sustain.

We admit we are still thinking our way through this. We are doing so with the aid of our evolving historical perspective about African American responses to oppression. At the same time, we are aware of the work African Americans from all walks of life are presently engaged in as they try to reconnect with others and to strengthen the black community. People like the former police officer Don Jackson and the former pro football player Jim Brown have been working with young people, including gang members. Politicians, businessmen, teachers, writers, filmmakers are all engaged in this search in the black community for approaches that work.

This is taking place in an atmosphere in which many Americans seemed engaged in remembering and reevaluating the American past. Nostalgia? Or something more profound? Scholars of American culture have noted during the past few years a phenomenon in which people are apologizing for their past mistakes and asking forgiveness. This phenomenon has crossed racial lines. President Clinton invited survivors of the Tuskegee Study to the White House to offer them a formal apology on behalf of the United States government. A religious denomination apologized for its past racism. The state of Florida apologized to the survivors of the Rosewood massacre and made restitution to the survivors.

At the same time, names from the past are suddenly back in the news. The Black Panther Geronimo Pratt, who has been serving time for murder, now hopes for a new trial. Before his recent death, James Earl Ray, who was convicted of assassinating Martin Luther King, won the support of the King family in his efforts to obtain his day in court. Louis Farrakhan has made his public peace with Malcolm X's family.

Everyday there is another reminder of the past—We think all of this remembering is a healthy sign.

Not long ago a writer who lives in Washington, D.C., was telling one of us about her library-sponsored afterschool program with inner city children. She and the kids do "quilting stories." Each of them brings in a piece of cloth and tells a story about it—the kind of activity African American women used to engage in as they patched together a quilt from pieces of recycled cloth. This writer is helping the children to put together a book of their stories—their collected memories.

We think that it is important that African Americans from all walks of life remember and explore our collective past in order to understand our present.

CRIME, JUSTICE, AND MEMORY

In preparing her notes for the argument she intended to make to the court about self-representation in her trial, Angela Davis (1971: 249) wrote:

> I begin by directing the court's attention to the fact that as the accused in this case, I find myself at an enormous disadvantage. As a Black woman, I must view my own case in the historical framework of the fate which has usually been reserved for my people in America's halls of justice.

The argument we make here is that African Americans are at a disadvantage if they do not know and apply their history to their theorizing about issues of crime and justice and to their activism around these issues. We began this book by discussing the themes that recur in African American social history and asserting that these themes continue to affect the responses of African Americans to crime and justice. We find evidence of not only a hostile environment in which African Americans have sought "safe spaces" but of a variety of perceptions that have shaped their searches. Thus from the colonial time to the present, blacks have ranged along a continuum from passive to assertive, from accommodative to rebellious.

We should mention again the complexity of human behavior. For example, was Booker T. Washington as self-serving in his accommodation of white power as his critics claimed? Or did he make a pragmatic assessment of the racial environment and make a good faith effort to act in the best interest of his people? Did he decide that in his time and place some gains (economic) could be made and others (social) were less feasible? Did he also serve the cause of resistance by being the "acceptable" black leader whose requests of white leaders seemed moderate and reasonable when compared to the demands of a "militant" such as Du Bois?

In the 1960s, in his letter from Birmingham jail to the white clergymen, Martin Luther King argued that it was better that the white South deal with him than with more radical blacks. He used the implied threat of more militant action as a strategy for achieving his goals. Of course, there were limits to this strategy. But Martin Luther King was more effective because of the more threatening presence of Malcolm X and of Stokely Carmichael.

These leaders and their strategies of resistance remain a part of the lore of African American culture. Their images are conjured up during rituals and celebrations. Each is a hero to some segment of our ethnic community. Because of our past and our heroes—and our designated villains—African Americans bring perspectives to their responses to crime and justice issues that are sometimes different from those of many white Americans. But just as whites are not a homogeneous group, neither are African Americans. African Americans as a group share an American experience—but we are also shaped by our individual experiences of race, class, and gender. We venture to say that this is true of other historically oppressed groups in America, such as Native Americans, Latinos, and Asian Americans.

In the case of black Americans our responses to crime and justice issues are constantly held up for scrutiny and debate. We do not enjoy the luxury of privacy as an ethnic community. When the police officers in the Rodney King beating case were acquitted, the rest of America waited with bated breath for our reaction. When O. J. Simpson was acquitted, television networks provided instantaneous split screen comparisons of our reactions and those of white Americans.

In such an environment in which we have so little space that is free from intrusion, we struggle to discover and understand our past. Some white Americans wait for the outcome of our struggle. In fact, they want progress reports. Have you forgotten about slavery yet? Will you admit that slavery is over now and, if some of your people are still living in poverty in ghetto slums, it's because they're too lazy to do better? Will you admit that some black males are not victims of society but rather vicious offenders? Will you stop going on about sentences for crack cocaine and about the death penalty and admit we have to do something about criminals whether they are black or white? Will you please just admit that? And don't tell us we're being racists!

Stop going on about the past and live in the present? Our past flows into our present and helps to shape our future. As David Roediger (1997) writes:

> A telling joke that has made the rounds among African American scholars comments on the distance between academic trends in writing on race and life in the "real world." "I have noticed," the joke laments, "that my research demonstrating that race is merely a social and ideological construction helps little in getting taxis to pick me up late at night."

As Roediger observes, the joke is an ironic comment on "the fact that race may be more easily demystified on paper than disarmed in everyday life" (345). Therefore, we believe it is important that we examine the racial myths we have lived by. We are not advocating critical race theory or any other approach as the optimal way of conceptualizing race, crime, and justice. However, we do think it is important that we understand enough about the historical context of American race relations to be able to detect the subtext and avoid the pretext when we engage in conversations about race and crime.

What we have attempted to do in this book is to begin to explore how African Americans have understood and responded to the issues of crime and justice. We conclude that for all African Americans the struggle for social justice has shaped—in one fashion or another—their response to these issues.

As Lyman (1994: 116) observed in an essay on history and memory, African Americans really have only two choices. We can "abolish history altogether and begin life de novo." Or, the other choice

> as in fact has been the case with four generations of black historians, to plunge into that heritage not merely to gather and order its data, but to arrange its interpretation so that guilt, shame, embarrassment, and any other degrading sensibility is removed from its interpretation.

As social scientists and African Americans, we advocate the latter course.

NOTES

1. See Turner (1993: 111–112). Also see Jones (1993).
2. A *New York Times* article reports

> a phenomenon that doctors, medical researchers and patient advocates say they had encountered repeatedly among blacks across the nation: a deeply held mistrust of the medical establishment, particularly concerning AIDS and its treatment. (Richardson, 1997, A1)

See also Stryker (1997: 24) about the legacy of the Tuskegee syphilis research.

3. For example, in a segment of the *Eyes on the Prize* documentary dealing with the killing of the Chicago Black Panther leader Fred Hampton during a police raid, the black FBI informant who infiltrated the Panther organization talks about his assignment and how he carried it out. See also Kornweibel (1987) on the FBI's use of Negro informants during the "Red Scare."

4. See Waters (1997) on conspiracy theories as ethnosociologies ("the theories that people use to explain social phenomena"). Waters asserts, "Sociologists should avoid lumping all conspiracy theories together as equally unbelievable and should evaluate, instead, both the context of the explanation and the effects of the explanation" (122). She points out that " 'conspiracies' may be more metaphoric than literal" (122).

5. See Anderson (1997) for his discussion of "decent" and "street" cultures.

Bibliographical Essay

Throughout the text and in the bibliography are references to the sources that we used in preparing this book. However, we thought that for the reader who is interested in exploring the subject further, it would be useful if we pointed out some of the works that illustrate the themes we discussed in the Introduction and have developed throughout the book.

The hostile environment in which African Americans live has been examined by many scholars from a variety of perspectives. We have already mentioned Gunnar Myrdal's *An American Dilemma: The Negro Problem and Modern Democracy* (New York: Pantheon Books, 1944). Volume 2 of the study includes an analysis of the criminal justice system, black institutions, and social trends. More recent examinations of race relations in Americans include Andrew Hacker's *Two Nations, Black and White, Separate, Hostile, and Unequal* (New York: Charles Scribner's Sons, 1992) and Kenneth O'Reilly's *Nixon's Piano: Presidents and Racial Politics from Washington to Clinton* (New York: Free Press, 1995). Works focusing specifically on the relationship between African Americans and the American criminal justice system include Jewell Taylor Gibbs *Race and Justice: Rodney King and O. J. Simpson in a House Divided* (San Francisco: Jossey-Bass, 1996), and Kenneth O'Reilly and David Galle, eds. *Black Americans: The FBI Files* (New York: Carroll & Graf, 1994). In his recent book, *Race, Crime, and the Law* (New York: Pantheon Books, 1997), Randall Kennedy attempts to find common ground between "competing ideological camps" and to examine the history of racial discrimination, injustice, and failure to protect that has made blacks "suspicious, if not antagonistic" toward the criminal justice system. This history of racial discrimination and injustice has been discussed in this book. The reader will also find historical studies such as Philip J. Schwarz's *Twice Condemned: Slaves and the Criminal Laws of Virginia, 1705–1865* (Baton Rouge: Louisiana State University Press, 1988); David M. Oshinsky's *"Worse Than Slavery": Parchman Farm and the Ordeal of Jim Crow Justice* (New York: Free Press, 1996); and Eric Rise's *The Martinsville Seven: Race, Rape, and Capital Punishment* (Charlottesville: University Press of Virginia, 1995) useful in examining various aspects of this history. Several scholars have focused on violence in the black urban community. Among these scholars, Roger Lane, in *Roots of Violence in Black Philadelphia 1860–1900* (Cambridge: Harvard University Press, 1986), argues that economic and social exclusion from the Industrial Revolution taking place in urban Philadelphia had a negative and long-lasting impact on black communities and contributed to the level of violence in them. Dealing with more recent history, Harold M. Rose and Paula D. McClain's *Race, Place, and Risk: Black Homicide in Urban America* (Albany: State University of New York Press, 1990) focuses on the microlevel and macrolevel structural factors that contribute to the high-risk homicide environments in black urban communities. In *All God's Children: The Bosket Family and the American Tradition of Violence* (New York: Alfred A. Knopf, 1995), an intriguing and perhaps controversial work, the journalist Fox Butterfield, exploring the family history of one black offender, traces the roots of black urban violence to the antebellum code of "honor" that existed among white southerners. Images of black violence have been one aspect of the popular culture that have served to maintain and perpetuate stereotypes of blacks. In *Toms, Coons, Mulattoes, Mammies, & Bucks: An Interpretative History of Blacks in American Films* (New York: Continuum, 1993), the film scholar Donald Bogle looks at the racial stereotypes of African Americans in popular films, beginning with the violent mulatto rapist of *The Birth of a Nation.*

Of course, one aspect of the hostile environment of black Americans has been the violence of white Americans toward them. In *Anatomy of a Lynching: The Killing of Claude Neal* (Baton Rouge: Louisiana State University Press, 1982), James R. McGovern offers a case study of an incident of white vigilante justice that occurred in Jackson County, Florida, in 1934 and attracted national attention. Herbert Shapiro's *White Violence and Black Response: From Reconstruction to Montgomery* (Amherst: The University of Massachusetts Press, 1988) offers a detailed overview of the role of violence in perpetuating white supremacy in white America. The matter of black response to white violence is addressed in this book and also in Mary Frances Berry's *Black Resistance White Law: A History of Constitutional Racism in America* (New York: Penguin Publishing, 1994). The apex of black resistance was during the civil rights era of the 1960s, but this activism had its roots in black history. Works such as Floyd B. Barbour's *The Black Revolt* (Boston: Extending Horizon Books, 1968), a collection of essays covering the period from 1619 to the 1960s and focusing on the historical development of the concept of black power, and William Chace and Peter Collier's *Justice Denied: The Black Man in White America* (New York: Harcourt, Brace & World, 1970), an anthology focusing on black advocates for justice from Frederick Douglass to the Black Panthers, provide the reader with an introduction to this topic. Other works of interest include Taylor Branch's *Parting the Waters: America in the King Years 1954–63* (New York: Simon & Schuster, 1988); John Egerton's *Speak Now against the Day: The Generation before the Civil Rights Movement in the South* (New York: Knopf, 1996); and Charles M. Payne, *I've Got the Light of Freedom: The Organizing Tradition and the Mississippi Freedom Struggle* (Berkeley: University of California Press, 1995). With regard to the efforts of black Americans to find their place in American society and carve out a safe space, we suggest the reader explore some of the literature on the black family, black education, and the black church. Andrew Billingsley examines the black family as a complex social system in *Black Families in White America* (Englewood Cliffs, NJ: Prentice-Hall, 1968). In *Climbing Jacob's Ladder: The Enduring Legacy of African-American Families* (New York: Simon & Schuster, 1992), Billingsley presents a wealth of information about black family life in America. The education of black children has always been a matter of paramount concern to black families, and in *The Education of Blacks in the South, 1860–1935* (Chapel Hill: The University of North Carolina Press, 1988), Anderson examines the development of black education in the aftermath of slavery and the efforts by white philanthropists and others to forward a model of industrial education for blacks. In *Black Religion and Black Radicalism: An Interpretation of the Religious History of Afro-American People*, 2nd ed. (Maryknoll, NY: Orbis Books, 1993), Gayraud S. Gilmore addresses the role of black theology in the black struggle against oppression.

One aspect of this struggle was the migration of black Americans to urban areas. Richard Wright's *12 Million Black Voices* (New York: Thunder's Mouth Press, 1941) is a folk history of blacks in America in photographs and narrative, concluding with a description of life in the urban ghetto in Chicago. In the 1960s, Kenneth B. Clark in *Dark Ghetto: Dilemmas of Social Power* (New York: Harper & Row, 1965) focused on Harlem as symbolic of all black American ghettoes. James R. Grossman's *Land of Hope: Chicago, Black Southerners, and the Great Migration* (Chicago: The University of Chicago Press, 1989) is one of the more recent examinations of migration to the urban ghetto from the perspective of the participants. In *On the Edge: A History of Poor Black Children and Their American Dream* (New York: Basic Books, 1993), Carl Husemoller Nightingale chronicles the history of poor black children in American ghettos, focusing on their rejection by and subsequent alienation from mainstream America.

In the post–civil rights era of the 1970s, more black Americans were able to move out of urban ghettos and into the economic mainstream. In *The Fruits of Integration: Black Middle-Class Ideology and Culture, 1960–1990* (Jackson: University Press of Mississippi, 1994), Charles Banner-Haley explores the changes that took place in African American society over a thirty-year period. However, a decade earlier, Alphonso Pinkney had challenged *The*

Myth of Black Progress (Cambridge: Cambridge University Press, 1984), pointing to the continuation of racial oppression.

In this regard, the 1960s and 1970s marked the emergence of a new generation of black Americans who would challenge white cultural hegemony. In an edited volume, Joyce Ladner brings together an impressive group of black social scientists, writers, and scholars who predict *The Death of White Sociology* (New York: Vintage Books, 1973). More recently, Jerry Gafio Watts has offered an intellectual case study of Ralph Ellison as symbolic of the "political and aesthetic dilemmas" confronting black intellectuals in *Heroism and the Black Intellectual* (Chapel Hill: The University of North Carolina Press, 1994). Culture conflicts and political dilemmas are also examined in Thomas Kochman's *Black and White Styles in Conflict* (Chicago: The University of Chicago Press, 1981); Theodore Rueter, ed., *The Politics of Race: African Americans and the Political System* (Armonk: M. E. Sharpe, 1995); Kathy Russell, Midge Wilson, and Ronald Hall *The Color Complex: The Politics of Skin Color among African Americans* (New York: Harcourt Brace Jovanovich, 1992); and Adam Sexton, ed., *Rap on Rap: Straight-up Talk on Hip-Hop Culture* (New York: Dell Books, 1995).

Throughout this book, we have discussed the relationship between black past and present. Among the works the reader might turn to for a sense of this past and its relevance to the present are James Mellon, ed., *Bullwhip Days: The Slaves Remember* (New York: Weidenfeld & Nicholson, 1988), which was drawn from the 1930s Federal Writers' Project interviews with former slaves. Dorothy Sterling, ed., *We Are Your Sisters: Black Women in the Nineteenth Century* (New York: W. W. Norton, 1984), provides a documentary history of black women during enslavement, emancipation, and Reconstruction. Malaika Adero, ed., *Up South: Stories, Studies, and Letters of This Century's Black Migration* (New York: The New Press at CUNY, 1993), brings the collective experiences of black Americans into the twentieth century. In *The Evidence of Things Not Seen* (New York: Holt, Rinehart, & Winston, 1985), the novelist–essayist James Baldwin ranges from discussion of Wayne Williams and the Atlanta child murders (1981) to memories of growing up in Harlem in the 1920s and 1930s. Finally, in *Mississippi: An American Journey* (New York: Alfred A. Knopf, 1995), Anthony Walton chronicles his return to his parents' southern home to try to understand the South of his parents and what led them and others to migrate north.

But what of the status of black Americans in the cities of the 1990s? In a recent book, *Turning Back: The Retreat from Racial Justice in American Thought and Policy* (Boston: Beacon Press, 1995), Stephen Steinberg asserts that there has been a backlash in race relations since the civil rights era. In the 1960s, social structure and the politics of race/ethnicity were implicated in the riots in urban America that Joe R. Feagin and Harlan Hahn discuss in *Ghetto Revolts: The Politics of Violence in American Cities* (New York: Macmillan, 1973). These factors were also present in the post–Rodney King riots examined in Mark Baldassare, ed., *The Los Angeles Riots: Lessons for the Urban Future* (Boulder, CO: Westview Press, 1994).

As these works will reveal to the interested reader, much has changed for African Americans since the seventeenth century. However, the search for space and place in a hostile environment continues.

DOCUMENTARY FILMS

The *Eyes on the Prize* series is a particularly useful resource for those who would like to examine more closely the history of the civil rights movement. Part 1 of this comprehensive documentary covers the period from 1954 to 1966. Archival footage is used extensively in this prize-winning six-part documentary. *Eyes on the Prize, Part II*, covers the period from 1964 to the mid-1980s. It examines the movement of the civil rights struggle from the South to the North and includes issues of power in the schools, police confrontations, and urban poverty.

We would also like to recommend *W.E.B. Du Bois: A Biography in Four Voices* (California Newsreel: San Francisco, CA, 1995). This video interweaves the story of Du Bois's personal life (as husband and father) and his career (as scholar, civil rights activist, editor, peace activist, and Pan Africanist) with United States and world history from the nineteenth century to 1963. Each of the four sections is narrated by an African American writer and includes rich reminiscences about Du Bois by his relatives, friends, and associates. The video captures the triumphs and the tragedies of Du Bois's life, including his editorship of the NAACP journal, the *Crisis*, his efforts when he was at Atlanta University to unite the Historically Black Colleges and Universities (HBCUs) into a consortium for the study of African American life, and his confrontation with the United States government during the McCarthy era of Communist "witch-hunting."

POPULAR FILMS

Although a number of popular films are mentioned in passing or discussed in the text, we thought it would be helpful to discuss briefly other films that we have found useful reference points in understanding various aspects of our topic. In the early days of filmmaking, as we have noted, black characters were played by white actors in "blackface." In fact, in *The Jazz Singer* (1927), the first feature-length "talkie," Al Jolson performs "My Mammy" in black grease paint. When black actors did begin to appear in films, they were generally limited to "walk-on" roles, usually as servants. But, in 1939, Hattie McDaniel would give an Oscar-winning performance—as Scarlett O'Hara's black Mammy.

During this era, blacks did appear in starring roles in "all-black" films such as *The Green Pastures* (1936) based on Marc Connelly's Pulitzer Prize–

winning play about stories from the Old Testament. The forces of good and evil also vied for a poor black man's soul in *Cabin in the Sky* (1943). *Carmen Jones* (1954) offered an adaptation of Bizet's opera *Carmen*, with Harry Belafonte as a soldier and Dorothy Dandridge as a light-skinned femme fatale. It was in one of these early films that Paul Robeson gave one of his finest performances, as a Pullman porter who establishes himself as the ruler of a Caribbean island, in *The Emperor Jones* (1933). These movies were made by white Hollywood and reflected the stereotypes of blacks common in American society. At the same time, by providing a showcase for talented African Americans performers such as Lena Horne, Rex Ingram, Brock Peters, and Ethel Waters, the films allowed these performers to push for greater cultural inclusion.

Since World War II, African Americans in real life have been becoming more assertive of their right to be full participants in American life. In the movies of the postwar period, African Americans were more visible as soldiers. But *Native Son* (1950), the film version of Richard Wright's novel, starring the author himself in the role of Bigger Thomas, was a reminder that many blacks were still trapped in urban ghettos. On the positive side, the decade of the 1950s marked the appearances of film biographies of two black cultural heroes, *The Jackie Robinson Story* (1950), starring Robinson as himself, and *St. Louis Blues* (1958), starring Nat "King" Cole as W. C. Handy, "the father of the blues." In this same decade, Sidney Poitier offered one of his more riveting performances in *The Defiant Ones* (1958) as a black prisoner who escapes from a southern chain gang—handcuffed to a white prisoner (Tony Curtis).

Filmmakers had not given up their attachment to the black woman as nurturer. But an actor such as Ethel Waters in *Member of the Wedding* (1952) could transcend stereotypes. In *A Raisin in the Sun* (1959), based on Lorraine Hansberry's play, the focus was again on a black woman—but this time the family she scolded and nurtured was her own. By the 1960s, new images of black men in films such as *Nothing but a Man* (1963) and *One Potato, Two Potato* (1964), challenged assumptions about their relationships with women (black and white). Also breaking new ground with perceptive and thoughtful portrayals of black life were *The Learning Tree* (1969), a coming-of-age story directed by the black photographer Gordon Parks, and *Sounder* (1972), a touching family saga about a black sharecropping family in the 1930s in which the father of the family is sent to prison. Two years later, Cicely Tyson, who had starred as the mother in *Sounder*, would also star in *The Autobiography of Miss Jane Pittman* (1974), the film version of Ernest J. Gaines's novel about a woman who is born into slavery and lives to see the early days of the civil rights movement. A number of other films focused on young people who were born during the civil rights era. Among the more memorable were *Cornbread, Earl, and Me* (1975), in which a young high school basketball star is mistakenly shot by police officers who attempt a cover-up, and *A Hero Ain't Nothin' but a Sandwich* (1978), based on the novel by Alice Childress, about an alienated ghetto youth who starts to use drugs.

The presence of drugs was an almost taken for granted element of the plot line in those films of the late 1960s and 1970s that came to be known as "blaxploitation films." Fascinating and controversial, aimed at a black audience, these films dealt with inner city crime, violence, and survival: *Shaft*, *Super Fly*, *Across 110th Street*, *Sweet Sweetback's Baadasss Song*, *Coffy*, and *Three the Hard Way*. The 1980s brought the premise of a new generation of black urban films (many by young African American filmmakers) such as *New Jack City*, *Straight out of Brooklyn*, *Menace II Society*, *Juice*, *Dead Presidents*, *Clockers*, and *Sugar Hill*. The issues raised by these urban films include (1) the images they present, (2) the impact of such images on audience, (3) the possibility of reinforcing—or refuting—stereotypes, (4) Hollywood's perception of market and marketing techniques for films, (5) black actors, writers, and filmmakers and their roles in resisting oppression.

Many of the films of the past two decades have treated criminal justice issues. Black actors have appeared as victims, offenders, cops, lawyers, and con artists. In *Criminal Justice* (1990), Forrest Whitaker plays an ex-con accused of attacking a woman (Rosie Perez) and encouraged by his attorney to accept a plea bargain. In *Devil in a Blue Dress* (1996), the moody film noir based on Walter Mosley's mystery, the setting is late 1940s Los Angeles, and the plot involves not only murder but racial deception. Also set in the 1940s, *A Soldier's Story* (1984), based on a Pulitzer Prize–winning play by Charles Fuller, deals with racism and its impact on the soldiers who are at the heart of the murder mystery.

Two very different films of 1989 captured the range of black portrayals in popular films. *Driving Miss Daisy*, a warm, tender film about a white southern Jewish woman and her black chauffeur, won the Academy Award for best picture. The other film, *Do the Right Thing*, was Spike Lee's commentary on race relations in a black neighborhood in Brooklyn. The final scenes depict the events that lead up to a race riot. Somewhere between *Driving Miss Daisy* and *Do the Right Thing* were the films that offered Hollywood renditions of events from the African American past. These films included *Glory* (1989), a Civil War saga about the 54th Massachusetts, the famous black infantry unit, led by a white officer. More recently, *Ghosts of Mississippi* (1997), about the efforts of a young white prosecutor to bring the assailant of civil rights leader Medgar Evers to justice, and *Rosewood* (1997), an action adventure version of the true story of the destruction of a prosperous black community by whites searching for a black alleged rapist, have at least brought these events to public awareness. *Amistad* (1998), a collaboration between Steven Spielberg and the African American actor Debbie Allen, reached deeper in its effort to tell the story of the slave ship uprising from the perspective of the black captives. But films such as *Sankofa* (1993), directed by Haile Gerima, about the slaves on a Caribbean island sugar plantation who must choose between accommodation to slavery and rebellion, and *Get on the Bus* (1997), Spike Lee's film about black men from different walks of life who choose to travel to the Million Man March, capture even more vividly the choices African Americans in slavery and in the present must make about self-determination and survival.

Bibliography

Abraham, J., ed. (1996). *Postmortem: The O. J. Simpson Case: Justice Confronts Race, Domestic Violence, Lawyers, Money, and the Media*. New York: Basic Books.

Abrahams, R. D. (1964). *Deep Down in the Jungle . . . Negro Narrative Folklore from the Streets of Philadelphia*. Hatsboro, PA: Folklore Associates.

Abreu, M. (1996). Slave Mother and Freed Children: Emancipation and Female Space in Debates on the "Free Womb" Law, Rio de Janeiro, 1871. *Journal of Latin American Studies* 28, part 3 (October): 567–580.

Adamson, C. R. (1983). Punishment after Slavery: Southern State Penal Systems, 1865–1890. *Social Problems* 30, no. 5 (June): 555–568.

Almaguer, T. (1994). *Racial Fault Lines: The Historical Origins of White Supremacy in California*. Berkeley: University of California Press.

Anderson, E. (1997). Violence and the Inner-City Street Code. Pp. 1–30 in J. McCord, ed., *Violence and Childhood in the Inner City*. New York: Cambridge University Press.

Anderson, J. (1981). *This Was Harlem: A Cultural Portrait, 1900–1950*. New York: Farrar, Straus, Giroux.

Anderson, J. D. (1988). *The Education of Blacks in the South, 1860–1935*. Chapel Hill: The University of North Carolina Press.

Andolsen, B. H. (1986). *"Daughters of Jefferson, Daughters of Bootblacks": Racism and American Feminism*. Macon, GA: Mercer University Press.

Angell, S. W. (1992). *Bishop Henry McNeal Turner and African-American Religion in the South*. Knoxville: The University of Tennessee Press.

Angelou, M. (1969). *I Know Why the Caged Bird Sings*. New York: Bantam.

Aptheker, H. (1971). *Afro-American History: The Modern Era*. New York: The Citadel Press.

Aptheker, H. (1977 [1943]). *American Negro Slave Revolts*. New York: International Publishers.

Aptheker, H. (1992). *Anti-Racism in U.S. History: The First Two Hundred Years*. New York: Greenwood Press.

Archer, L. C. (1973). *Black Images in the American Theatre: NAACP Protest Campaigns—Stage, Screen, Radio & Television*. New York: Pageant-Poseidon.

Armstead, M.B.Y. (1992). *Dimensions of African-American Community Life in Saratoga Springs, New York, 1930–1989*. Saratoga Springs, New York: Historical Society of Saratoga Springs.

Atkins, B. M. and H. R. Glick, eds. (1972). *Prisons, Protest, and Politics*. Englewood Cliffs, NJ: Prentice-Hall.

Attica: The Official Report of the New York State Special Commission on Attica. (1972) New York: Bantam Books.

Aulette, K. (1982). *The Underclass*. New York: Random House.

Austin, R. L. (1992). "Race, Female Headship, and Delinquency: A Longitudinal Analysis. *Justice Quarterly* 9, no. 4 (Dec.): 585–607.

Axelrod, A. and Phillips, C. (1992). *What Every American Should Know about American History*. Holbrook, MA: Bob Adams.

Ayers, E. L. (1984). *Vengeance and Justice: Crime and Punishment in the 19th Century American South*. New York: Oxford University Press.

Bailey, F. Y. (1986). *Boundary Maintenance, Interest-Group Conflict, and Black Justice in Danville, VA, 1900–1930*. Ph.D. dissertation, State University of New York at Albany.

Bailey, F. Y. (1991). *Out of the Woodpile: Black Characters in Crime and Detective Fiction*. Westport, CT: Greenwood Press.

Bailey, F. Y. (1996). The "Tangle of Pathology" and the Lower Class African-American Family: Historical and Social Science Perspectives. Pp. 49–71 in M. J. Lynch and E. B. Patterson, eds., *Justice With Prejudice: Race and Criminal Justice in America*. Guilderland, NY: Harrow & Heston.

Bailey, F. Y. (1999) *Blanche on the Lam*: The Invisible Woman Speaks. In K. G. Klein, ed. *Diversity and Detective Fiction*. Bowling Green, OH: Bowling Green State University Popular Press.

Bailey, R. C. (1979). *Popular Influence upon Public Policy: Petitioning in Eighteenth Century Virginia*. Westport, CT: Greenwood Press.

Baker, H. A., Jr., ed. (1972). *Twentieth Century Interpretations of Native Son*. Englewood Cliffs, NJ: Prentice-Hall.

Baldassare, M., ed. (1994). *The Los Angeles Riots: Lesson for the Urban Future*. Boulder, CO: Westview Press.

Baldwin, J. (1985). *The Evidence of Things Not Seen*. New York: Holt, Rinehart & Winston.

Barak, G. (1991). Cultural Literacy and a Multicultural Inquiry into the Study of Crime and Justice. *Journal of Criminal Justice* 2: 173–192.

Barak, G., ed. (1996). *Representing O.J.: Murder, Criminal Justice, and Mass Culture*. Guilderland, NY: Harrow & Heston.

Bardolph, R., ed. (1970). *The Civil Rights Record: Black Americans and the Law, 1849–1970*. New York: Thomas Y. Crowell.

Barrows, I. C., ed. (1969 [1890–1891]). *First Mohonk Conference on the Negro Question*. New York: Negro Universities Press.

Bates, M. J. (1996). *The Wars We Took to Vietnam: Cultural Conflict and Storytelling*. Berkeley: University of California Press.

Bederman, G. (1995). *Manliness & Civilization: A Cultural History of Gender and Race in the United States*. Chicago and London: The University of Chicago Press.

Belenko, S. R. (1993). *Crack and the Evolution of Anti-Drug Policy*. Westport, CT: Greenwood.

Bellah, R. N., R. Madsen, W. M. Sullivan, A. Swidler, and S. M. Tipton (1986 [1985]). *Habits of the Heart: Individualism and Commitment in American Life*. New York: Perennial Library.

Bender, D. L., ed. (1989). *American Values: Opposing Viewpoints*. San Diego: Greenhaven Press.

Benedict, H. (1992). *Virgin or Vamp: How the Press Covers Sex Crimes*. New York: Oxford University Press.

Bennett, L., Jr. (1968). *Pioneers in Protest*. Chicago: Johnson Publishing.

Bennett, L., Jr. (1975). *The Shaping of Black America*. Chicago: Johnson Publishing.

Benson, J. and D. Lyons (1991). *Strutting and Fretting: Standards for Self-Esteem*. Ninot, CO: University Press of Colorado.

Berg, B. L. and R. L. Bing, III (1990). Mentoring Members of Minorities: Sponsorship and "The Gift." *Journal of Criminal Justice Education* 1, no. 2 (Fall): 153–165.

Berlin, I. (1974). *Slaves without Masters: The Free Negro in the Antebellum South*. New York: Pantheon Books.

Berry, M. F. (1977). *Military Necessity and Civil Rights Policy: Black Citizenship and the Constitution, 1861–1868*. Port Washington, NY: Kennikat Press.

Berzon, J. R. (1978). *Neither White nor Black: The Mulatto Character in American Fiction*. New York: New York University Press.

Bethel, E. R. (1981). *Promiseland: A Century of Life in a Negro Community*. Philadelphia: Temple University Press.

Billingsley, A. (1968). *Black Families in White America*. Englewood Cliffs, NJ: Prentice-Hall.

Birmingham, S. (1977). *Certain People: America's Black Elite*. Boston: Little, Brown.

Black, D. (1993). *The Social Structure or Right and Wrong*. San Diego: Academic Press.

Blackwell, J. E. and M. Janowitz, eds. (1974). *Black Sociologists: Historical and Contemporary Perspectives*. Chicago: University of Chicago Press.

Blassingame, J. W. (1979). *The Slave Community: Plantation Life in the Antebellum South*, revised and enlarged ed. New York: Oxford University Press.

Blight, D. W. (1994). W.E.B. Du Bois and the Struggle for American Historical Memory. Pp. 45–71 in G. Fabre and R. O'Meally, eds., *History and Memory in African-American Culture*. New York: Oxford University Press.

Blockson, C. L. (1987). *The Underground Railroad*. New York: Prentice-Hall.

Boardman, F. W., Jr. (1972). *America and the Gilded Age, 1876–1900*. New York: Henry Z. Walck.

Bogle, D. (1993). *Toms, Coons, Mulattoes, Mammies, & Bucks: An Interpretative History of Blacks in American Films*. New York: Continuum.

Boland, O. N. (1995). Proto-Proletarians? Slave Wages in the Americas: Between Slave Labour and Free Labour. Pp. 123–147 in M. Turner, ed., *From Chattel Slaves to Wage Slaves: The Dynamics of Labour Bargaining in the Americas*. London: James Curry.

Boles, J. B. (1983). *Black Southerners, 1619–1869*. Lexington: The University Press of Kentucky.

Boles, J. B., ed. (1988). *Masters and Slaves in the House of the Lord: Race and Religion in the American South, 1740–1870*. Lexington: The University Press of Kentucky.

Bolster, W. J. (1990). "To Feel Like a Man": Black Seamen in the Northern States, 1800–1860. *The Journal of American History* 76, no. 4 (March): 1173–1199.

Bolton, C. C. (1994). *Poor Whites of the Antebellum South: Tenants and Laborers in Central North Carolina and Northeast Mississippi*. Durham, NC: Duke University Press.

Boney, F. W. (1984). *Southerners All*. Macon, GA: Mercer University Press.

Boorstin, D. J. (1987). *Hidden History*. New York: Harper & Row.

Boskin, J. (1986). *Sambo: The Rise and Demise of an American Jester*. New York: Oxford University Press.

Boston City Council (1969 [1889]). *A Memorial of Crispus Attucks, Samuel Maverick, James Caldwell, Samuel Gray, and Patrick Carr, from the City of Boston*. Miami, FL: Mnemosyne Publishing.

Boston University Art Gallery (1994). *Black Boston: Documentary Photography and the African American Experience*. Boston, MA, March 5–April 10.

Brandt, N. (1996). *Harlem at War: The Black Experience in WW II*. New York: Syracuse University Press.

Breeden, J. O., ed. (1980). *Advice among Masters: The Ideal in Slave Management in the Old South*. Westport, CT: Greenwood Press.

Breen, W. J. (1978). Black Women and the Great War: Mobilization and Reform in the South. *The Journal of Southern History* 44, no. 3 (Aug.): 421–440.

Brent, L. (1973 [1861]). *Incidents in the Life of a Slave Girl*. New York: Harvest/HBJ.

Breslaw, E. G. (1996). *Tituba, Reluctant Witch of Salem: Devilish Indians and Puritan Fantasies*. New York and London: New York University Press.

Brigham, W. (1996). "Whatup in the 'Hood?": The Rage of African-American Filmmakers. Pp. 91–106 in R. R. Curry and T. L. Allison, eds., *States of Rage: Emotional Eruption, Violence, and Social Change*. New York: New York University Press.

Brown, S. (1937). *The Negro in American Fiction*. Albany, NY: J. B. Lyon Press.

Bruce, D. D., Jr. (1979). *Violence and Culture in the Antebellum South*. Austin and London: University of Texas Press.

Bullard, S., ed. (1991). Box Office Propaganda. P. 19 in *The Ku Klux Klan: A History of Racism and Violence*, 4th ed. Montgomery, AL: The Southern Poverty Law Center.

Burns, S. (1990). *Social Movements of the 1960s: Searching for Democracy*. Boston: Twayne Publishers.

Butler, P. (1995). Racially Based Jury Nullification: Black Power in the Criminal Justice System. *Yale Law Journal* 105: 677–725.

Bynum, V. E. (1992). *Unruly Women: The Politics of Social and Sexual Control in the Old South*. Chapel Hill and London: The University of North Carolina Press.

Byrne, W. A. (1994). Slave Crime in Savannah, Georgia. *The Journal of Negro History*, 7979, no. 4 (Fall): 352–362.

Cade, T., ed. (1970). *The Black Woman: An Anthology*. New York: New American Library.

Calhoun, F. S. (1989). *The Lawmen: United States Marshals and Their Deputies, 1789–1989*. New York: Penguin Books.

Campbell, E.D.C., Jr. (1981). *The Celluloid South: Hollywood and the Southern Black.* Knoxville: The University of Tennessee Press.

Capeci, D. J., Jr. and J. C. Knight (1996). Reckoning with Violence: W.E.B. Du Bois and the 1906 Atlanta Race Riot. *The Journal of Southern History* 62, no. 4 (Nov.): 727–766.

Carroll, C. (1900, reprinted 1991). *The Negro a Beast.* Salem, NH: Ayer.

Carter, D. T. (1979). *Scottsboro: A Tragedy of the American South*, rev. ed. Baton Rouge: Louisiana State University Press.

Cary, F. C., ed. (1996). *Urban Odyssey: A Multicultural History of Washington, D.C.* Washington and London: Smithsonian Institute Press.

Cash, F. B. (1991). Radicals or Realists: African American Women and the Settlement House Spirit in New York City. *Afro-Americans in New York Life and History* 15, no.1 (Jan.): 7–17.

Cashin, J. E. (1991). *A Family Venture: Men and Women on the Southern Frontier.* New York: Oxford University Press.

Chambers, J. A. (1993). *Philosophy, Slavery and Socio-Economic Disorders: An Analysis of a Political Economy.* Langley Park, MD: IASS Publishers.

Chambers, J. A. (1995) *Blacks and Crime: A Function of Class.* Westport, CT: Praeger.

Cheek, W. F. (1970). *Black Resistance before the Civil War.* Beverly Hills, CA: Glencoe Press.

Clark, E. B. (1995). "The Sacred Rights of the Weak": Pain, Sympathy, and the Culture of Individual Rights in Antebellum America. *The Journal of American History* 82, no.2 (Sept.): 463–492.

Clark, K. B. (1965). *Dark Ghetto: Dilemmas of Social Power.* New York: Harper & Row.

Clarke, J. H., ed. (1968). *William Styron's Nat Turner: Ten Black Writers Respond.* Boston: Beacon Press.

Clark-Lewis, E. (1996). For a Real Better Life: Voices of African American Women Migrants, 1900–1930. Pp. 97–112 in F. C. Cary, ed., *Urban Odyssey: A Multicultural History of Washington, D.C.* Washington and London: Smithsonian Institute Press.

Cleaver, E. (1992 [1968]). *Soul on Ice.* New York: Dell Publishing.

Clinton, C. (1984). *The Other Civil War: American Women in the Nineteenth Century.* New York: Hill & Wang.

Cockett, L. S. and J. R. Kleinberg (1994). Periodical Literature for African-American Young Adults: A Neglected Resource. Pp. 115–142 in K. P. Smith, ed., *African-American Voices in Young Adult Literature: Tradition, Transition, Transformation.* Metuchen, NJ: The Scarecrow Press.

Colasanto, D. (1988). Black Attitudes. *Public Opinion* (Jan./Feb.): 45–49.

Collins, P. H. (1990). *Black Feminist Thought: Knowledge, Consciousness, and the Politics of Empowerment.* New York: Routledge.

Condé, M. (1994 [1986]). *I, Tituba, Black Witch of Salem.* Translated by R. Philcox. New York: Ballantine Books.

Conrad, P. (1997). Public Eyes and Private Genes: Historical Frames, News Constructions, and Social Problems. *Social Problems* 44, no. 2 (May): 139–154.

Crenshaw, K. N. Gotanda, G. Peller, and K. Thomas, eds. (1995). *Critical Race Theory: The Key Writings That Formed the Movement.* New York: The New Press.

Cripps, T. (1983). *Amos 'n' Andy* and the Debate over American Racial Integration.

Pp. 33–54 in J. E. O'Connor, ed., *American History/American Television: Interpreting the Video Past*. New York: Frederick Ungar Publishing.

Crist, T.A.J., D. G. Roberts, R. H. Pitts, J. P. McCarthy, and M. Parrington (1997). The First African Baptist Church Cemeteries: African American Mortality and Trauma in Antebellum Philadelphia. Pp. 19–49 in D. A. Poirier and N. F. Ballantoni, eds., *In Remembrance: Archaeology and Death*. Westport, CT: Bergin & Garvey.

Crouch, B. A. (1994a). A Spirit of Lawlessness: White Violence, Texas Blacks, 1865–1868. *Journal of Social History* 18, no. 2 (Winter): 217–232.

Crouch, B. A. (1994b). The "Chords of Love": Legalizing Black Martial and Family Rights in Postwar Texas. *The Journal of Negro History* 79, no. 1 (Fall): 334–351.

Crowder, R. L. (1991). "Don't Buy Where You Can't Work": An Investigation of the Political Forces and Social Conflict within the Harlem Boycott of 1934. *Afro-Americans in New York Life and History* 15, no. 2 (July): 7–41.

Crunden, R. M. (1994). *A Brief History of American Culture*. New York: Paragon House.

Cummins, E. (1994). *The Rise and Fall of California's Radical Prison Movement*. Stanford, CA: Stanford University Press.

Dabney, V. (1987). *Pistols and Pointed Pens: The Dueling Editors of Virginia*. Chapel Hill, NC: Algonquin Books.

Dailey, J. (1997). Deference and Violence in the Postbellum South: Manners and Massacres in Danville, Virginia. *The Journal of Southern History* 63, no. 3 (Aug.): 553–590.

Dance, D. C. (1987). *Long Gone: The Mecklenburg Six and the Theme of Escape in Black Folklore*. Knoxville: The University of Tennessee Press.

Daniels, R. (1990). *Coming to America: A History of Immigration and Ethnicity in American Life*. New York: HarperCollins.

Davidson, J. W. and M. L. Lytle (1982). *After the Fact: The Art of Historical Detection*. New York: Alfred A. Knopf.

Davis, A. L. and B. L. Graham (1995). *The Supreme Court, Race, and Civil Rights*. Thousand Oaks, CA: Sage Publications.

Davis, A. P. and M. W. Peplow (1975). *The New Negro Renaissance: An Anthology*. New York: Holt, Rinehart & Winston.

Davis, A.Y. (1971). *If They Come in the Morning: Voices of Resistance*. New Rochelle, NY: Third Press Publishers.

Davis, A. Y. (1983 [1981]). *Women, Race & Class*. New York: Vintage Books.

Davis, M. D. and H. R. Clark (1992). *Thurgood Marshall: Warrior at the Bar, Rebel on the Bench*. New York: Birch Lane Press.

Davis, O. (1992 [1965]). On Malcolm X. Pp. 457–460 in Malcolm X and Alex Haley, *The Autobiography of Malcolm X*. New York: Ballantine Books.

Delany, S. L. and A. E. Delany with A. M. Hearth (1993). *Having Our Say: The Delany Sisters' First 100 Years*. New York: Dell.

Demos, V. (1990). Black Family Studies in the Journal of Marriage and the Family and the Issue of Distortion: A Trend Analysis. *Journal of Marriage and the Family* 52 (Aug.): 603–612.

Derber, C. (1996). *The Wilding of America: How Greed and Violence Are Eroding Our Nation's Character*. New York: St. Martin's Press.

Dickson, L. (1993). The Future of Marriage and Family in Black America. *Journal of Black Studies* 23, no. 4 (June): 427–491.

Dillon, M. L. (1990). *Slavery Attacked: Southern Slaves and Their Allies, 1619–1865*. Baton Rouge and London: Louisiana State University Press.

Dinnertstein, L., R. L. Nichols, and D. M. Reimers (1990). *Natives and Strangers: Blacks, Indians, and Immigrants in America*, 2nd ed. New York: Oxford University Press.

Dixon, T., Jr. (1905). *The Clansman: An Historical Romance of the Ku Klux Klan*. New York: Grosset & Dunlap.

Douglas, G. H. (1992). *All Aboard! (The Railroad American Life)*. New York: Paragon House.

Douglass, F. (Jan. 1867). Appeal to Congress for Impartial Suffrage. The University of Oklahoma Law Center @http://www.law.uoknor.edu/hist/suff.html.

Douglass, F. (1968 [1855]). *My Bondage and My Freedom*. New York: Arno Press.

Douglass, F. (1988 [1845]). *Narrative of the Life of Frederick Douglass, An American Slave, Written by Himself*. Cambridge, MA: The Belknap Press.

Douglass, F. (1995). Oration, Delivered in Corinthian Hall, Rochester, July 5, 1852. Pp. 203–218 in F. L. Hord and J. S. Lee, eds., *I Am Because We Are: Readings in Black Philosophy*. Amherst: University of Massachusetts Press.

Downey, D. B. and R. M. Hyser (1991). *No Crooked Death: Coatesville, Pennsylvania and the Lynching of Zachariah Walker*. Urbana and Chicago: University of Illinois Press.

Doyle, B. (1971 [1937]). *The Etiquette of Race Relations: A Study in Social Control*. New York: Schocken Books.

Du Bois, W.E.B. (1968). *The Autobiography of W.E.B. Du Bois: A Soliloquy on Viewing My Life from the Last Decade of Its First Century*. No city: International Publishers.

Du Bois, W.E.B. (1968 [1909]). *The Negro American Family*. New York: Arno Press.

Du Bois, W.E.B. (1969 [1901]). *The Black North in 1901: A Social Study*. New York: Arno Press.

Du Bois, W.E.B. (1969 [1903]). *The Souls of Black Folk*. New York: New American Library.

Du Bois, W.E.B. (1996 [1899]). *The Philadelphia Negro: A Social Study*. Philadelphia: University of Pennsylvania Press.

Du Bois, W.E.B. (1997). *John Brown*. Introduction by J. D. Smith. Armonk, NY: M.E. Sharpe.

Dunier, M. (1992). *Slim's Table: Race, Respectability, and Masculinity*. Chicago: The University of Chicago Press.

Dyson, M. E. (1993). *Reflecting Black: African—American Cultural Criticism*. Minneapolis: University of Minnesota Press.

Dyson, M. E. (1997). *Race Rules: Navigating the Color Line*. New York: Vintage Books.

Earl, R. R., Jr. (1993). *Dark Symbols, Obscure Signs: God, Self, and Community in the Slave Mind*. Maryknoll, NY: Orbis Books.

Elkins, S. N. (1963). *Slavery: A Problem in American Institutional and Intellectual Life*. New York: Grosset & Dunlap.

Ellis, E. (1990). *Developing an Afro Centric Model for Social Change*. A Criminal Justice

Discussion Paper prepared for Black History Month Legislative Conference, Greenhaven Prison, Stormville, New York.

Ellis, M. (1992). "Closing Ranks" and "Seeking Honors": W.E.B. Du Bois in World War I. *The Journal of American History* 79, no. 1 (June): 96–124.

Ely, M. P. (1991). *The Adventures of Amos 'n' Andy: A Social History of an American Phenomenon.* New York: The Free Press.

Engram, E. (1982). *Science, Myth, Reality: The Black Family in One-Half Century of Research.* Westport, CT: Greenwood Press.

Engs, R. F. (1979). *Freedom's First Generation: Black Hampton, VA, 1861–1890.* Philadelphia: University of Pennsylvania Press.

Equiano, O. (1969 [1789]). *The Life of Olaudah Equiano, or Gustavus Vassa, the African.* New York: Negro Universities Press.

Fabian, A. (1990). *Card Sharps, Dream Books & Bucket Shops: Gambling in 19th Century America.* Ithaca and London: Cornell University Press.

Factor, R. L. (1970). *The Black Response to America: Men, Ideals and Organizations from Frederick Douglass to the NAACP.* Reading, MA: Addison-Wesley.

Faulkner, A. O., M. A. Heisel, W. Holbrook, and S. Geismar (1982). *When I Was Comin' Up: An Oral History of Aged Blacks.* Hamden, CT: Archon Books.

Faust, D. G. (1992). *Southern Stories: Slaveholders in Peace and War.* Columbia and London: University of Missouri Press.

Feldstein, R. (1994). "I Wanted the Whole World to See": Race, Gender, and Constructions of Motherhood in the Death of Emmett Till. Pp. 263–303 in J. Meyerowitz, ed., *Not June Cleaver: Women and Gender in Postwar America, 1945–1960.* Philadelphia: Temple University Press.

Ferguson, L. (1992). *Uncommon Ground: Archaelogy and Early African American, 1650–1800.* Washington: Smithsonian Institution Press.

Finkelman, P. (1993). The Crime of Color. *Tulane Law Review* 67, no. 6 (June): 2063–2112.

Finkelman, P. (1996). *Slavery and the Founders: Race and Liberty in the Age of Jefferson.* Armonk, NY: M.E. Sharpe.

Finkelman, P., ed. (1988). *Fugitive Slaves and American Courts: The Pamphlet Literature,* 4 vols. New York & London: Garland Publishing.

Fishbein, L. (1982). Dress Rehearsal in Race Relations: Pre–World War I American Radicals and the Black Question. *Afro-Americans in New York Life and History* 6, no. 1 (Jan.): 6–15.

Fisher, M. M. (1990 [1953]). *Negro Slaves Songs in the United States.* New York: Citadel Press.

Flateau, J. (1996). *The Prison Industrial Complex: Race, Crime and Justice in New York.* New York: Medgar Evans College Press.

Fogel, R. W. (1989). *Without Consent or Contract: The Rise and Fall of American Slavery.* New York: W.W. Norton & Company.

Foner, E. (1996). *Freedom's Lawmakers: A Directory of Black Officeholders during Reconstruction,* rev. ed. Baton Rouge: Louisiana State University Press.

Foster, F. S. (1994 [1979]). *Witnessing Slavery: The Development of Antebellum Slave Narratives, 2nd ed.* Madison, WI: The University of Wisconsin Press.

Fox, S. R. (1970). *The Guardian of Boston: William Monroe Trotter.* New York: Atheneum.

Franklin, E. F. (1932). *The Free Negro Family: A Study of Family Origins before the Civil War*. Nashville, TN: Fisk University Press.

Franklin, H. B. (1978). *The Victim as Criminal and Artist: Literature from the American Prison*. New York: Oxford University Press.

Franklin, J. H. (1956). *The Militant South, 1800–1861*. Cambridge, MA: The Belknap Press of Harvard.

Franklin, J. L. (1994). Black Southerners, Shared Experience, and Place: A Reflection. *The Journal of Southern History* 60, no. 1 (Feb.): 3–18.

Franklin, V. P. (1984). *Black Self-Determination: A Cultural History of the Faith of the Fathers*. Westport, CT: Lawrence Hill.

Frazier, E. F. (1932). *The Free Negro Family: A Study of Family Origins before the Civil War*. Nashville, TN: Fisk University Press.

Frehill-Rowe, L. M. (1993). Postbellum Race Relations and Rural Land Tenure: Migration of Blacks and Whites to Kansas and Nebraska, 1870–1890. *Social Forces* 72, no. 1 (Sept.): 77–92.

Frey, S. R. (1991). *Water from the Rock: Black Resistance in a Revolutionary Age*. Princeton, NJ: Princeton University Press.

Frye, C. A. (1980). The Bad Man Be Stylin' for Days: The Symposium Overview. Pp. 2–11 in C.A. Frye, ed., *Values in Conflict: Blacks and the American Ambivalence toward Violence*. Washington: University Press of America.

Fukurai, H., E. W. Butler, and R. Krooth (1993). *Race and the Jury: Racial Disenfranchisement and the Search for Justice*. New York and London: Plenum Press.

Fukurai, H., R. Krooth, and E. W. Butler (1994). The Rodney King Beating Verdicts. Pp. 73–102 in M. Baldassare, ed., *The Los Angeles Riots: Lessons for the Urban Future*. Boulder, CO: Westview Press.

Gaines, K. K. (1996). *Uplifting the Race: Black Leadership, Politics and Culture in the Twentieth Century*. Chapel Hill: The University of North Carolina Press.

Gates, H. L., Jr., A. P. Griffin, D. E. Lively, R. C. Post, W. B. Rubenstein, and N. Strossen (1994). *Speaking of Race, Speaking of Sex: Hate Speech, Civil Rights, and Civil Liberties*. New York and London: New York University Press.

Genovese, E. D. (1976 [1972]). *Roll, Jordan, Roll: The World the Slaves Made*. New York: Vintage Books.

Genovese, E. D. (1979). *From Rebellion to Revolution: Afro-American Slave Revolts in the Making of the Modern World*. Baton Rouge and London: Louisiana State University Press.

Genovese, E. D. (1991). Black Plantation Preachers in the Slave South. *Southern Studies*, 2, no. 3/4 (Fall and Winter): 203–228.

George, L. (1992). *No Crystal Stair: African-Americans in the City of Angels*. London: Verso.

Gerber, D. A. (1976). *Black Ohio and the Color Line, 1860–1950*. Urbana: University of Illinois Press.

Gerteis, L. S. (1973). *From Contraband to Freedman: Federal Policy Toward Southern Blacks, 1861–1865*. Westport, CT: Greenwood Press.

Gibbs, J. T., ed. (1988). *Young, Black, and Male in America: An Endangered Species*. Dover, MA: Auburn House.

Gibbs, J. T. (1996). *Race and Justice: Rodney King and O. J. Simpson in a House Divided*. San Francisco: Jossey-Bass.

Gibson, J. W. (1994). *Warrior Dreams: Paramilitary Culture in Post-Vietnam America*. New York: Hill & Wang.

Giddings, P. (1984). *When and Where I Enter: The Impact of Black Women on Race and Sex in America*. New York: Bantam Books.

Gilmore, A-T. (1975). *Bad Nigger! The National Impact of Jack Johnson*. Port Washington, NY: Kennikat Press.

Gilmore, A-T., ed. (1978). *Revisiting Blassingame's* The Slave Community: *The Scholars Respond*. Westport, CT: Greenwood Press.

Gilmore, D. D. (1990). *Manhood in the Making: Cultural Concepts of Masculinity*. New Haven, CT: Yale University Press.

Gimenez, M. E. (1990). The Feminization of Poverty: Myth or Reality. *Social Justice* 17, no. 3 (Fall): 43–69.

Giroux, H. A. (1996). *Fugitive Cultures: Race, Violence, and Youth*. New York: Routledge.

Goldfield, D. R. (1990). *Black, White, and Southern: Race Relations and Southern Culture 1940 to the Present*. Baton Rouge: Louisiana State University Press.

Goldman, R. and D. Gallan (1992). *Thurgood Marshall: Justice for All*. New York: Carroll & Graf.

Gomez, M. A. (1994). Muslims in Early America. *The Journal of Southern History* 60, no. 4 (Nov.): 671–710.

Goodheart, L. B. (1984). "The Chronicles of Kidnapping in New York": Resistance to the Fugitive Slave Law, 1834–1835. *Afro-Americans in New York Life and History*, 8, no. 1 (Jan.): 7–15.

Gooding-Williams, R., ed. (1993). *Reading Rodney King, Reading Urban Uprising*. New York: Routledge.

Goodman, J. (1994). *Stories of Scottsboro*. New York: Pantheon Books.

Goodstein, A. S. (1989). *Nashville, 1780–1860: From Frontier to City*. Gainesville: University of Florida Press.

Gordon, L. (1991). Black and White Visions of Welfare: Women's Welfare Activism, 1890–1945. *The Journal of American History* 78, no. 2 (Sept.): 559–590.

Goss, L. and M. E. Barnes, ed. (1989). *Talk That Talk: An Anthology of African-American Storytelling*. New York: Simon & Schuster.

Gossett, T. F. (1985). *Uncle Tom's Cabin and American Culture*. Dallas: Southern Methodist University Press.

Grantham, D. W. (1988). *The Life and Death of the Solid South: A Political History*. Lexington: The University Press of Kentucky.

Gray, B. C. (1993). *Black Female Domestics During the Depression in New York City, 1930–1940*. New York and London: Garland Publishing.

Gray, H. (1995). *Watching Race: Television and the Struggle for "Blackness."* Minneapolis: University of Minneapolis Press.

Green, D. S. and E. D. Driver, eds. (1978). *W.E.B. Du Bois on Sociology and the Black Community*. Chicago: The University of Chicago Press.

Greenberg, C. (1992). The Politics of Disorder: Reexamining Harlem's Riots of 1935 and 1943. *Journal of Urban History* 18, no. 4 (Aug.): 395–441.

Greenberg, K. S. (1996). *Honor and Slavery*. Princeton, NJ: Princeton University Press.

Greene, J. L. (1980). Violence in Black American Literature. Pp. 40–52 in C. A.

Frye, ed., *Values in Conflict: Blacks and the American Ambivalence toward Violence*. Washington, DC: University Press of America.

Grier, W. H. and P. M. Cobbs (1968). *Black Rage*. New York: Basic Books.

Griffin, F. J. (1995). *"Who Set You Flowin'?" The African-American Migration Narrative*. New York and Oxford: Oxford University Press.

Gross, T. L. (1971). *The Heroic Ideal in American Literature*. New York: The Free Press.

Grover, K. (1994). *Making a Way Somehow: African-American Life in a Northern Community, 1790–1965*. New York: Syracuse University Press.

Gutman, H. G. (1976). *The Black Family in Slavery and Freedom, 1750–1925*. New York: Pantheon Books.

Gutman, H. G. (1989). *Who Built America? Working People and the Nation's Economy, Politics, Culture & Society*, Vol 1. New York: Pantheon Books.

Hacker, A. (1995). The Crackdown on African-Americans. *The Nation* (July 10): 45–49.

Hall, E. T. (1969 [1966]). *The Hidden Dimension*. Garden City, NY: Anchor Books.

Hall, G. M. (1971). *Social Control in Slave Plantation Societies: A Comparison of St. Domingue and Cuba*. Baltimore and London: The John Hopkins Press.

Hall, J. D. (1993). *Revolt against Chivalry: Jessie Daniel Ames and the Women's Campaign against Lynching*. New York: Columbia University Press.

Haller, J. S., Jr. (1995). *Outcasts from Evolution: Scientific Attitudes of Racial Inferiority 1859–1900*. Carbondale: Southern Illinois University Press.

Haller, M. (1991). Policy Gambling, Entertainment, and the Emergence of Black Politics: Chicago from 1900 to 1940. *Journal of Social History* 24, no. 4 (Summer): 719–739.

Hamilton, C. V. (1991). *Adam Clayton Powell, Jr.: The Political Biography of an American Dilemma*. New York: Atheneum.

Harding, V. (1983). *There Is a River: The Black Struggle for Freedom in America*. New York: Vintage Books.

Hardwick, K. R. (1993). "Your Old Father Abe Lincoln Is Dead and Damned": Black Soldiers and the Memphis Race Riot of 1866. *Journal of Social History* 27, no. 1: 109–128.

Harley, S. (1995). *The Timetable of African-American History: A Chronology of the Most Important People and Events in African-American History*. New York: Simon & Schuster.

Harper, P. B. (1996). *Are We Not Men? Masculine Anxiety and the Problem of African-American Identity*. New York: Oxford University Press.

Harring, S. L. (1983). *Policing a Class Society: The Experience of American Cities, 1865–1915*. New Brunswick, NJ: Rutgers University Press.

Harris, T. (1984). *Exorcising Blackness: Historical and Literary Lynching and Burning Rituals*. Bloomington: Indiana University Press.

Harris, T. (1982). *From Mammies to Militants: Domestics in Black American Literature*. Philadelphia: Temple University Press.

Harwell, F. (1980). *A True Deliverance*. New York: Alfred A. Knopf.

Haskins, J. and K. Benson (1978). *Scott Joplin*. New York: Doubleday.

Hawke, D. F. (1988). *Everyday Life in Early America*. New York: Harper & Row.

Hawkins, D. F., ed. (1995). *Ethnicity, Race, and Crime: Perspectives across Time and Place*. Albany: State University of New York Press.

Hay, D., P. Linebaugh, J. G. Rule, E. P. Thompson, and C. Winslow (1975). *Albion's Fatal Tree: Crime and Society in Eighteenth-Century England*. New York: Pantheon Books.

Heard, C. A. and R. L. Bing, III (1993). African-American Faculty and Students on Predominantly White University Campuses. *Journal of Criminal Justice* 4, no. 1: 1–13.

Heaton, T. B. and C. K. Jacobson (1994). Race Differences in Changing Family Demographics in the 1980s. *Journal of Family Issues* 15, no. 2 (June): 290–308.

Heaton, W. C. (1932). A Statement by the N.A.A.C.P. on the Scottsboro Cases. *The Crisis* (March): 82–83.

Henri, F. (1975). *Black Migration: Movement North 1900–1920*. Garden City, NY: Anchor Press.

Henry, C. P. (1990). *Culture and African American Politics*. Bloomington and Indianapolis: Indiana University Press.

Hickey, N. and E. Edwin (1965). *Adam Clayton Powell and the Politics of Race*. New York: Fleet Publishing.

Higginbotham, A. L., Jr. (1996). *Shades of Freedom: Racial Politics and Presumptions of the American Legal Process*. New York: Oxford University Press.

Higginbotham, A. L., Jr., A. B. Francois, and L. Y. Yueh (1997). The O. J. Simpson Trial: Who Was Improperly "Playing the Race Card"? Pp. 31–56 in T. Morrison and C. B. Lacour, eds., *Birth of a Nation'hood: Gaze, Script, and Spectacle in the O. J. Simpson Case*. New York: Pantheon Books.

Hill, A. F. and E. C. Jordan, eds. (1995). *Race, Gender, and Power in America: The Legacy of the Hill–Thomas Hearings*. New York: Oxford University Press.

Hill, F. (1995). *A Delusion of Satan: The Full Story of the Salem Witch Trials*. New York: Doubleday.

Himes, C. (1965). *Cotton Comes to Harlem*. New York: Dell Publishing.

Himes, C. (1985 [1957]). *Rage in Harlem*. London and New York: Allison & Busby.

Hinks, P. P. (1997). *To Awaken My Afflicted Brethren: David Walker and the Problem of Antebellum Slave Resistance*. University Park, PA: The Pennsylvania State University Press.

Historical Almanack (1997). People; African American; *Introduction to Colonial African-American Slave Life*. http://www.history.org/people/african/aaintro.htm.

Historical Almanack (1997). People; Biographies; Patrick Henry. http://www.history.org/people/bios/biohen.htm.

Hoffer, P. C., ed. (1984). *Criminal Proceedings in Colonial Virginia [Records of] Fines, Examination of Criminals, Trials of Slaves, etc. from March 1710 [1711] to [1754] [Richmond County, Virginia]*. Athens: The University of Georgia Press.

Holder, C. B. (1980). The Rise of the West Indian Politician in New York City, 1900–1952. *Afro-Americans in New York Life and History* 4, no. 1 (Jan.): 45–59.

Holifield, E. B. (1989). *Era of Persuasion and American Thought and Culture 1521–1680*. Boston: Twayne Publishers.

Holt, S. A. (1994). "Making Freedom Pay": Freedpeople Working for Themselves, North Carolina, 1865–1900. *The Journal of Southern History* 60, no. 2 (May): 229–262.

Holt, T. (1977). *Black Over White: Negro Political Leadership in South Carolina during Reconstruction*. Urbana: University of Illinois Press.

hooks, b. (1995). *Killing Rage: Ending Racism*. New York: Henry Holt.

Hord, F. L. and J. S. Lee, eds. (1995). *I Am Because We Are: Readings in Black Philosophy*. Amherst: University of Massachusetts Press.

Horne, G. (1995). *Fire This Time: The Watts Uprising and the 1960s*. Charlottesville: University Press of Virginia.

Hornsby, A., Jr. (1972). *The Black Almanac: From Involuntary Servitude (1619–1860) to the Age of Disillusionment*. Woodbury, NY: Barron's Educational Series.

Horton, J. O. and L. E. Horton (1979). *Black Bostonians: Family Life and Community Struggle in the Antebellum North*. New York: Holmes & Meier.

Hurston, Z. N. (1969 [1937]). *Their Eyes Were Watching God*. Greenwich, CT: Fawcett.

Hutchinson, E. O. (1996). *Betrayed: A History of Presidential Failure to Protect Black Lives*. Boulder, CO: Westview Press.

Hutton, F. (1993). *The Early Black Press in America, 1827 to 1860*. Westport, CT: Greenwood Press.

Innis, L. and J. R. Feagin (1989). The Black "Underclass" Ideology in Race Relations Analysis. *Social Justice* 16, no. 4 (Winter): 13–34.

Jackson, A. W., ed. (1982). *Black Families and The Medium of Television*. Ann Arbor: The University of Michigan.

Jackson, G. (1970). *Soledad Brother; The Prison Letters of George Jackson*. New York: Coward-McCann.

Jackson, R. L., II (1997). Black "Manhood" as Xenophobe: An Ontological Exploration of the Hegelian Dialetic. *Journal of Black Studies* 27, no. 6 (July): 731–750.

Jacobs, J. B. (1977). *Statesville: The Penitentiary in Mass Society*. Chicago and London: The University of Chicago Press.

JACYL [*Journal of African Children's & Youth Literature*]. *Special Issue: African American Children's Literature*, O. Osa, ed., Vol. 3, 1991/1992.

Jaher, F. C. (1985). White America Views Jack Johnson, Joe Louis, and Muhammad Ali. Pp. 145–192 in D. Spivey, ed., *Sport in America: New Historical Perspectives*. Westport, CT: Greenwood Press.

James, A. W. (1995). A Black Demand for Racial Equality: The 1970 Black Student Protest at the University of Mississippi. *The Journal of Mississippi History* 57, no. 2 (Summer): 97–120.

Jankowski, M. S. (1991). *Islands in the Street: Gangs and American Urban Society*. Berkeley: University of California Press.

Jefferson, T. (1955). *Notes on the State of Virginia*. Ed. with Introduction by William Peden. Chapel Hill: University of North Carolina Press.

Jewell, K. S. (1993). *From Mammy to Miss America and Beyond: Cultural Images and the Shaping of U.S. Social Policy*. London and New York: Routledge.

Johnson, D. (1990). *Telling Tales: The Pedagogy and Promise of African American Literature for Youth*. New York: Greenwood Press.

Johnson, J. (1992). *Jack Johnson—In the Ring—and Out*. New York: Citadel Press.

Johnson, J. W. (1951 [1927]). *The Autobiography of an Ex-Coloured Man*. New York: Alfred A. Knopf.

Johnson, M. P. and J. L. Roarke (1984). *Black Masters: A Free Black Family of Color in the Old South*. New York: W.W. Norton.

Johnson, S. L. (1993). Racial Imagery in Criminal Justice Cases. *Tulane Law Review* 67, no. 6 (June): 1739–1805.

Jones, B. A. (1974). The Tradition of Sociology Teaching in Black Colleges: The Unheralded Professionals. Pp. 121–163 in J. E. Blackwell and M. Janowitz, eds., *Black Sociologists: Historical and Contemporary Perspectives*. Chicago: The University of Chicago Press.

Jones, H. (1987). *Mutiny on the Amistad*. New York: Oxford University Press.

Jones, J. A. (1993). *Bad Blood: The Tuskegee Syphilis Experiment*. New York: Free Press.

Jones, L. (1963). *Blues People: Negro Music in White America*. New York: Morrow Quill Paperbacks.

Jones, N.T. (1990). Slave Religion in South Carolina: A Heaven in Hell. *Southern Studies* 1, no. 1 (Spring): 5–32.

Jones, N. T., Jr. (1992). The Black Family as a Mechanism of Planter Control. Pp. 162–187 in J. W. Harris, ed., *Society and Culture in the Slave South*. London and New York: Routledge.

Jordan, E. L., Jr. (1995). *Black Confederates and Afro-Yankees in Civil War Virginia*. Charlottesville: University Press of Virginia.

Jordan, W. D. (1977 [1968]).*White over Black: American Attitudes toward the Negro, 1550–1812*. New York: W.W. Norton.

Joyner, C. (1984). *Down by the Riverside: A South Carolina Slave Community*. Urbana and Chicago: University of Illinois Press.

Kane, G. P. (1997). An Apology for Slavery? Try Atonement. *Albany Times Union*, June 23: A7. Katz, J. (1988). *Seductions of Crime: Moral and Sensual Attractions in Doing Evil*. New York: Basic Books.

Katz, W. L. (1996 [1987]). *The Black West*. New York: Touchstone.

Katzman, D. M. (1978). *Seven Days a Week: Women and Domestic Service in Industrializing America*. New York: Oxford University Press.

Kelley, R.D.G. (1994). *Race Rebels: Culture, Politics, and the Black Working Class*. New York: The Free Press.

Kelley, R.D.G. (1992). The Riddle of the Zoot: Malcolm Little and Black Cultural Politics during World War II. Pp. 155–182 in J. Wood, ed., *Malcolm X in Our Own Image*. New York: St. Martin's Press.

Kennedy, R. (1997). *Race, Crime, and the Law*. New York: Pantheon Books.

Kenzer, R. C. (1993). The Black Business Community in Post Civil War Virginia. *Southern Studies* 4, no. 3 (Fall): 229–252.

Keve, P. W. (1986). *The History of Corrections in Virginia*. Charlottesville: University Press of Virginia.

Kimmel, M. (1996). *Manhood in America: A Cultural History*. New York: The Free Press.

King M. (1963). I Have a Dream. Pp. 217–220 in J. M. Washington, ed., *A Testament of Hope: The Essential Writings of Martin Luther King, Jr*. New York: HarperCollins.

King, M. L., Jr. (1968). The Role of the Behaviorial Scientist in the Civil Rights Movement. *Journal of Social Issues* 24, no. 1: 1–12.

King, W. (1995). *Stolen Childhood: Slave Youth in Nineteenth-Century America*. Bloomington and Indianapolis: Indiana University Press.

Kirby, J. T. (1986). *Media-Made Dixie: The South in the American Imagination*, revised ed., Athens and London: The University of Georgia Press.

Kissman, K. and J. A. Allen (1993). *Single-Parent Families*. Newbury Park, CA: Sage.

Klein, H. S. (1995). African Women in the Atlantic Slave Trade. Pp. 67–75 in D. C. Hine, W. King, and L. Reed, eds., *"We Specialize in the Wholly Impossible": A Reader in Black Women's History*. Brooklyn, NY: Carlson Publishing.

Kobrin, D. (1975 [1971]). *The Black Minority in Early New York*. Albany: University of the State of New York.

Kornweibel, T., Jr. (1987). Black on Black: The FBI's First Negro Informants and Agents and the Investigation of Black Radicalism during the Red Scare. Pp. 121–136 in *Criminal Justice History*: An International Annual Vol. 8. Westport, CT: Meckler Corporation.

Kreiling, A. (1993). The Commercialization of the Black Press and the Rise of Race News in Chicago. Pp. 176–203 in W. S. Solomon and R. W. McChesney, eds., *Ruthless Criticism: New Perspectives in U.S. Communication History*. Minneapolis: University of Minnesota Press.

LaFree, G. and K. K. Russell (1993). The Argument for Studying Race and Crime. *Journal of Criminal Justice Education* 4, no. 2 (Fall): 251–289.

Lane, R. (1967). *Policing the City: Boston 1822–1855*. Cambridge: Harvard University Press.

Langum, D. J. (1994). *Crossing over The Line: Legislating Morality and the Mann Act*. Chicago: University of Chicago Press.

Laver, J. (1966). *Manners and Morals in the Age of Optimism, 1848–1914*. New York: Harper & Row.

Leaming, H. P. (1995). *Hidden Americans: Maroons of Virginia and the Carolinas*. New York: Garland Publishing.

Lee, E. B. and L. A. Browne (1995). Effects of Television Advertising on African American Teenagers. *Journal of Black Studies* 25, no. 5 (May): 523–536.

Lemelle, A. J. (1995). *Black Male Deviance*. Westport, CT: Greenwood Publishing.

Levine, D. (1997). A Single Standard of Civilization: Black Private Social Welfare Institutions in the South, 1880s-1920s. *The Georgia Historical Quarterly* 81, no. 1 (Spring): 52–77.

Levine, L. (1977). *Black Culture and Black Consciousness: Afro-American Folk Thought From Slavery to Freedom*. New York: Oxford University Press.

Levine, L. (1993). *The Unpredictable Past: Explorations in American Cultural History*. New York: Oxford University Press.

Levy, E. (1973). *James Weldon Johnson: Black Leader Black Voice*. Chicago and London: The University of Chicago Press.

Lewis, D. L. (1997 [1979]). *When Harlem Was in Vogue*. New York: Penguin.

Lewis, E. (1991). Expectations, Economic Opportunities, and Life in the Industrial Age: Black Migration to Norfolk, Virginia, 1910–45. Pp. 22–45 in J. Trotter, ed., *The Great Migration in Historical Perspective: New Dimensions of Race, Class, and Gender*. Bloomington and Indianapolis: Indiana University Press.

Lewis, N. A. (1997). For Black Scholars Wedded to Prism of Race, New and Separate Goals. *The New York Times* (May 5): B9.

Lichtenstein, A. (1993). Good Roads and Chain Gangs in the Progressive South: "The Negro Convict Is a Slave." *The Journal of Southern History* 59, no. 1 (Feb.): 85–110.

Liebow, E. (1967). *Tally's Corner: A Study of Negro Streetcorner Men.* Boston: Little, Brown.

Lincoln, C. E. (1996). *Coming through the Fire: Surviving Race and Place in America.* Durham and London: Duke University Press.

Link, A. S., ed. (1978). *The Papers of Woodrow Wilson,* Vol. 28. 1913. Princeton, NJ: Princeton University Press.

Link, A. S., ed. (1979). *The Papers of Woodrow Wilson,* Vol. 31, Sept. 6–Dec. 31, 1914. Princeton, NJ: Princeton University Press.

Littlejohn-Blake, S. M. and C. A. Darling (1993). Understanding the Strengths of African American Families. *Journal of Black Studies* 23, no. 4 (June): 460–471.

Litwack, L. F. (1979). *Been in the Storm So Long.* New York: Alfred A. Knopf.

Litwack, L. F. (1986). "Blues Falling Down Like Hail": The Ordeal of Black Freedom. Pp. 109–127 in R. H. Abzug and S. E. Maizlish, eds., *New Perspectives on Race and Slavery in America.* Lexington: The University Press of Kentucky.

Lomax, A. (1960). *The Folk Songs of North America.* Garden City, NY: Doubleday.

Long, C. H. (1980). "The Archetypal Significance of the Bad Man." Pp. 24–39 in C. Frye, ed., *Values in Conflict: Blacks and the American Ambivalence toward Violence.* Washington, DC: University Press of America.

Los Angeles Times (1992). *Understanding the Riots: Los Angeles before and after the Rodney King Case.* Los Angeles: Los Angeles Times.

Lyman, S. M. (1994). *Color, Culture, and Civilization: Race and Minority Issues in American Society.* Urbana: University of Illinois.

Lynes, R. (1985). *The Lively Audience: A Social History of the Visual and Performing Arts in America, 1890–1950.* New York: Harper & Row.

Mabee, C. (1979). *Black Education in New York State: From Colonial to Modern Times.* Syracuse, NY: Syracuse University Press.

Mabee, C. (1990). Sojourner Truth Fights Dependence on Government: Moves Freed Slaves off Welfare in Washington to Jobs in Upstate New York. *Afro-Americans in New York Life and History* 14, no. 1 (Jan.): 7–27.

MacCann, D. and G. Woodard, eds. (1972). *The Black American in Books for Children: Readings in Racism.* Metuchen, NJ: The Scarecrow Press.

MacDonald, J. F. (1983). *Blacks and White TV: Afro-Americans in Television since 1948.* Chicago: Nelson-Hall.

Mackey, P. E. (1982). *Hanging in the Balance: The Anti-Capital Punishment Movement in New York State, 1776–1861.* New York: Garland Publishing.

MacLean, N. (1994). *Behind the Mask: The Making of the Second Ku Klux Klan.* New York: Oxford University Press.

Maish, A., J. C. Rose, and M. K. Marks (1997). Cedar Grove: African-American History in Rural Arkansas. Pp. 19–49 in D. A. Poirier and N. F. Bellantoni, eds., *In Remembrance: Archaeology and Death.* Westport, CT: Bergin & Garvey.

Malcolm X (1995). Speech on Black Revolution (New York, April 8, 1964). Pp. 272–284 in F. L. Hord and J. S. Lee, eds., *I Am Because We Are: Readings in Black Philosophy.* Amherst: University of Massachusetts Press.

Malcolm X and A. Hailey (1992 [1964]). *The Autobiography of Malcolm X.* New York: Ballantine Books.

Mancini, M. J. (1996). *One Dies, Get Another: Convict Leasing in the American South, 1866–1928.* Columbia, SC: University of South Carolina Press.

Mann, C. R. (1993). *Unequal Justice: A Question of Color*. Bloomington: Indiana University Press.

Mann, C. R. and M. S. Zatz, eds. (1998). *Images of Color, Images of Crime*. Los Angeles, CA: Roxbury Publishing.

Marable, M. (1995). Million Man March: An Analysis. *The New York Amsterdam News*, Sept. 2: 12.

Martin, J. M. and E. P. Martin (1985). *The Helping Tradition in the Black Family and Community*. Silver Springs, MD: National Association of Social Workers.

Massood, P. J. (1996). Mapping the Hood: The Genealogy of City Space in *Boyz N the Hood* and *Menace II Society*. *Cinema Journal*, 35, no. 2 (Winter): 85–97.

Mays, B. E. (1969 [1938]). *The Negro's God (as Reflected in His Literature)*. Westport, CT: Greenwood Press.

McAdoo, H. P., ed. (1988). *Black Families*, 2nd ed. Newbury Park, CA: Sage.

McAneny, L. (1993). The Rodney King Case: Federal Trial's Split Verdicts Leave Black Americans Disheartened. *The Gallup Poll Monthly* (April): 27–29.

McColley, R. (1986). Slavery in Virginia, 1619–1660: A Reexamination. Pp. 11–24 in R. H. Abzug and S. E. Maizlish, eds., *New Perspectives on Race and Slavery in America*. Lexington: The University Press of Kentucky.

McDonnell, L. T. (1988). Money Knows No Master: Market Relations and the American Slave Community. Pp. 31–44 in W.W.B. Moore, Jr., J. F. Tripp, and L. G. Tyler, Jr., eds., *Developing Dixie: Modernization in a Traditional Society*. New York: Greenwood Press.

McKenzie, R. T. (1993). Freedmen and the Soil in the Upper South: The Reorganization of Tennessee Agriculure, 1865–1880. *The Journal of Southern History* 59, no.1 (Feb.) 63–84.

McLaurin, M. A. (1991). *Celia, A Slave*. New York: The University of Georgia Press.

McMillan, T.J. (1994). Black Magic, Witchcraft, Race, and Resistance in Colonial New England. *Journal of Black Studies* 25, no. 1 (Sept.): 99–117.

Meier, A. (1988 [1963]). *Negro Thought in America, 1880–1915*. Ann Arbor: The University of Michigan Press.

Meier, A. and E. Rudwick (1986). *Black History and the Historical Profession, 1915–1980*. Urbana and Chicago: University of Illinois Press.

Meier, A. and J. H. Bracey, Jr. (1993). The NAACP as a Reform Movement, 1909–1965: "To Reach the Conscience of America." *The Journal of Southern History* 59, no. 1 (Feb.): 3–30.

Mellon, J., ed. (1988). *Bullwhip Days: The Slaves Remember (an Oral History)*. New York: Weidenfeld & Nicolson.

Meriwether, L. (1989 [1970]). *Daddy Was a Number Runner*. New York: The Feminist Press.

Merton, R. (1972). Insiders and Outsiders: A Chapter in the Sociology of Knowledge. Pp. 9–47 in R. Merton, ed., *Varieties in Political Expression in Sociology*. Chicago: University of Chicago Press.

Messenger, The (Jan. 1918). The Hanging of the Negro Soldiers.

Messenger, The (Dec. 1920). An Open Letter to America on the Ku Klux Klan, 166–168.

Messner, S. F. and R. Rosenfeld (1994). *Crime and the American Dream*. Belmont, CA: Wadsworth Publishing.

Meyerowitz, J. (1994). Beyond the Feminine Mystique: A Reassessment of Postwar

Mass Culture, 1946–1958. Pp. 229–262 in J. Meyerowitz, ed., *Not June Cleaver: Women and Gender in Postwar America, 1945–1960*. Philadelphia: Temple University Press.

Miller, J. C. (1995 [1977]). *The Wolf by the Ear: Thomas Jefferson and Slavery*. Charlottesville and London: The University Press of Virginia.

Miller, K. D. (1992). *Voice of Deliverance: The Language of Martin Luther King, Jr., and Its Sources*. New York: The Free Press.

Mintz, S. W. and R. Price (1976). *An Anthropological Approach to the Afro-American Past: A Caribbean Perspective*. Philadelphia: Institute for the Study of Human Issues.

Mitchell, J., Jr. (1902). Shall the Wheels of Race Agitation Be Stopped? *The Colored American Magazine* 5, no. 5 (Sept.): 386–391.

Mohl, R. A. (1993). Shifting Patterns of American Urban Policy since 1900. Pp. 1–45 in A. R. Hirsch and R. A. Mohl, eds., *Urban Policy in Twentieth-Century America*. New Brunswick, NJ: Rutgers University Press.

Montgomery, K. C. (1989). *Target: Prime Time (Advocacy Groups and the Struggle over Entertainment Television)*. New York: Oxford University Press.

Montgomery, W. E. (1993). *Under Their Own Vine and Fig Tree: The African American Church in the South, 1865–1900*. Baton Rouge: Louisiana State University Press.

Moore, W. B., Jr. and J. F. Tripp (1989). *Looking South: Chapters in the Story of an American Region*. Westport, CT: Greenwood Press.

Morgan, E. S. (1975). *American Slavery, American Freedom: The Ordeal of Colonial Virginia*. New York: W. W. Norton.

Morgan, H. W., ed. (1963). *The Gilded Age: A Reappraisal*. Syracuse, NY: Syracuse University Press.

Morris, R. L. (1980). *Wait until Dark: Jazz and the Underworld, 1880–1940*. Bowling Green, OH: Bowling Green University Popular Press.

Morris, T. D. (1974). *Free Men All: The Personal Liberty Laws of the North, 1780–1861*. Baltimore and London: The John Hopkins University Press.

Morris, T. D. (1996). *Southern Slavery and the Law, 1619–1860*. Chapel Hill: The University of North Carolina Press.

Morrison, P. A. and I. S. Lowry (1994). A Riot of Color: The Demographic Setting. Pp. 1–17 in M. Baldassare, ed., *The Los Angeles Riots: Lessons for the Urban Future*. Boulder, CO: Westview Press.

Morrison, T., ed. (1992). *Race-ing Justice, En-gendering power: Essays on Anita Hill, Clarence Thomas, and the Construction of Social Reality*. New York: Pantheon Books.

Morrison, T. and C. B. Lacour, eds. (1997). *Birth of a Nation 'hood: Gaze, Script, and Spectacle in the O. J. Simpson Case*. New York: Pantheon Books.

Morton, P. (1991). *Disfigured Images: The Historical Assault on Afro-American Women*. New York: Praeger.

Mosley, W. (1990). *Devil in a Blue Dress*. New York: Pocket Books.

Moynihan, D. P. (1965). *The Negro Family: The Case for National Action*. Washington, DC: Office of Policy Planning and Research, U.S. Department of Labor.

Moynihan, D. P. (1986). *Family and Nation: The Godkin Lectures, Harvard University*. New York: Harcourt Brace Jovanovich.

Mullen, B., ed. (1995). *Revolutionary Tales: African American Women's Short Stories from the First Story to the Present*. New York: Laurel Books (Dell Publishing).

Mullen, R. W. (1973). *Blacks in American Wars: The Shift in Attitudes from the Revolutionary War to Vietnam*. New York: Monad Press.

Murray, C. (1994 [1984]). *Losing Ground: American Social Policy, 1950–1980*. New York: Basic Books.

Murray, L. (1979). *The Celluloid Persuasion: Movies and the Liberal Arts*. Grand Rapids, MI: William B. Eerdmans Publishing.

Myers, M. A. and J. L. Massey (1991). Race, Labor, and Punishment in Postbellum Georgia. *Social Problems* 38, no. 2 (May): 267–287.

Myrdal, G. (1962 [1944]). *An American Dilemma: The Negro Problem and Modern Democracy*, Vol. II. New York: Pantheon Books.

Nash, G. B. (1988). *Forging Freedom: The Formation of Philadelphia's Black Community, 1720–1840*. Cambridge and London: Harvard University Press.

Nash, G. B. (1990). *Race and Revolution*. Madison, WI: Madison House Publishers.

Neverdon-Morton, C. (1989). *Afro-American Women of the South and the Advancement of the Race, 1895–1925*. Knoxville: The University of Tennessee Press.

Newman, D. L. (1995). Black Women in the Era of the American Revolution in Pennsylvania. Pp. 211–224 in D. C. Hine, W. King, and L. Reed, eds., *"We Specialize in the Wholly Impossible": A Reader in Black Women's History*. Brooklyn, NY: Carlson Publishing.

Nieman, D. G. (1989). Black Political Power and Criminal Justice: Washington County, Texas, 1868–1884. *The Journal of Southern History* 55, no. 3 (Aug.): 391–420.

Nisbett, R. E. and D. Cohen (1996). *Culture of Honor: The Pychology of Violence in the South*. Boulder, CO: Westview Press.

Nobles, W. W. (1989). Public Policy and the African-American Family. Pp. 93–120 in *Race: Twentieth Century Dilemmas—Twenty-First Century Prognoses*. Milwaukee: The University of Wisconsin.

Nobles, W. W. and L. L. Goddard (1984). *Understanding the Black Family: A Guide for Scholarship and Research*. Oakland, CA: The Institute for the Advanced Study of Black Family Life and Culture.

Nye, D. E. and C. Pedersen, eds. (1991). *Consumption and American Culture*. Amsterdam: VU University Press.

Oakes, J. (1990). *Slavery and Freedom: An Interpretation of the Old South*. New York: Alfred A. Knopf.

Oates, S. B. (1975). *The Fires of Jubilee: Nat Turner's Fierce Rebellion*. New York: Harper & Row.

O'Kane, J. M. (1992). *The Crooked Ladder: Gangsters, Ethnicity, and the American Dream*. New Brunswick, NJ: Transaction Publishers.

Okur, N. A. (1995). Underground Railroad in Philadelphia, 1830–1860. *Journal of Black Studies* 25, no. 5 (May): 537–557.

O'Meally, R. and G. Fabre (1994). Introduction. Pp. 3–17 in G. Fabre and R. O'Meally, eds., *History and Memory in African American Culture*. New York: Oxford University Press.

Omolade, B. (1994). *The Rising Song of African American Women*. New York and London: Routledge.

O'Reilly, K. (1995). *Nixon's Piano: Presidents and Racial Politics from Washington to Clinton*. New York: The Free Press.

Oshinsky, D. M. (1997 [1996]). *"Worse Than Slavery": Parchman Farm and the Ordeal of Jim Crow Justice*. New York: Free Press.

Ostendorf, B. (1982). *Black Literature in White America*. Sussex: The Harvester Press.

Osunleye, T. (1997). African American Folklore: Its Role in Reconstructing African American History. *Journal of Black Studies* 27, no. 4 (March): 435–455.

Oswald, R. G. (1972). *Attica—My Story*. New York: Doubleday.

Ottley, R. (1968 [1943]). *New World A-Coming*. New York: Arno Press and The New York Times.

Ownby, T. (1990). *Subduing Satan: Religion, Recreation, and Manhood in the Rural South, 1865–1920*. Chapel Hill: University of North Carolina Press.

Painter, N. (1977). *Exodusters: Black Migration to Kansas after Reconstruction*. New York: Alfred A. Knopf.

Painter, N. (1996). *Sojourner Truth: a Life, a Symbol*. New York: W.W. Norton.

Palmer, C. A. (1994). *The First Passage: Blacks in the Americas, 1502–1617*. New York: Oxford Press.

Parish, P. J. (1989). *Slavery: History and Historians*. New York: Harper & Row.

Parker, F. L. (1993). *Running for Freedom: Slave Runaways in North Carolina 1775–1840*. New York: Garland Publishing.

Patterson, O. (1982). *Slavery and Social Death: A Comparative Study*. Cambridge, MA: Harvard University Press.

Pauly, T. H. (1990). Black Images and White Culture during the Decade before the Civil Rights Movement. *American Studies* 31, no. 2 (Fall): 101–119.

Payne, C. M. (1995). *"I've Got the Light of Freedom": The Organizing Tradition and the Mississippi Freedom Struggle*. Berkeley: University of California Press.

Pearson, E. W., ed. (1969 [1906]). *Letters from Port Royal, 1862–1868*. New York: Arno Press.

Pedersen, C. (1991). Black Responses to Consumption: From Frederick Douglass to Booker T. Washington. Pp. 194–203 in D. E. Nye and C. Pedersen, eds., *Consumption and American Culture*. Amsterdam: VU University Press.

Perata, D. D. (1997–98). Those Pullman Blues. *American Educator* 21, no. 4, Winter: 29–42.

Peretti, B. W. (1997). *Jazz in American Culture*. Chicago: Ivan R. Dee.

Persons, S. (1987). *Ethnic Studies at Chicago, 1905–45*. Urbana: University at Illinois Press.

Pescosolido, B. A., E. Grauerholz, and M. A. Milkie (1997). Culture and Conflict: The Portrayal of Blacks in U.S. Children's Picture Books through the Mid- and Late-Twentieth Century. *American Sociological Review* 62 (June): 443–464.

Petry, A. (1964). *Tituba of Salem Village*. New York: Thomas Y. Crowell.

Petry, A. (1974 [1946]). *The Street*. Boston-Houghton Mifflin.

Pfeffer, P. F. (1990). *A. Philip Randolph, Pioneer of the Civil Rights Movement*. Baton Rouge: Louisiana State University Press.

Phillips, C. (1993). The Roots of Quasi-Freedom: Manumission and Term Slavery in Early National Baltimore. *Southern Studies* 4, no. 1 (Spring): 39–66.

Piersen, W. D. (1993), *Black Legacy: America's Hidden Heritage*. Amherst: The University of Massachusetts Press.

Pieterse, J. N. (1992). *White on Black: Images of Africa and Blacks in Western Popular Culture*. New Haven and London: Yale University Press.

Platt, A. M. (1971). *The Politics of the Riot Commissions, 1917–1970*. New York: Collier Books.

Pomerance, A. (1988). *Repeal of the Blues: How Black Entertainers Influenced Civil Rights*. New York: Carol Publishing.

Quarles, B. (1969). *Black Abolitionists*. New York: Da Capo Press.

Quarles, B. (1989 [1953]). *The Negro in the Civil War*. New York: Da Capo Press.

Quarles, B. (1996). *The Negro in the Making of America*, 3rd ed. New York: Touchstone.

Rainwater, L. and W. L. Yancey (1967). *The Moynihan Report and the Politics of Controversy*. Cambridge, MA: The MIT Press.

Randolph, A. P. (March 1919). Lynching: Capitalism Its Causes, Socialism Its Cure. *The Messenger*, 9–12.

Ransby, B. (1995). A Righteous Rage and a Grassroots Mobilization. Pp. 45–52 in G. Smitherman, ed., *African American Women Speak Out on Anita Hill–Clarence Thomas*. Detroit: Wayne State University.

Ransom, R. L. (1989). *Conflict and Compromise: The Political Economy of Slavery, Emancipation, and the American Civil War*. Cambridge: Cambridge University Press.

Raybon, P. (1989). A Case of 'Severe Bias.' *Newsweek* Oct. 2, 11.

Report of the Committee of Merchants for the Relief of Colored People, Suffering from the Late Riots in the City of New York. African American Perspectives: Pamphlets from the Daniel A. P. Murray Collection, 1818–1907. Library of Congress, http:/cweb2./oc.gov/ammen/aap/aaphome.html.

Report of the National Advisory Commission on Civil Disorders (1968). New York: E.P. Dutton.

Reston, J., Jr. (1977). *The Innocence of Joan Little: A Southern Mystery*. New York: Times Books.

Rice, D. (1975). *The Rise and Fall of Black Slavery*. New York: Harper & Row.

Richards, J. and J. M. Mackenzie (1986). *The Railway Station: A Social History*. Oxford and New York: Oxford University Press.

Richardson, L. (1997). An Old Experiment's Legacy: Distrust of AIDS Treatment. *The New York Times, April 21*, A1/B4.

Risbane, R. H. (1983 [1974]). *Black Activism*. Valley Forge, PA: Judson Press.

Rise, E. W. (1995). *The Martinsville Seven: Race, Rape, and Capital Punishment*. Charlottesville: University Press of Virginia.

Roberts, R. R. (1963). Gilt, Gingerbread, and Realism. Pp. 169–195 in H. W. Morgan, ed., *The Gilded Age: A Reappraisal*. Syracuse, NY: Syracuse University Press.

Robinson, J. L. (1995). *Racism or Attitude? The Ongoing Struggle for Black Liberation and Self-Esteem*. New York and London: Basic Books.

Roediger, D. (1997). Introduction: From the Social Construction of Race to the Abolition of Whiteness. Pp. 247–277 in E. N. Gates, ed., *Race Classification and History*. New York: Garland.

Rogers, G. C., Jr. (1969). *Charleston in the Age of the Pinckneys*. Norman: University of Oklahoma.

Rome, D. M. (1992). Race, Media, and Crime: A Content Analysis of *The New York*

Times, The Atlanta Constitution, and *The Los Angeles Times*, 1950–1988. Doctoral dissertation. Washington State University.

Rose, W. L. (1976). *Rehearsal for Reconstruction: The Port Royal Experiment*. London, Oxford, and New York: Oxford University Press.

Rotunda, E. A. (1993). *American Manhood: Transformations in Masculinity from the Revolution to the Modern Era*. New York: Basic Books.

Rousey, D. C. (1996). *Policing the Southern City, New Orleans, 1805–1889*. Baton Rouge and London: Louisiana State University Press.

Rowe, G. S. (1989). Black Offenders, Criminal Courts, and Philadelphia Society in the Late Eighteenth-Century. *Journal of Social History* 22, no. 1 4 (Summer): 685–712.

Rury, J. L. (1985). Philanthropy, Self Help, and Social Control: The New York Manumission Society and Free Blacks, 1785–1810. *Phylon* 46, no. 3 (Sept.): 231–241.

Russell, K., M. Wilson, and R. Hall (1993). *The Color Complex: The Politics of Skin Color among African Americans*. New York: Anchor Books.

Sann, P. (1967). *The Lawless Decade*. New York: Crown Publishing.

Savage, W. S. (1976). *Blacks in the West*. Westport, CT: Greenwood Press.

Savitt, T. L. (1978). *Medicine and Slavery: The Diseases and Health Care of Blacks in Antebellum Virginia*. Urbana, Chicago, and London: University of Illinois Press.

Scheter, W. (1970). *The History of Negro Humor in America*. New York: Fleet Press.

Schwarz, P. J. (1988). *Twice Condemned: Slaves and the Criminal Laws of Virginia, 1705–1865*. Baton Rouge: Louisiana State University Press.

Scott, E. (1969 [1920]). *Negro Migration during the War*. New York: Arno Press and the New York Times.

Scruggs, C. (1993). *Sweet Home: Invisible Cities in the Afro-American Novel*. Baltimore: The Johns Hopkins University Press.

Sellin, J. T. (1976). *Slavery and the Penal System*. New York: Elsevier.

Selnow, G. W. and R. R. Gilbert (1993). *Society's Impact on Television: How the Viewing Public Shapes Television Programming*. Westport, CT: Praeger.

Senate Report, No. 579. *Alleged Outrages in Danville, Va*. Committee on Privileges and Elections, 48th Congress, 1st Session, 1884.

Senna, C. (1993). *The Black Press and the Struggle for Civil Rights*. New York: The African-American Experience.

Shapiro, H. (1988). *White Violence and Black Response: From Reconstruction to Montgomery*. Amherst: The University of Massachusetts Press.

Shaw, S. J. (1986). *Black Women in White Collars: A Social History of Lower-Level Professional Black Women Workers, 1870–1954*, Vols. 1 and 2. Ph.D. dissertation, The Ohio State University. Ann Arbor, MI: University Microfilms.

Shi, D. E. (1985). *The Simple Life: Plain Living and High Thinking in American Culture*. New York: Oxford University Press.

Sidran, B. (1971). *Black Talk: How the Music of Black America Created a Radical Alternation to the Values of Western Literary Tradition*. New York: Holt, Rinehart, & Winston.

Silberman, C. E. (1978). *Criminal Violence, Criminal Justice*. New York: Random House.

Silk, C. and J. Silk (1990). *Racism and Anti-Racism in American Popular Culture: Por-*

trayals of African-Americans in Fiction and Film. Manchester, England: Manchester University Press.

Simon, T. W. (1997). Jurisprudential Indeterminacy: The Case of Hate Speech Regulation. Pp. 293–309 in S. W. Griffin and Moffat R.C.L., eds., *Radical Critiques of the Law*. Lawrence: University Press of Kansas.

Slaughter, T. P. (1991). *Bloody Dawn: The Christiana Riot and Racial Violence in the Antebellum North*. New York: Oxford University Press.

Smith, C. E. (1993). Black Muslims and the Development of Prisoners' Rights. *Journal of Black Studies* 24, no. 2 (Dec.): 131–146.

Smith, P. (1985). *America Enters the World: A People's History of the Progressive Era and World War I*, Vol 7. New York: McGraw-Hill.

Smith, P. (1987). *Redeeming the Time: A People's History of the 1920s and the New Deal*, Vol. 8. New York: McGraw-Hill.

Smitherman, G. (1994). *Black Talk: Words and Phrases from the Hood to the Amen Corner*. Boston: Houghton Mifflin.

Smitherman, G., ed. (1995). *African American Women Speak Out on Anita Hill–Clarence Thomas*. Detroit: Wayne State University Press.

Snowden, F. M., Jr. (1983). *Before Color Prejudice: The Ancient World View of Blacks*. Cambridge, MA: Harvard University Press.

Sobel, M. (1987). *The World They Made Together: Black and White Values in Eighteenth Century Virginia*. Princeton, NJ: Princeton University Press.

Sorin, G. S. and J. W. Rehl (1992). *Honorable Work: African Americans in the Resort Community of Saratoga Springs, 1870–1970*. Saratoga Springs: Historical Society of Saratoga Springs.

Spear, A. H. (1967). *Black Chicago: The Making of a Negro Ghetto, 1890–1920*. Chicago: The University of Chicago Press.

Spivey, D., ed. (1985). *Sport in America: New Historical Perspectives*. Westport, CT: Greenwood Press.

Staff Report to the Subcommittee on Civil Rights of the Committee on Labor and Public Welfare (1954). *Employment and Economic Status of Negroes in the United States*. United States Senate, Eighty-Third Congress, Second Session.

Staples, R. (1978 [1973]). *The Black Woman in America*. Chicago: Nelson-Hall.

Staples, R. and L. B. Johnson (1993). *Black Families at the Crossroads*. San Francisco: Jossey-Bass.

Staples, R., ed. (1991). *The Black Family*, 4th ed. Belmont, CA: Wadsworth Publishing.

Starkey, M. L. (1950). *The Devil in Massachusetts: A Modern Inquiry into the Salem Witch Trials*. New York: Alfred A. Knopf.

Starobin, R. S., ed. (1988 [1974]). *Blacks in Bondage: Letters of American Slaves*, 2nd ed. New York: Markus Wiener Publishing.

Stein, J. (1986). *The World of Marcus Garvey: Race and Class in Modern Society*. Baton Rouge and London: Louisiana State University Press.

Steinberg, S. (1995). *Turning Back: The Retreat from Racial Justice in American Thought and Policy*. Boston: Beacon Press.

Stetson, E. and L. David (1994). *Glorying in Tribulation: The Lifework of Sojourner Truth*. East Lansing, MI: Michigan State University Press.

Stone, A. E. (1992). *The Return of Nat Turner: History, Literature, and Cultural Politics in Sixties America*. Athens: The University of Georgia Press.

Stowe, S. M. (1987). *Intimacy and Power in the Old South: Ritual in the Lives of the Planters*. Baltimore and London: The Johns Hopkins University Press.

Striefford, D. M. (1979). The American Colonization Society: An Application of Republican Ideology to Early Antebellum Reform. *The Journal of Southern History* 45, no. 2: 201–220.

Stuckey, Sterling (1987). *Slave Culture: Nationalist Theory and the Foundations of Black America*. New York: Oxford University Press.

Styrker, J. (1997). Tuskegee's Long Arm Still Touches a Nerve. *The New York Times* April 13, 4.

Styron, W. (1993 [1966]). *The Confessions of Nat Turner*. New York: Vintage Books.

Sullivan, L. (1996). The Demise of Black Civil Society: Once upon a Time When We Were Colored Meets the Hip-Hop Generation. *Social Policy* 27, no. 2 (Winter): 6–16.

Sullivan, P. (1996). *Days of Hope: Race and Democracy in the New Deal Era*. Chapel Hill: The University of North Carolina Press.

Sulton, A., ed. (1994). *African-American Perspectives On: Crime Causation, Criminal Justice Administration and Crime Prevention*. Englewood, CO: Sulton Books.

Sundquist, E. J. (1992). *The Hammers of Creation: Folk Culture in Modern African-American Fiction*. Athens and London: The University of Georgia Press.

Swift, D. E. (1989). *Black Prophets of Justice: Activist Clergy before the Civil War*. Baton Rouge: Louisiana State University Press.

Takaki, R. T. (1979). *Iron Cages: Race and Culture in Nineteenth-Century America*. New York: Alfred A. Knopf.

Taylor, E. (1989). *Prime Time Families: Television Culture in Postwar America*. Berkeley: University of California Press.

Taylor, H. (1995). "The Griot from Tennessee": The Saga of Alex Haley's *Roots*. *Critical Quarterly* 37, no. 2 (Summer): 46–62.

Taylor, R. A. (1991). Crime and Race Relations in Jacksonville, 1884–1892. *Southern Studies* 2, no. 1 (Spring): 17–37.

Taylor, W. R. (1961). *Cavalier and Yankee: The Old South and American National Character*. New York: George Braziller.

Tierney, K. J. (1994). Property Damage and Violence: A Collective Behavior Analysis. Pp. 149–173 in M. Baldassare, ed. *The Los Angeles Riots: Lessons for the Urban Future*. Boulder, CO: Westview Press.

Tindall, G. B. (1966). *South Carolina Negroes, 1877–1900*. Baton Rouge: Louisiana State University Press.

Tolnay, S. E. and E. M. Beck (1995). *A Festival of Violence: An Analysis of Southern Lynchings, 1882–1930*. Urbana and Chicago: University of Illinois Press.

Trotter, J. W., ed. (1991). *The Great Migration in Historical Perspective: New Dimensions of Race, Class, and Gender*. Bloomington: Indiana University Press.

Tucker, L. R. and H. Shah (1992). Race and the Transformation of Culture: The Making of the Television Miniseries *Roots*. *Critical Studies in Communication* 9: 325–336.

Turner, M., ed. (1995). *From Chattel Slaves to Wage Slaves: The Dynamics of Labour Bargaining in the Americas*. London: James Curry.

Turner, P. A. (1993). *I Heard It through the Grapevine: Rumor in African-American Culture*. Berkeley: University of California Press.

Turner, P. A. (1994). *Ceramic Uncles and Celluloid Mammies: Black Images and Their Influence on Culture*. New York: Anchor Books.

Van Deburg, W. L. (1992). *New Day in Babylon: The Black Power Movement and American Culture, 1965–1975*. Chicago: The University of Chicago Press.

Van Deburg, W. L. (1997). *Black Camelot: African-American Cultural Heroes in Their Times, 1960–1980*. Chicago and London: The University of Chicago Press.

Van Horne, W. A., ed. (1989). *Race: Twentieth Century Dilemma—Twenty-First Century Prognoses*. Milwaukee: The University of Wisconsin.

Van Vechten, C. (1926). *Nigger Heaven*. New York: Grosset & Dunlap.

Vinson, R. T. (1996). The Law as Lawbreaker: The Promotion and Encouragement of the Atlantic Slave Trade by the New York Judiciary System, 1857–1862. *Afro-Americans in New York Life and History* 20, no. 2 (July): 35–58.

Vold, G. B., T. J. Bernard, and J. B. Snipes (1998). *Theoretical Criminology*, 4th ed. New York: Oxford University Press.

Wade, R. C. (1964). *Slavery in the Cities: The South 1820–1860*. New York: Oxford University Press.

Walden, D., ed. (1972). *W.E.B. Du Bois: The Crisis Writings*. Greenwich, CT: Fawcett Publications.

Waldrep, C. (1996). Substituting Law for the Lash: Emancipation and Legal Formalism in a Mississippi County Court. *The Journal of American History* 82, no. 4 (March): 1425–1451.

Walker, R. H. (1967). *Everyday Life in the Age of Enterprise 1865–1900*. New York: G. P. Putnam's Sons.

Walsh, L. S. (1995). Work and Resistance in the New Republic: The Case of the Chesapeake 1770–1820. Pp. 97–122 in M. Turner, ed. *From Chattel Slaves to Wage Slaves: The Dynamics of Labour Bargaining in the Americas*. London: James Curry.

Walters, R. G. (1976). *The Antislavery Appeal: American Abolition after 1830*. Baltimore and London: The Johns Hopkins University Press.

Ware, G. (1976). *From the Black Bar: Voices for Equal Justice*. New York: G.P. Putnam's Sons.

Warren, K. W. (1993). *Black and White Strangers: Race and American Literary Realism*. Chicago and London: The University of Chicago Press.

Washington, B. T. (1915 [1901]). *Up from Slavery: An Autobiography*. Garden City, NY: Doubleday.

Waters, A. M. (1997). Conspiracy Theories as Ethnosociologies: Explanation and Intention in African American Political Culture. *Journal of Black Studies* 28, no. 1 (Sept): 112–125.

Waters, D. J., ed. (1983). *Strange Ways and Sweet Dreams: Afro-American Folklore from the Hampton Institute*. Boston: G.K. Hall.

Webber, T. L. (1978). *Deep Like the Rivers: Education in the Slave Quarter Community*. New York: W.W. Norton.

Weiner, M. F. (1996). Mistresses, Morality, and the Dilemmas of Slaveholding: The Ideology and Behavior of Elite Antebellum Women. Pp. 278–298 in P. Morton, ed., *Discovering the Women in Slavery: Emancipating Perspectives on the American Past*. Athens: The University of Georgia Press.

Wells-Barnett, I. B. (1969). *On Lynchings: Southern Horrors; A Red Record; Mob Rule in New Orleans*. New York: Arno Press.

West, C. (1993). *Race Matters*. New York: Vintage Books.

Wheeler, C. G. (1993). 30 Years Beyond "I Have a Dream." *The Gallup Poll Monthly* (Oct.): 2–10.

White, S. and G. White (1995). Slave Hair and African American Culture in the Eighteenth and Nineteenth Centuries. *The Journal of Southern History* 61, no. 1 (Feb.): 45–76.

White, W. (1935). U.S. Department of (White) Justice. *The Crisis* (Oct.): 309–310.

White, W. (1969 [1948]). *A Man Called White*. New York: Arno Press.

Whitfield, S. J. (1991 [1988]). *A Death in the Delta: The Story of Emmett Till*. Baltimore: The Johns Hopkins University Press.

Whitman, S. T. (1993). Industrial Slavery at the Margin: The Maryland Chemical Works. *The Journal of Southern History* 61, no. 1 (Feb.): 31–62.

Wiggins, D. K. (1985). Leisure Time on the Southern Plantation: The Slaves' Respite from Constant Toil, 1810–1860. Pp. 25–50 in D. Spivey, ed., *Sport in America: New Historical Perspectives*. Westport, CT: Greenwood Press.

Wiggins, W. H., Jr. (1983). The Black Folk Church. Pp. 144–154 in R. M. Dorson, ed., *Handbook of American Folklore*. Bloomington: Indiana University Press.

Williams, J. K. (1980). *Dueling in the Old South: Vignettes of Social History*. College Station and London: Texas A & M University Press.

Williams, L. S. (1977). Attica Prisoners Seek Aid from N.A.A.C.P. (A Note and Document). *Afro-Americans in New York Life and History* 1, no. 2 (July): 211–212.

Williams-Myers, A. J. (1994). *Long Hammering: Essays on the Forging of an African American Presence in the Hudson River Valley to the Early Twentieth Century*. Trenton, NJ: African World Press.

Williamson, J. (1990). *After Slavery: The Negro in South Carolina during Reconstruction, 1861–1877*. Hanover, NH: University Press of New England.

Wilmore, G. S. (1983). *Black Religion and Black Radicalism: An Interpretation of the Religious History of Afro-American People*, 2nd ed. Maryknoll, NY: Orbis Books.

Wilson, M. and K. Russell (1996). *Divided Sisters: Bridging the Gap between Black Women and White Women*. New York: Doubleday, Anchor Books.

Wilson, W. J. (1978). *The Declining Significance of Race: Blacks and Changing American Institutions*. Chicago and London: The University of Chicago Press.

Wilson, W. J. (1987). *The Truly Disadvantaged: The Inner City, the Underclass, and Public Policy*. Chicago: The University of Chicago Press.

Winch, J. (1988). *Philadelphia's Black Elite: Activism, Accommodation, and the Struggle for Autonomy, 1787–1848*. Philadelphia: Temple University Press.

Wintz, C. D. (1988). *Black Culture and the Harlem Renaissance*. Houston: Rice University Press.

Wolfe, C. and K. Lornell (1992). *The Life and Legend of Leadbelly*. New York: HarperCollins.

Wood, B. (1995). "Never on a Sunday?": Slavery and the Sabbath in Lowcountry, Georgia, 1750–1830. Pp. 79–96 in M. Turner, ed., *From Chattel Slavery to Wage Slaves: The Dynamics of Labour Bargaining in the Americas*. London: James Curry.

Wood, F. G. (1990). *The Arrogance of Faith: Christianity and Race in America from the Colonial Era to the Twentieth Century*. New York: Alfred A. Knopf.

Woodruff, N.E. (1994). Mississippi Delta Planters and Debates over Mechanization,

Labor, and Civil Rights in the 1940s. *The Journal of Southern History* 60, no.2 (May): 263–284.

Woodward, C.V. (1974 [1955]). *The Strange Career of Jim Crow*, 3rd rev. ed. New York: Oxford University Press.

Woodward, C. V. (1993). Look Away, Look Away. *The Journal of Southern History* 59, no. 3 (Aug.): 487–507.

Wright, G. C. (1984). The Billy Club and the Ballot: Police Intimidation of Blacks in Louisville, Kentucky, 1880–1930. *Southern Studies* 22, no. 1 (Spring): 20–41.

Wright, R. (1987 [1940]). Man of All Work. Pp. 117–162 in *Eight Men*. New York: Thunder's Mouth Press.

Wright, R. (1992 [1940]). *Native Son*. New York: Harper Perennial.

Wright, R. (1993 [1938]). *Uncle Tom's Children*. New York: Harper Perennial.

Wyatt-Brown, B. (1982). *Southern Honor: Ethics and Behavior in the Old South*. New York: Oxford University Press.

Young, M. E. (1993). *Mules and Dragons: Popular Culture Images in the Selected Writings of African American and Chinese American Women Writers*. Westport, CT: Greenwood Press.

Young, R. J. (1994). The Political Economy of Black Abolitionists. *Afro-Americans in New York Life and History* 18, no. 1 (Jan.): 47–71.

Young, R. J. (1996). *Antebellum Black Activists: Race, Gender, and Self*. New York: Garland.

Ziglar, W. (1992). "Community on Trial": The Coatesville Lynching of 1911. Pp. 323–348 in P. Finkelman, ed., *Race, Law, and American History, 1700–1990, Vol. 9: Lynching, Racial Violence, and Law*. New York and London: Garland Publishing.

Zipf, K. L. (1997). "Among These American Heathens": Congregationalist Missionaries and African American Evangelicals during Reconstruction, 1865–1878. *The North Carolina Historical Review* 74, no. 2: 111–134.

Index

Abernathy, Ralph, 145–46, 152 n.12

Abolitionists, 13 n.17, 33; free blacks as, 33, 43 n.26; literature as incendiary, 38; moral suasion, 37; regarding Port Royal Experiment, 57–58 n.5; vigilance committees, 39; work with Underground Railroad, 38. *See also* Blacks, free; Douglass, Frederick; Slavery, abolition of; Truth, Sojourner

Acquired immunodeficiency syndrome (AIDS), and blacks, 173, 182, 186 n.2

Adams, John, 62

African Americans, as a new people, 19

Alabama, 69, 94–95, 136. *See also* Scottsboro Boys

Albany, New York, 39

Alinsky, Saul, Woodlawn Project, 149

Allen, Richard, 32, 35, 41 n.5

American Colonization Society, 36

American Missionary Society, 58 n.6

American Psychological Association, speech to by Martin Luther King, Jr., 152–53 n.13

American Revolution, 3–5, 9, 10, 32, 63

Ames, Jessie Daniel, 72 n.11, 130 n.6

Amistad, mutiny, 43 n.21. *See also* Conspiracies, slave; Rebellions, slave

Amos 'n' Andy, 101–2, 108 n.1

Angelou, Maya, 120 n.1, 130 n.2

Association for the Study of Negro Life and History. *See* Woodson, Charles Goodwin

Atlanta, Georgia, 56, 67, 96, 97, 114, 119. *See also* Du Bois, W.E.B.; Riots, race

Attica: letter from prisoners, 117–18; riot, 149–51. *See also* Prisons

Attucks, Crispus: death in Boston Massacre, 61; Frederick Douglass on, 62–63; honored in ceremony, 61–63. *See also* American Revolution

Aulette, Ken, *The Underclass*, 157

Aunt Jemima, 106, 110 n.10. *See also* Stereotypes, of black women

Back to Africa movement. *See* Garvey, Marcus

Badman, black, 77–78

Baker, Ella, 146, 169 n.10

Baker, Josephine, 105

Baraka, Amiri, on black migration, 75

Barry, Marion, 167, 170 n.25, 172

Bell, Derrick. *See* Critical race theory

Birmingham, Alabama, 101, 114, 138,

About the Authors

FRANKIE Y. BAILEY is an Associate Professor in the School of Criminal Justice, University at Albany, State University of New York. Her research and teaching focus on issues of race, class, gender, and social conflict in the fields of crime and American culture and crime history. She is the author of *Out of the Woodpile: Black Characters in Crime and Detective Fiction* (Greenwood, 1991) and the coeditor of *Popular Culture, Crime, and Justice* (with Donna C. Hale, 1998).

ALICE P. GREEN is the founder and Executive Director of the Center for Law and Justice, a community-based organization that serves as a clearinghouse for information on legal and criminal justice systems for members of low-income communities and those of color. An activist/criminologist, she monitors criminal justice programs and lectures extensively on social policy, race, crime, and the impact of incarceration on African Americans and their communities.